Representative and Responsible Government

# Representative and Responsible Government

## AN ESSAY ON
## THE BRITISH CONSTITUTION

### BY A. H. BIRCH

*Professor of Political Studies
in the University of Hull*

UNIVERSITY OF TORONTO PRESS

© *George Allen & Unwin Ltd, 1964*

*Published in Canada by*
*University of Toronto Press*

PRINTED IN GREAT BRITAIN
*in 10 point Times Roman type*
BY UNWIN BROTHERS LIMITED
WOKING AND LONDON

*To Dorothy*

# ACKNOWLEDGEMENTS

This book was conceived and largely written while I was a member of the Department of Government at Manchester University, and it owes a great deal to the stimulating intellectual atmosphere of that Department. Professor W. J. M. Mackenzie has read the entire typescript in the final draft and has commented on it in his usual thoughtful and erudite fashion. But I am grateful to him not only (or mainly) for this but also for many years of friendship, encouragement, and unobtrusive guidance. I am also indebted to Mr J. W. Grove, Professor A. M. Potter, and Dr C. R. Rose, each of whom has commented on parts of the book, and to the students who attended my seminar on 'Political Theory and Practice in Modern Britain' between 1958 and 1961.

Outside Manchester, my thanks go to Professor Wilfrid Harrison of Liverpool University, who gave me much valuable advice and encouragement in the early stages of the work, and to Dr R. E. Dowse and Dr W. H. Greenleaf of Hull University, each of whom has commented on particular chapters. Of course none of those mentioned is responsible for the faults which remain.

My greatest debt of all is to my wife, to whom I dedicate the book. Not only did she create the conditions in which I could write; in addition she read the entire manuscript day by day as it was written, and sharpened the arguments, corrected the grammar, and made numerous stylistic improvements. In a very real sense it is her book as well as mine.

A.H.B.

# CONTENTS

# PART I
# INTRODUCTION

## CHAPTER 1

## Representation and Responsibility in Politics

Everyone knows that the British constitution provides for a system of representative and responsible government. These characteristics are almost universally regarded as both desirable and important. Their existence is often said to make the British political system, like those of other liberal democracies, different in kind from the political systems of countries behind the Iron Curtain and of certain under-developed countries, which are generally described as autocratic or dictatorial. The concepts of representation and responsibility are, indeed, invoked in almost every modern discussion of how countries ought to be governed.

Though constantly used, these terms are rarely defined with any care. In fact each of them has several usages and shades of meaning and a good deal of confusion arises in public discussion because these are not always distinguished from one another. The purpose of this introductory chapter is to examine the ways in which the terms are most commonly used so as to provide a basis for the subsequent discussion of the theory and practice of representative and responsible government in Britain.

### REPRESENTATION

It is generally agreed that a political system can properly be described as a system of representative government if it is one in which representatives of the people share, to a significant degree, in the making of political decisions. The description would not be extended to a system in which power is concentrated in the hands of one man who claimed to represent the people, either in virtue of a supposed contract, as in the case of Hobbes's imagined sovereign, or in virtue of an actual plebiscite, as in the case of the Emperor Napoleon. Most students of politics agree that the variety of interests and opinions

13

within a society is too great for them to be adequately represented by any one man. The necessary condition of representative government is therefore said to be the existence of a fair number of representatives of the people, meeting together in some kind of council or assembly.

But what is a representative of the people? This is a question to which answers vary, not in the sense that they are contradictory but in the sense that they emphasize different qualities which a representative ought to possess. The countless discussions which have taken place on this topic cannot be understood unless it is realized that the term 'representative' is commonly used in three different ways.

In the first place, the term is used to denote an agent or delegate, a person whose function is to protect and if possible advance the interests of the individual or group on whose behalf he is acting. Ambassadors are representatives in this sense, and so are commercial travellers and barristers. This is not to say that these people all function in the same way: the ambassador is generally allowed more discretion than the salesman, and the barrister representing his client in court has more freedom than the ambassador. The point is that all these people are representatives in the sense that, irrespective of who they are, how they are chosen, or how much discretion they are allowed, their function is to look after the interests of the organization, group or person that they represent.

Representatives of this kind fill many roles in British politics. Royal commissions hear evidence from representatives of the interests that may be affected by the commission's proposals. Government departments confer regularly with officials of trade associations that represent their respective industries. The social service departments and the public utilities have a host of local advisory committees which are composed partly of representatives of local organizations. Until quite recently the legislative assemblies of many British colonies included representatives of racial minorities or commercial interests, who were generally nominated by the Governor. And many other examples could easily be cited.

We may note in passing that it is in this sense of the term that the idea of representation is loosely bound up with the idea of consent. Since an agent acts on behalf of his principal, it is generally assumed that the agent's agreement to a proposal can be taken to imply the consent of the principal. The House of Commons owes its origins to the King's need to secure the consent of the Commons to financial exactions: the knights of the shires were assumed to be able to consent on behalf of the residents of the shires, and the citizens and burgesses to be able to do the same on behalf of townsfolk. There are various theoretical problems about this kind of assumption which need not detain us; the point to be noted is that the connection between representation and consent (whatever it is) is only a connection between one kind of representation and consent, and cannot properly be invoked when the term is used in other ways.

In the second place, the term is commonly used to describe persons and assemblies who have been freely elected:[1] in this usage the characteristic of a representative would seem to be the manner of his selection rather than his behaviour. But there is a difficulty about this, because not all elected persons can be regarded as representatives. The Pope is elected, but he is not to be regarded as a representative of the College of Cardinals. Equally, in most American states judges are elected, but it would not be accurate to describe them as representatives of their electors. It would seem that elected persons can be described as representatives only if their election involves some obligation, however slight, to advance the interests and opinions of their electors. It follows that in strict logic this second usage of the term is not clearly separable from the first usage.

Nevertheless, in practice the two usages are distinguishable, because the conventions of politics do not compel an elected representative to act as an agent or delegate of his constituents. In Britain only a small minority of politicians have argued that M.P.'s should behave as delegates, and the accepted view has been exactly the opposite. In Campion's words: 'As to the way in which it exercised the function of representation, the House claimed to be its own judge; it prohibited the publication of debates lest this should be an admission of its accountability to the electors.' And though this prohibition has not been enforced since 1771 (except occasionally during wartime) it 'has not been explicitly withdrawn'.[2]

There can be no doubt that in the prevailing view an M.P. is regarded as being the Parliamentary representative of his constituency whether or not he takes any notice of the views of his constituents. So long as he has been elected, and is dependent on his constituents for re-election, he is looked upon as their representative. It may be that the ultimate justification of the electoral process is that it tends to make M.P.'s act in the interests (and further the opinions) of their constituents, but in common usage the process itself—the manner of choice—entitles the M.P. and the assembly to the description of 'representative'.

There is a third usage of the term which is different again, and is

[1] The word 'freely' is included here because freedom of choice is normally assumed when people refer to representatives in this sense of the term. The question of what constitutes a free election involves complicated problems which are outside the scope of this book. On this, see W. J. M. Mackenzie, *Free Elections* (London, 1958).

[2] G. Campion (ed.), *Parliament: a Survey* (London, 1952), p. 13.

also very common. In this usage the term signifies that a person is or a group of people are typical of a class. A small body is said to be representative of a large one if it mirrors the main characteristics of the larger one. Statisticians use the word in this sense when they speak of a representative sample. Students of politics do the same when they discuss the extent to which the composition of the executive committee of a trade union or political party is representative of the membership. The Leader of the Parliamentary Labour Party used the word in this way when he claimed recently that Labour M.P.'s are more representative of the electorate as a whole than Conservative M.P.'s are.

These three usages of the term indicate different ways in which members of a committee or assembly can represent a larger group of people: by virtue of their activities, by virtue of the manner of their selection, or by virtue of their personal characteristics. To put this in another form, it can be said that a group of citizens can be represented in an assembly in three alternative ways: if one or more of the members of the assembly conceive one of their duties to be the protection of the citizens' interests; if one or more of the members have been elected by the citizens; or if one or more of the members are the same sort of people as the citizens. In the case of representation by election it is the process that is important and not the behaviour of any particular citizen; so that a person is said to be represented in this sense if he had the right to vote, even though he may actually have abstained or voted against the candidate who was elected.

It is clear that assemblies which are representative in one of these senses of the term need not be representative in other senses, though it is sometimes suggested that they ought to be. Thus, the representatives of minority groups in colonial legislatives were there to look after the interests of their groups, and this function was not obscured by the fact that in most cases they were nominated by the Governor. Sometimes it was claimed that they would do the job better if they were representatives in the second sense of the term as well as in the first sense; that is, if they were elected; but this was a separate argument.

To cite a slightly different example, ambassadors are representatives in the sense that they act as agents of their governments, and it is not necessary for an ambassador to share the characteristics of members of his government. In 1945 some supporters of the Labour Party suggested that Lord Halifax, as an aristocrat of Conservative views, was not the most suitable man to represent the Labour Government and the British nation in Washington, but the Foreign Secretary refused to accept this argument. Equally, the modern House

16

of Commons is a representative institution because it is freely elected, and it does not follow that its members are, or should be, similar to their constituents. Critics sometimes suggest that the House would be improved if it were also a social microcosm of the nation, but this is an independent and somewhat doubtful proposition. The doubt arises because it is extremely unlikely that a process of free election would ever yield members who constituted a cross-section of the electors, just as it is unlikely that a representative sample can be obtained by asking for volunteers. In practice it is virtually impossible for an assembly to be fully representative in both the second and third senses of the term, as we have defined them, although some assemblies are further away from this position than others.

In western democracies representation by election has come to be regarded as the most important form of representation, and indeed as the only proper basis of a political system. Nobody would now disagree with Lord Brougham's remark: 'We mean by a representative government one in which the body of the people . . . elect their deputies to a chamber of their own.'[1] This is hardly a complete definition; we need to add that the chamber must occupy a powerful position in the political system and that the elections to it must be free, with all that this implies in the way of freedom of speech and political organization. But it indicates the main point, which is that it is the manner of choice of members of the legislative assembly, rather than their characteristics or their behaviour, which is generally taken to be the criterion of a representative form of government.

Despite this, it would not be right, either in principle or in practice, simply to equate representation with election. Electoral systems are not self-justifying: their function is to afford a means of appointing representatives who are expected to behave in certain ways. How these expectations are described varies from country to country and from time to time, but most descriptions involve one of the other senses in which the term 'representative' is used. Alternatively, or in addition, the descriptions involve the concept of political responsibility, which we must now examine.


## RESPONSIBILITY

The concept of political responsibility, like that of representation, is somewhat ambiguous. In political discussion the concept is commonly invoked in three quite distinct ways.

In the first place, the term 'responsible' is commonly used to describe a system of government in which the administration is

---

[1] *The British Constitution* (London, 1862), p. 89.

responsive to public demands and movements of public opinion. It is in this sense that the term is sometimes used to distinguish between liberal or democratic régimes, which recognize an obligation to be responsive to public opinion, and dictatorial or autocratic régimes, which may be responsive for reasons of prudence but generally regard leadership as a greater virtue than responsiveness. The difference of emphasis is clearly reflected in the attitudes taken to censorship: in liberal systems censorship is thought to be wrong because it distorts the public opinion on which government is presumed to be based, whereas in autocratic systems censorship is often regarded as a permissible weapon to use against groups who try to undermine public confidence in the wisdom of those in power.

Ideally, governments which are responsible in this sense take heed of the views of all groups within society when determining their policies; they are the servants of the public, not its masters. This state of affairs is generally regarded by democrats as desirable, though it cannot easily be defined in terms precise enough to serve as a guide to action or a criterion of good government. To do this, it would be necessary to define what is meant by public opinion, to explain how public opinion can be known, and to make clear how a government should act when that opinion appears to consist of a set of mutually incompatible views. These difficulties will be discussed in later chapters; at present it is sufficient to note that one of the things expected of a responsible government is that it should be generally responsive to public demands. It will be convenient to use the term responsiveness to denote this meaning of political responsibility.

In the second place, the term is used in a quite different way, which invokes the concepts of duty and moral responsibility. The headmaster is responsible for the welfare of his pupils. The prison governor is responsible for seeing that prisoners do not escape or kill themselves or attack the guards. In the same way, the ministers in office are responsible for seeing that the government pursues a wise policy, whether or not what they do meets with the immediate approval of the public. L. S. Amery used the term in this way when he said:

'The word "responsibility" . . . connotes a state of mind, which weighs the consequence of action and then acts, irrespective, it may be, of the concurrence or approval of others. It is the strength of our constitutional system that it encourages and fosters responsibility in that higher sense. . . . The combination of responsible leadership by government with responsible criticism in Parliament is the essence of our Constitution.'[1]

[1] *Thoughts on the Constitution* (London, 1947), pp. 31 and 32.

And in 1962 Lord Hailsham used the term in exactly the same way in his speech on the Budget:

'When a Government has to choose between a run on the pound and its own popularity, it has only one choice it can make. It makes it unwillingly. It must face unpopularity, loss of by-elections and even, if need be, defeat at a later general election. This is the price of responsible government.'[1]

The precise significance of this usage of the term can best be understood by considering cases when it is used in a negative form. A good example is the allegation commonly made that Sir Anthony Eden's decision to intervene at Suez in 1956 was irresponsible. On inspection, this allegation appears to have been based on two distinct grounds. One ground is that the decision was made recklessly, without full consultation with diplomatic and military experts, and without careful consideration of the difficulties involved in launching the expedition quickly enough for it to achieve its objects. The other ground is that the decision to intervene was inconsistent with other important British policies, notably that of retaining the full support and friendship of the United States. In short, the allegation of irresponsibility can be broken down into an allegation of imprudence and an allegation of inconsistency.

These usages of the term are common in political life. One familiar historical example is Gladstone's Midlothian campaign, in which Disraeli's foreign policy was attacked by his rival as irresponsible, by which was meant that it was reckless. Another is the widespread criticism of the decision to revert to the gold standard at pre-war parity in 1925, in which the Chancellor of the Exchequer and the Governor of the Bank of England were accused of being irresponsible in the sense of failing to consider the full effects of this move on the British economy. A more recent example is the charge of irresponsibility in regard to Gaitskell's pledges in the 1959 general election that a Labour government would increase the benefits paid to old-age pensioners and others without increasing income tax or purchase tax. The Conservative press said, rightly or wrongly, that these pledges were both imprudent and mutually inconsistent. A government spokesman in 1955 had used the term in much the same way when he said: 'We should all like to reduce the period of National Service, but it is irresponsible to suggest that we can afford to do so at the present time.'

Although there is a distinction between imprudence and inconsistency it is not so sharp as to invalidate the procedure adopted here of

[1] Speech in the House of Lords reported in *The Guardian*, April 24, 1962.

grouping them together as comprising a second meaning of the concept of irresponsibility, and therefore of responsibility, in politics.

There is a third usage of the term 'responsibility' which is more common in Britain than in most other countries. This is its usage to signify the accountability of ministers, or of the government as a whole, to an elected assembly. In Britain individual ministers are responsible to Parliament for the work of their departments, and the cabinet is collectively responsible for government policy. In principle this implies that ministers should resign (or be ready to resign) when serious mistakes by their departments are disclosed, and that the government should resign when the confidence of Parliament is withdrawn. In practice resignations of this kind are relatively rare, but the convention of ministerial responsibility is nevertheless an essential feature of modern British government. Its value was well described by John Stuart Mill. Writing in 1864, he said: 'It should be apparent to all the world who did everything, and through whose default anything was left undone. Responsibility is null when nobody knows who is responsible. . . . To maintain it at its highest there must be one person who receives the whole praise of what is well done, the whole blame of what is ill.'[1] It is in this sense of the term that the boards of nationalized industries are partially irresponsible, for the ministers concerned are answerable to Parliament only on questions of general policy, and not on questions of day-to-day administration.

It is clear that people who regard political responsibility as a virtue generally want their government to be responsible in all these three senses of the term: they want it to be responsive to public opinion, to pursue policies which are prudent and mutually consistent, and to be accountable to the representatives of the electors. It is also clear that the first and second of these objectives are not always compatible. The public's opinions on a set of issues do not normally add up to a coherent programme which the government could follow. On some issues it is meaningless to speak of public opinion in the singular, for there is nothing but a patchwork of conflicting opinions held by different groups in society. On other issues there may be a prevailing view, an opinion shared by the majority of those who have any opinion on the subject; but a government which followed the prevailing view on each question as it arose would quickly find itself pursuing contradictory policies. It is not only that different sets of people are articulate on different topics, but also that the same people may hold incompatible views in their various roles as producers, consumers, taxpayers, parents, church members and so on. To quote

[1] *Considerations on Representative Government*, ed. R. B. McCallum (Oxford, 1946), p. 264.

the most obvious example, the prevailing view might be simultaneously in favour of increasing government expenditure, reducing taxation, and securing a budgetary surplus. It is the job of the government, but not of the ordinary citizen, to strike a balance between these objectives.

It follows that a government which wishes to pursue consistent policies must continually be arranging compromises between the conflicting demands of sections of the public. It must also, on occasion, initiate policies which it conceives to be in the best interests of the nation, even though they are unpopular. It must educate the public so that they accept the need for these compromises and unattractive policies. In this way it may hope to secure support for its actions when the public next have the opportunity to express their approval or disapproval by the direct method of casting votes.

## RESPONSIBILITY AND THE REPRESENTATIVE SYSTEM

In this process the representative system plays a vital role. It is largely through this system that public demands are expressed, modified, and presented to the government. The political parties absorb a wide variety of opinions on controversial issues and merge them, with varying degrees of success, into a limited number of alternative policies. Political leaders use party conferences and election meetings to increase public understanding of their programmes. Periodic elections ensure that some weight is given to the opinions of inarticulate and unorganized citizens, as well as to those of people who know how to make their views felt. A representative system thus provides a way of bridging the gulf between the policies a government would follow if it responded to the varying day-to-day expressions of public opinion and those it must follow if its policies are to be coherent and mutually consistent: in some degree, a representative system enables a government to be responsible in both these senses of the term.

In what manner and to what extent it does this depends on the nature of the representative system. Thus, a good deal of current discussion implies that the British national government is generally more consistent in its policies than the American national government, but less responsive to movements of public opinion. If there is any truth in this view, the difference results from differences in the representative systems of the two countries, the British system being more rigid than the American and providing for greater party discipline. Another contrast that is sometimes drawn is between ministerial responsibility in Britain as it is today and as it was a century ago. This reflects differences in the representative systems of the two periods: if the accountability of the administration to Parliament is less of a worry to ministers than it used to be, this is largely a consequence of the centralization of political power than has followed the extension of the suffrage and the emergence of political parties with mass memberships.

The character of a country's representative system is shaped by a number of factors. These include the extent to which the country is socially homogeneous and the nature of its social divisions. They also include the climate of political ideas in the country and the attitudes people have to their parties, elections, and representatives. In Britain these ideas and attitudes have their roots in certain traditional doctrines about the purpose and ideal nature of a representative system. These doctrines were established in the period between the middle years of the eighteenth century and the later years of the nineteenth century, when representation was the subject of almost continuous political debate. Though they differ sharply from one another, they are nearly all based on assumptions about the nature of society which would not be accepted today, and for this reason it could be maintained that they are out of date. But doctrines which form part of the common stock of ideas about British government, and which are continually referred to in political discussions, cannot be dismissed in this way. They are not modern doctrines, based squarely on the facts of contemporary life, but they are not out-of-date doctrines either. They are traditional doctrines, and unless they are understood it is impossible to grasp the nature of the British representative system and the current controversies about it. These doctrines will therefore be outlined in Part II of the book.

# THE TRADITIONAL DOCTRINES

## CHAPTER 2

# Tory and Whig Attitudes to Representation

In considering the traditional doctrines of representation in Britain it must be remembered that they emerged in the course of debates about relatively specific issues, and as the practice of representation changed, so did the issues and the focus of discussion. During much of the period with which we are concerned there was a fairly continuous trend towards the liberalization of the representative system. Proposals that were radical in one generation often seemed moderate in the next, and the positions taken up by the opponents of change became successively untenable as the tide of reform flowed on. In this shifting debate there were few fixed points of reference, and it is not easy to group the antagonists into clearly defined schools of thought. Thus Disraeli was a disciple of Burke, and was separated from John Stuart Mill by a fundamental difference of political attitude; yet Disraeli's arguments in the 1860's were closer to Mill's than they were to Burke's, simply because the climate of opinion in the mid-Victorian era differed so much from that of the late eighteenth century.

The great watershed in this debate is the reform movement which culminated in the Reform Act of 1832. Before that, almost all members of Parliament took the view that the main function of the House of Commons was to represent the various communities and economic interests within the nation. The extent of the franchise was not regarded as important, for all citizens were thought to be represented, or 'virtually represented', through this system. On one hand they were represented 'through the land on which they lived',[1] by the Members for their county or borough. On the other hand they were represented, or virtually represented, by the Members who regarded it as their concern to protect the interests of the trade or

[1] L. B. Namier, *England in the Age of the American Revolution* (London, 1930), p. 28.

industry or type of farming in which the citizens were engaged. 'Virtual representation', wrote Burke, 'is that in which there is a communion of interests, and a sympathy in feelings and desires, between those who act in the name of any description of people, and the people in whose name they act, though the trustees are not actually chosen by them.'[1] Before 1832 there were differences of view between groups of M.P.'s about the deliberative and decision-making functions of Parliament, but there was little real difference of view about its representative function.

After the Reform Act, a quite different view of Parliamentary representation, which had been canvassed by Radicals for many years, became increasingly prominent. This regarded the individual citizen as the unit to be represented, rather than the community or interest, and it regarded the opinions of the citizen as being of equal importance to, or greater importance than, his economic interests or status. Once this view was widely accepted, the concept of virtual representation tended to disappear, and the extent of the franchise became the main subject of debate. Many of the arguments and concepts that were current in the earlier period were still used in the later, but the change of emphasis is clear enough to make 1832 a natural point of division in the analysis.

The dominant ideas about representation in the earlier period can conveniently be divided into the two categories of Tory and Whig, and will be considered under these headings. A third category consists of Radical theories, which were widely discussed in the late eighteenth century but were not widely accepted until after 1832. These theories will be considered in later chapters.

### TORY AND WHIG IDEAS

Before discussing these ideas we must face a difficulty of terminology. It is now many years since L. B. Namier exploded the view that eighteenth-century politics could be interpreted in terms of a two-party struggle between Tories and Whigs, and presented us instead with a picture of a complicated interplay between factions, personal connections, and independent Members. If the idea of a two-party struggle is a gross over-simplification, so must be the idea that there were two theories of government in this period, one held by each party.

Nevertheless, it is fairly clear that (if we exclude Radical theories) ideas about the functions of Parliament between 1688 and 1832 can

---

[1] *Letter to Sir Hector Langrishe*, 1797, reprinted in Burke's *Works* (Bohn's Standard Library, London, 1887), vol. III, p. 334. (All subsequent references to Burke's *Works* are to this edition.)

be divided into two broad categories. Giving these categories the names of Tory and Whig is misleading in so far as it seems to imply that politicians could be divided into Tories who subscribed consistently to one view and Whigs who subscribed consistently to the other. If our main concern was with the history of eighteenth-century ideas these titles would probably have to be abandoned and a more elaborate classification would have to be devised. But since the main concern of this book is with more modern ideas it seems unnecessary to indulge in this kind of experiment, particularly since it might divert attention from the arguments which follow. In this chapter we shall therefore keep to the familiar names of Tory and Whig, with the warning that this is not meant to imply anything about the loyalties or activities of the people who, at various times, subscribed to these ideas.[1]

Tory ideas were derived partly from medieval notions about society and partly from experience of government in the days of the Tudors. From medieval thought was taken the belief that the nation was a unity greater than the sum of its parts, an organic whole which could be personified by a monarch whose authority had divine sanction. From the practice of Tudor government was derived the assumption that the administration should be firmly in the hands of the King, who would summon Parliament when he needed consent to the imposition of taxes or the introduction of laws, but would not expect Parliament to take the initiative in major questions of state.

Whig ideas were derived partly from medieval doctrines of contractual obligation, partly from ecclesiastical doctrines of representation, and partly from experience of the incompetence and arrogance of Stuart rule. Those who subscribed to these ideas believed that the authority of the sovereign should be limited and that the nation's representatives in Parliament should share fully in the responsibility for governing the country. In 1688 Whigs emphasized the limits of royal power and the right of citizens to resist if these limits were ignored: by the Hanoverian succession of 1714 the emphasis had shifted to an assertion of the importance of a balanced constitution in which ultimate supremacy lay with Parliament.

In each of these bodies of ideas there was implicit a theory of representation, or at any rate an attitude to representation. It is not suggested that these attitudes were very well defined, or that all Tories subscribed to one and all Whigs to another. But an examination

---

[1] Among the many discussions of Tory and Whig ideas, the following are particularly helpful: P. A. Gibbons, *Ideas of Political Representation in Parliament, 1651–1832* (Oxford, 1914) and S. H. Beer, 'The Representation of Interests in British Government: Historical Background', in *American Political Science Review*, vol. 51 (1957).

of eighteenth-century opinions about representation shows clearly enough that the two kinds of attitude existed. The essence of the Tory attitude was the belief that the function of Parliamentary representatives was not to take part in the formulation of policy but to express the grievances and represent the interests of their constituents: in Namier's words, to declare 'the sense of the commonalty in questions which most patently and directly concerned them'.[1] The essence of the Whig attitude was the belief that Parliament should have a large share in the responsibility of governing the country, and that Members of Parliament should be as much concerned with debating the national interest as with representing the various sectional interests within society.

## THE TORY ATTITUDE TO REPRESENTATION

The Glorious Revolution of 1688 was a challenge to Tory principles which might, in other circumstances, have provoked an eloquent and coherent statement of the Tory position. But as it happened, the Tories were so divided and confused during much of the eighteenth century that no such statement was made. After the accession of George I in 1714, the Tories were in the embarrassing position of wishing to reassert the powers and dignity of the Crown while they disliked the King. Some of the Tories resented his accession so much that they rallied to the Jacobite cause and supported the Pretender's fruitless attempt to place himself on the throne in 1715. The majority, believing in both the virtues of obedience and the need to uphold the Protestant church, reluctantly accepted the Hanoverian succession. But of the two most eminent Tory politicians, Oxford was imprisoned in the Tower, and Bolingbroke fled to France to accept a position in the Pretender's Court. In the election of 1716 the Tory representation in the House of Commons was considerably reduced. The departments of government came under a Whig domination that was to last until 1760, and Tory supporters who remained faithful to their cause could do no better than look to 'the Kingly power in the abstract, though not to the reigning King, as their only protection from an impending oligarchy'.[2]

In these circumstances most Tory politicians, when they wrote or spoke on constitutional matters, were concerned mainly to emphasize the limitations on the power of Parliamentarians. In the debates on the Septennial Bill in 1716 the Tories based their opposition to this measure on two principles. In the first place, they main-

[1] Namier, op. cit., p. 3.
[2] Benjamin Disraeli, *Vindication of the British Constitution* (1835), reprinted in *Whigs and Whiggism*, ed. W. Hutcheon (London, 1913) p. 215.

tained that the Members had no right to extend their own term of office: they had been authorized by the electors to act on their behalf for a period of three years, and they had no authority to do so after that period expired.[1] Secondly, they argued that frequent elections were necessary if the King, who was responsible for the government of the country, was to be properly informed of the opinions and interests of his subjects. Hutcheson said that he hoped to see the day when 'instead of triennial, we shall have annual new Parliaments. Then indeed the British liberties will be founded on a rock . . . and the Crown will be frequently and faithfully informed of the sentiments of the people.'[2] Similar views were expressed in 1734, when a number of Tories supported a motion for the repeal of the Septennial Act. In this debate Lord Noel Somerset claimed that 'This House is properly the grand inquest of the nation, they are to represent the grievances of the people to their sovereign'.[3]

Bolingbroke, the most eloquent of the Tory politicians, was not allowed to take his seat in the Lords when he returned from France, but he became joint editor of a weekly political journal[4] and he also wrote a number of essays and tracts. In all of these he re-stated the view that the initiative in government should not be taken by the leaders of Parliamentary factions, but by a King who would symbolize and represent the best interests of the whole nation. In his most ambitious work, *The Idea of a Patriot King*, he drew a picture of the characteristics and behaviour of a monarch who would truly be a father to his people. Such a monarch would 'begin to govern as he begins to reign', and he would appoint ministers who shared his principles. He would put the well-being of the nation above the interests of sections, and would 'distinguish the voice of his people from the clamour of a faction'. In their way they were noble sentiments, but Bolingbroke himself admitted that such a King would be 'a sort of standing miracle',[5] and the political influence of the essay was slight.

The Whig supremacy continued until the accession of George III, and, although some Tory leaders returned to office under that King, that were not moved to justify his reassertion of royal influence by reference to general principles. Indeed, although George III was in a sense a Tory, he did not govern according to Tory principles. Instead of trying to curtail the powers of Parliament, or destroy the well-

[1]This view was particularly well expressed by Archibald Hutcheson. See *Parliamentary History*, vol. 7, cols. 349–50.
[2]Ibid., col. 347.   [3]Op. cit., vol. 9, col. 421.
[4]*The Craftsman*, published from 1726 to 1736.
[5]*Letters on The Spirit of Patriotism, on The Idea of a Patriot King, and on The State of Parties at the Accession of King George the First* (London, 1749), pp. 138, 156, and 135.

organized system of corruption which had given the Whigs their Parliamentary majorities, he merely adopted similar methods to put his own favoured men into Parliament in place of the Whigs. As his reign dragged out its length, and reformist and Radical ideas gathered momentum, so the Tory view of government passed from the centre of the stage, and it was left to the more conservative of the Whigs, notably Edmund Burke, to make the most eloquent statements of the case against the reform of the representative system.

## THE WHIG ATTITUDE TO REPRESENTATION

The kernel of the Whig attitude to representation was the belief that Parliament should itself play a leading role in the process of decision-making. It should not only give expression to the various opinions, interests, and grievances within society, it should also try to reconcile them in policies which would serve the best interests of the nation. The Whigs admitted that there were innumerable groups and sections within the country, all with their own interests, and not all directly represented in Parliament. They admitted that many of the interests were opposed to each other and that it was not easy to find policies that would strike a satisfactory balance between them. To deal with these difficulties the Whigs emphasized two concepts that were of central importance in their attitude to representative government.

The first of these was the concept of virtual representation, which has already been mentioned. This could be applied to citizens who did not enjoy the franchise, but were said to be virtually represented by the Member for the area in which they lived. It could also be applied to communities and interests which were not directly represented in Parliament, but were said to be virtually represented by Members for other parts of the country which shared similar interests. The first aspect, the idea of representation through the land, was mainly emphasized by the Tories; the second aspect was mainly emphasized by the Whigs. It was this that enabled them to maintain that all the interests in the country were represented, virtually if not directly, in the eighteenth-century Parliament.

The other idea that the Whigs emphasized was that Members, once elected, should act according to their own judgement, and should not behave as delegates of their constituents. This was stated very clearly in the writings of Algernon Sidney, whose *Discourses Concerning Government* was published in 1698, some years after it was written. (Its author was beheaded in 1683.) Sidney contrasted the political unity of England with what we should now call the federal nature of Switzerland and the United Netherlands. In England, he maintained, 'every county does not make a distinct body, having in itself a sovereign power, but is a member of that great body which com-prehends the whole nation. It is not therefore for Kent or Sussex, Lewes or Maidstone, but for the whole nation, that the members chosen to serve in these places are sent to serve in Parliament. And though it be fit for them . . . to harken to the opinions of the electors for the information of their judgements, and to the end that what they say may be of more weight . . . yet they are not strictly and properly obliged to give account of their actions to any, unless the whole body of the nation for which they serve, and who are equally concerned in their resolutions, could be assembled. This being im-practicable, the only punishment to which they are subject, if they betray their trust, is scorn, infamy, hatred, and an assurance of being rejected, when they shall again seek the same honour.'[1]

This assertion that Members should be more or less independent of their constituencies, once they were elected, was essential to the Whig view of government. Only on this basis could they claim that Parliament was a deliberative as well as a representative body, and that the results of its deliberations were, or could be, something more than a mere aggregate of sectional demands. The point was made again and again by Whig politicians.

In the debate on the motion to repeal the Septennial Act in 1734, for instance, John Willis declared:

'After we are chosen, and have taken our seats in this House, we have no longer any dependence on our electors, at least in so far as regards our behaviour here. Their whole power is then devolved upon us, and we are in every question that comes before this House, to regard only the public good in general, and to determine according to our own judgements.'[2]

Sir William Yonge adopted a similar position, and asserted the independence of Members from their constituents in the same terms, and almost the same words, that Sidney had used half a century earlier.[3] Forty years later Edmund Burke echoed the same sentiments in the well-known speech which he made to the electors of Bristol. Parliament, he said, was

'not a *congress* of ambassadors from different hostile interests; which interests each must maintain, as an agent and advocate, against the other agents and advocates; but Parliament is a *deliberative* assembly of *one* nation, with *one* interest, that of the whole; where, not local purposes, not local prejudices ought to guide, but the general good, resulting from the general reason of the whole.'

---

[1] *Discourses concerning Government* (London, 1698), Chapter III, Section 44, p. 451.    [2] *Parliamentary History*, vol. 9, col. 435.    [3] Ibid., cols. 450–1.

Certainly a representative should keep in close touch with his constituents, and should even 'prefer their interests to his own. But his unbiassed opinion, his mature judgement, his enlightened conscience, he ought not to sacrifice to you . . . your representative owes you, not his industry only, but his judgement; and he betrays, instead of serving you, if he sacrifices it to your opinion'.[1]

In these ways the Whigs sought to demonstrate that the House of Commons was both a representative and a deliberative body, and that the results of its deliberations reflected the interests of the whole nation. Such a House, they claimed, could and should play a central part in the government of the country, together with the Lords, the King, and the King's Ministers. There was no suggestion that the Commons should bear the whole burden of representing the feelings of the nation. 'The King is the representative of the people', declared Burke: 'so are the Lords; so are the judges. They are all trustees for the people, as well as the Commons.'[2] Their trust, their responsibility, was to pursue the common good, and so to promote that 'happiness of the whole' which Burke regarded as the object of the state.[3]

In this way the Whig attitude had more in common with later views than the Tory attitude: it regarded the process of harmonizing popular demands in a common policy as one in which all the people's representatives should take part. The Whigs believed in responsible government in the sense that all the institutions of the national government were held to be involved in the process of ensuring that state policies were as responsive to public demands as was consistent with the welfare of the nation.

This was the dominant view of government in England throughout most of the eighteenth century, and it corresponded fairly well with political practice. The great majority of legislative measures were private bills, introduced for some such purpose as the enclosure of land or the acquisition of rights to build a canal or reservoir. These bills were frequently opposed by rival interests, and they were certainly of national, rather than of purely local concern. However, they did not affect the policies of the administration and were not the subject of ministerial decisions. They thus provided an opportunity for Parliament to resolve the conflicts and to play a vital part in the national government, side by side with the administration rather than

[1] From the speech at Bristol on being elected to Parliament for that city, November 1774. See *Works*, vol. I, p. 447.

[2] *Thoughts on the Cause of the Present Discontents*, ibid., vol. I, p. 345.

[3] Speech on the Petition of the Unitarians, May 11, 1792, ibid., vol. VI, p. 116. The idea that governments should promote happiness was a common theme in political discussion in the second half of the eighteenth century: it was not confined to the Utilitarians.

subservient to it, as the Tory view implied, or in control of it, as Radical theories were later to demand.

The Whig view also provided a justification of some of the aspects of the eighteenth-century representative system which, by modern standards, seem almost indefensible. Neither the extreme inequalities in the size of constituencies nor the existence of corrupt and rotten boroughs seemed, to the eighteenth-century Whigs, to constitute a serious defect in the Parliamentary system. No government lost office in the eighteenth century through the result of an election or a revolt of back-benchers, and the presence of a number of Members who represented only a handful of constituents did not therefore affect the maintenance of the government's majority, as it might today. Moreover, the existence of the corrupt and rotten boroughs enabled the *nouveaux-riches* in each generation to buy seats, and made it possible for bright young men to be given seats. Many of the most able Members were recruited in this fashion; without them, the House would have been dominated by landed gentlemen whose main concern was to criticize the administration rather than to take part in the government of the country.

During the last decades of the eighteenth century the progress of the industrial revolution led to changes in the social structure, in the relative importance of agricultural and commercial interests, and in the distribution of the population. As there were no corresponding changes in the constituencies, the feeling grew that the House of Commons no longer gave adequate representation to the varying interests within the nation and this was one of the factors which contributed to the movement for Parliamentary reform. In the prolonged though intermittent discussion of the case for reform, the Whig view of representation was used to support both sides of the argument, as will be seen in Chapter 4. However, the movement for reform derived its emotional and much of its intellectual force from quite a different set of principles, and it is to these Radical principles that we must now turn.

# CHAPTER 3

# The Early Radicals

## THE RADICAL ATTITUDE

The Tory and Whig views had this in common, that each of them was in essence a justification, in somewhat idealized terms, of a set of practices that were current at a particular period of English history. Radical theorists were not tied in this way for they were advocating an ideal system which might be created but which did not yet exist. This allowed their imaginations freer play than that enjoyed by Tory and Whig writers, and their doctrines were rather less coherent. For this reason it is desirable to outline the essential features of the Radical attitude before summarizing the historical development of Radical theories.

One of the features common to nearly all Radical thinkers from the English Revolution to the Reform Act is that they had no patience with the view, so brilliantly expounded by Burke, that political institutions are rooted in the history and customs of the community, and should not therefore be subjected to sudden change. They proposed 'to reform society anew, without reference to the special traditions and beliefs by which it [had] been hitherto bound together'.[1] It is true that some Radical thinkers in this period sought to strengthen their case by appealing to the myth that before the Norman invasion the Anglo-Saxon inhabitants of England had lived in conditions of political freedom and equality. Such thinkers suggested that the reform of the political system would restore to the people rights which they had enjoyed before the imposition of 'the Norman Yoke'.[2] But from the Levellers onwards, the more important and influential Radicals placed their main emphasis not on an appeal to mythology[3] but on an appeal to first principles.

The nature of these principles varied. To some writers the basic principles were principles of natural right, to others they were principles of utility. But they all believed that if a principle was valid, it should be applied universally, and this fundamental attitude to

[1] Leslie Stephen, *History of English Thought in the Eighteenth Century* (London, 1876), vol. 2, p. 253.

[2] Arguments of this kind are traced and analysed in Christopher Hill's essay on 'The Norman Yoke', reprinted in his *Puritanism and Revolution* (London, 1958).

[3] Which is, of course, itself very different from an appeal to tradition.

politics distinguished them from piecemeal reformers to whom the word 'radical' cannot be applied.

## THE IDEA OF POPULAR SOVEREIGNTY

One of the beliefs which Radicals of this period shared was that citizens who were obliged to obey a government were entitled to participate, directly or through their representatives, in the process by which the policies of that government were determined. Some Radicals went further and claimed that if citizens were denied the right to participate, they were thereby relieved of the obligation to obey. Others stopped short of this but maintained that the purposes of government could not be achieved unless the representative system were based on manhood suffrage. Such a view, often referred to as the doctrine of popular sovereignty, involves those who subscribe to it in a number of problems. The central problem is that of showing how a government can follow the dictates of the popular will without pursuing a set of contradictory policies. In the language of Chapter 1, it is the problem of showing how a government can be both responsive and consistent when it has, in some degree, surrendered its decision-making power to the public.

All those who subscribe to the doctrine of popular sovereignty are logically obliged to suggest an answer to this problem. To make the issue more clear, it may be helpful to preface a historical discussion of the early English Radicals by a brief consideration of the work of the most eloquent of all Radical philosophers.

Jean-Jacques Rousseau was one of the least systematic of political thinkers, but he was also one of the most perceptive. In his *Contrat Social* he not only adduced persuasive arguments in favour of a political system in which government would be based on the popular will but also indicated the difficulties inherent in such an arrangement and the special social and political conditions that would be required for its success. In Rousseau's view the most important of the necessary social conditions were that the community should be small, socially homogeneous, and united. Its members should be bound together not only by their agreement to accept the authority of the state, but also by their common acceptance of certain principles of 'civil religion'. There is, said Rousseau, 'a purely civil profession of faith of which the Sovereign should fix the articles, not exactly as religious dogmas, but as social sentiments without which a man cannot be a good citizen or a faithful subject. While it can compel no one to believe them, it can banish from the State whoever does not believe them . . . not for impiety, but as an anti-social being'.[1]

[1] *The Social Contract* (Everyman Edn., London, 1913), Bk. IV, Chap. 8, p. 121.

A political condition is that when a question of policy is put to the people it must be of such a nature and must be framed in such a way as to elicit what Rousseau called 'the general will'. It must be a question of general principle rather than of a particular application of a principle; the citizens must be asked whether they think the proposed measure would be to the advantage of the state, and not merely whether they like the proposal themselves; and to impede the formation of factions, which would substitute their private wills for the general will, the citizens must vote without any public discussion of the question. In making these points, Rousseau was not indulging in naïve optimism about the unselfishness of mankind. On the contrary, many passages in his writings show that he took a rather pessimistic view of the kind of behaviour that could be expected from his contemporaries.[1] His argument was of a conditional kind: for government based on popular participation to be successful, people must put the public good before their private interests. If for any reason people were not to do this, then the combination of political freedom and good government which he put forward as an ideal would not be achieved.

Rousseau insisted that citizens could not delegate their voting rights to representatives. Deputies could act as stewards of the people, but their proposals would have to be ratified by the sovereign assembly before they could become law. It follows that Rousseau was thinking of very small communities, like the city-state of Geneva in which he was born, where all the citizens could gather together in one place to pass legislation. His theory is not directly applicable to any modern state, and it certainly cannot be called a theory of representative government. It is nevertheless of central importance in any discussion of representation, for two reasons. The first is that its influence on democratic thought and practice has been immense, and it has served as an inspiration to reformers even in situations where a logical analysis would show it to be largely irrelevant. The other reason is that Rousseau, in describing the conditions necessary for the emergence of the general will, also indicated that in other conditions the 'will of the people', if it were sought, would prove to be no more than an aggregate of conflicting opinions and demands, which would not be a satisfactory basis for policy or legislation; and this argument is as relevant to representative as it is to direct democracy.

[1]The cautious and rather sceptical attitude Rousseau adopted when writing about problems of practical politics can be seen in the *Lettres écrite de la Montagne* (1764), in the *Projet de constitution pour la Corse* (1765), and in the *Considérations sur le gouvernement de Pologne* (written 1772, first published 1782), all of which are reprinted in C. E. Vaughan (ed.), *The Political Writings of Rousseau* (Cambridge, 1915).

The essential conditions, it may be repeated, are that the community must be small and united, that its members must share common values and must agree on fundamental issues, and that when they vote they must do so as citizens thinking of the public interest rather than as individuals thinking of their own private interests. In this way the potential conflict between public and private interests will be resolved in the mind of each citizen, and there will be a consensus of opinion on important issues. But if the 'social bond' is weak, and 'particular interests begin to make themselves felt' then this consensus may not emerge. Worse still, if 'in every heart the social bond is broken and the meanest interest lays hold of the sacred name of "public good", the general will becomes mute'. Men will be guided by secret motives, 'and iniquitous decrees directed solely to private interest get passed under the name of laws'.[1]

Seen in this light, Rousseau's ideas are both suggestive and helpful. It is true (and not surprising) that Rousseau's ideal society does not exist in the modern world. But his theory is an attractive one, supported by penetrating arguments, and accompanied by a clear acknowledgement of the difficulties of attaining the perfect state. In this sense Rousseau was a more perceptive thinker than those Radicals who, while staking a claim for popular sovereignty in Britain or America, ignored the difficulties inherent in this conception of government.

### ENGLISH RADICALS OF THE SEVENTEENTH CENTURY

English Radical theories before the Reform Act found their chief expression in four distinct movements. They were advanced by the Levellers of the seventeenth century; they next achieved prominence in the agitations set off by Wilkes's expulsion from Parliament; they were given more widespread publicity by the reformers and revolutionists who were inspired by the ideas of the American and French Revolutions; and they were espoused, in the early years of the nineteenth century, by Bentham, James Mill and their associates.

The Levellers were a group of soldiers and civilians who wanted to push Cromwell and the Parliamentarians very much further than the latter were prepared to go in the direction of republican democracy. They had no success in this, but they are important because they were the first English political group to advance a doctrine of popular sovereignty in an unambiguous form. Earlier writers had sometimes suggested that political authority was to be thought of as having its origin in the consent of the governed, but they did not give clear answers to the questions of how this consent was (or

[1]*The Social Contract*, Bk. IV, Chap. 1, p. 91.

should be) expressed, how it was to be recognized, and whether (and if so how frequently) it needed to be renewed. Fifty years before the Levellers, for instance, Richard Hooker had suggested that states derive their legitimacy from the consent of their citizens. But Hooker denied much practical significance to the idea by his assumption that the mere existence of a state showed that consent had been given to it.[1]

The Levellers insisted that the only proper basis for government was the consent of the ruled, expressed through the exercise of the right to take part in the election of Members of Parliament. They would not accept the view of many Parliamentarians that sovereignty rested with Parliament, for in the Levellers' view Members of the House of Commons were properly to be regarded as servants of their electors. Lilburne, who may be regarded as the leader of the Levellers, wrote in a pamphlet published in 1645 that the upholders of Parliamentary, rather than popular, sovereignty were claiming, in effect, that 'an ambassador had more power than the prince by whom he was sent'.[2]

These claims were based on an assertion of moral principle and a belief in the natural equality of all men as human beings and as citizens. The Levellers demanded that, since all citizens were affected by the laws, all should take part in the choice of legislators. During the debates in the Army council in 1647, Colonel Rainboro declared that 'Every man born in England, cannot, ought not, neither by the law of God nor the law of nature, to be exempted from the choice of those who are to make laws for him to live under and for ought I know, to lose his life under'.[3] The argument was put more fully by Wildman, an agent of the private soldiers, in the following terms:

'I conceive that the undeniable maxim of government is that all government is in the free assent of the people. If so, then upon that account there is no person that is under a just government or hath justly his own, unless he by his free consent be put under that government. This he cannot be unless he be consenting to it and therefore according to this maxim there is never a person in England but ought to have a voice in electing; there are no laws that in this strictness and vigour of justice any man is bound to that are not made by those whom he doth consent to.'[4]

The case for popular sovereignty was stressed by a number of

[1] See R. Hooker, *The Laws of Ecclesiastical Polity* (first published London, 1594).

[2] See G. P. Gooch, *Political Thought in England: from Bacon to Halifax* (London, 1914), p. 82.

[3] Quoted in A. D. Lindsay, *The Essentials of Democracy* (London, 2nd edn., 1935), p. 13.     [4] Ibid., p. 13.

speakers and pamphleteers, and was well expressed by Richard Overton in *An Appeal from the Commons to the Free People* (1647):

'For all just human powers are but betrusted, conferred, and conveyed by joint and common consent; for . . . by natural birth all men are equal, and alike born to propriety and freedom, every man by natural instinct aiming at his own safety and weal. . . . Now these premises considered . . . the transgression of our weal by our trustees is an utter forfeiture of their trust, and cessation of their power.'

It follows that 'an appeal from them (Parliament) to the people is not anti-parliamentary, anti-magisterial; not *from* that sovereign power, but *to* that sovereign power'.[1]

These arguments are clear as far as they go, but they do not amount to a full theory of representative government. They constitute a demand for manhood suffrage, a claim that citizens who are not enfranchised cannot be morally bound to obey the laws passed by Parliament, and an assertion that sovereignty rests with the people. In the three 'Agreements of the People' the Levellers asked for annual or biennial Parliaments and equal constituencies as well as for manhood suffrage; they declared that Parliament should be the agent of the popular will; and they maintained that the people possessed certain natural rights, such as religious freedom and equality before the law, which Parliament should not be entitled to curtail. But they did not explain what the relations should be between government and Parliament—indeed they paid virtually no attention to the need for an executive authority—and they gave no clear account of how the popular will was to be translated into government action. In this respect their theories were less complete than those of James Harrington, who drew up a plan for an ideal constitution in the *Oceana*, published in 1656. In this lengthy work he proposed a balanced system of government in which a senate, composed of the natural aristocracy of talent, would make proposals which a popular assembly, representing the people, would have power to accept or reject. The executive, or magistracy, would then carry into effect such proposals as were approved.

The ideas of the Levellers were backed by strong moral convictions and those of Harrington by the power of a very considerable intellect. For a short period they were the subject of widespread debate. But they were the product of the peculiar conditions of the revolutionary period, and after the Restoration of 1660 they lost currency except among a small minority of people in clerical and

[1] See A. S. P. Woodhouse (ed.) *Puritanism and Liberty* (London, 1938), p. 327.

academic circles.[1] They had some direct influence on affairs in the American colonies, where Harrington, in particular, was widely read and respected. The constitutions of Carolina (framed in 1669) and New Jersey (framed in 1676 and 1682) contained many features assembling those recommended in the *Oceana*.[2] The constitution of Pennsylvania, drawn up by Penn and Sidney in 1682, was even more radical, and included provision for manhood suffrage, equal constituencies, and the secret ballot. But in England the Radical ideas of the seventeenth century had no lasting influence on events, though they had some on subsequent political ideas.

## WILKES AND HIS SUPPORTERS

In the first years of George III's reign the apathy which had characterised the public's attitude to government during the previous half century was replaced by the growth of popular discontent. This was brought to a head in 1769 by the expulsion from Parliament of John Wilkes, a Member for Middlesex, on the ground that some years earlier he had published a seditious libel. Wilkes was promptly re-elected by his constituents, at once expelled again, re-elected for a second time, and expelled once more. When he was re-elected for a third time the House of Commons decided not to recognize his election and to seat in his place the candidate whom he had defeated. This action aroused fierce protests. Wilkes was elected an Alderman of the City of London, and later became Lord Mayor. The Aldermen of London petitioned the King, asking him to dissolve Parliament. A Society of Supporters of the Bill of Rights was formed—the first political society of its kind—to support Wilkes and to demand the dissolution of the 'corrupt Parliament'. London mobs, who had been out in force at each of the by-elections, held noisy demonstrations of protest. An anonymous but widely read journalist who called himself Junius attacked the government with scathing wit and a biting flow of invective.

These critics of government and Parliament quickly broadened their objectives. The Bill of Rights Society demanded annual Parliaments, equal constituencies, and the exclusion from Parliament of Members receiving salaries or pensions from the government. The Society claimed that Members should follow the instructions of their electors, and prepared a set of questionnaires to be presented to candidates at elections. In many constituencies instructions were

---

[1] Their continued currency in these circles has been traced by Caroline Robbins, in *The Eighteenth-Century Commonwealthman* (Cambridge, Mass., 1959).

[2] See G. P. Gooch, *English Democratic Ideas in the Seventeenth Century* (2nd edn., Cambridge, 1927), Appendix A (added by H. J. Laski).

sent to Members, though they were not always obeyed. A new society called the Constitutional Society was formed, and also demanded Parliamentary reform. Corresponding committees were set up in several towns, and in this way many citizens who did not enjoy the franchise were drawn into political activity. It was realized that public opinion, if properly mobilized, could influence the government through channels other than the electoral system.

In 1774 Wilkes was again elected for Middlesex, and this time he was permitted to take his seat. Two years later he introduced the first motion for Parliamentary reform. In this he claimed that the purpose of government is the good of the people and that they are the original source of political authority. Even the meanest mechanic or peasant had rights of liberty and of property that were affected by Parliamentary legislation, and all men were therefore entitled to some share in the legislative power. It followed that the rotten boroughs should be disfranchised and equal representation and manhood suffrage should be instituted.[1]

In the following years a number of resolutions on similar lines were passed by the newly formed political societies in the country. For instance, in 1780 the Sub-Committee of Westminster issued a report claiming that equal representation, annual Parliaments, and manhood suffrage were part of the English inheritance, since they had been enjoyed in medieval times. The report went on to outline a plan of reform which included not only these rights but also single-member constituencies, the secret ballot, the exclusion of office-holders and pensioners from Parliament, the payment of Members and the abolition of the property qualifications.[2] This report anticipated all the demands that the Chartists were to make some sixty years later. Somewhat more moderate claims were made by the Yorkshire Association, whose members were mainly country gentry, farmers, and clergy. In 1781 the Association demanded shorter Parliaments and more county Members, saying that Englishmen had ancient privileges which they had lost and which ought to be restored.[3] But after 1781 this phase of Radical activity gave way to a period of relative quiescence.

The political ideas of these reformers were somewhat more detailed and specific than those of the Levellers. They also obtained much wider currency and had a more enduring effect on the nation. But they did not add up to an adequate theory of representative govern-

[1] Parts of his speech are reprinted in S. MacCoby, *The English Radical Tradition 1763–1914* (London, 1952), pp. 28–32.

[2] Ibid., pp. 36–9.

[3] Ibid., pp. 39–42. See also I. R. Christie, 'The Yorkshire Association, 1780–4', in *The Historical Journal*, vol. 3 (1960).

ment, any more than their predecessors' ideas had done. The answer that the opponents of reform gave to the Radical demands was that if the representative system were transformed into one of perpetual canvass, with Members losing their financial independence through the crippling expense of frequent elections and their political independence through the need to follow the instructions of their constituents, there would be no hope of Parliament reconciling the conflicts within society and finding the national interest by a process of deliberation and compromise. To these arguments, repeated time and time again by Burke and the other exponents of the Whig theory,[1] the Radicals of that day had no effective reply.

## THE INFLUENCE OF AMERICAN AND FRENCH IDEAS

The period between 1760 and 1800 was one in which revolutionary ideas circulated throughout the western world. It is appropriate to associate these ideas with the two countries in which major revolutions occurred. But the ideas were not confined to America and France, and these countries were not the only ones to experience political upheaval. There were also revolutions in Poland in 1794, in Milan in 1796, in Rome in 1797, and in Naples in 1798. There were agitations elsewhere in Europe and in the western hemisphere. These developments were connected rather in the way that the revolutionary changes in Africa since 1945 have been connected. It is not so much that an upheaval in one territory led directly to agitation in another as that a set of revolutionary ideas spread irresistibly across the continents, leading to similar consequences wherever the conditions were similar. In Africa since 1945 the operative ideas have been a rejection of imperialism and a belief in the right of each society to govern itself. In Europe and America in the late eighteenth century the operative ideas were a rejection of aristocratic rule and a belief in the doctrine of popular sovereignty.

The main influence of these ideas on English political thought was to popularize the notion of abstract rights. The Westminster Sub-Committee and the Yorkshire Association had thought it appropriate to strengthen their demands by somewhat dubious references to the historic rights of Englishmen. Richard Price, Tom Paine and their followers based their claims on the natural rights of man. During the forty years after the French Revolution the combination of an appeal to natural rights and a protest against obvious abuses

[1] Good examples are Burke's speeches on a Bill for Shortening the Duration of Parliaments, and on a Motion for a Committee to Enquire into the state of the Representation of the Commons in Parliament, May 7, 1782. Both are reprinted in vol. VI of Burke's *Works*.

proved an effective means of agitating the unenfranchised classes to the point when they could exercise a decisive influence on Parliamentary action.

The revolutionary ideas of this period were derived in part from Rousseau, and Rousseau's ideas were introduced to the English by two middle-class dissenters, Joseph Priestley and Richard Price. It is of course not surprising that dissenters, who were denied certain civil rights simply on account of their religion, should have been attracted to a theory which stressed the natural equality of all men.[1] Priestley published his *Essay on the First Principles of Government* in 1768 and acknowledged his debt to the French writer. He maintained that men are by nature both free and equal, and that government is founded on a contract by which every man surrenders part of his natural freedom in exchange for a certain degree of influence on the decisions of the government. It followed that all men were entitled to that influence, and could not otherwise be obliged to obey the state. In the subsequent development of his argument Priestley parted company with Rousseau. He held that complete freedom of religion was desirable, and that a good society was one in which there existed a great variety of beliefs. If this meant that it would be only occasionally that a majority would be found for action by the government, this would be all to the good; for Priestley was one of the early believers in the principle of *laissez-faire*.[2]

Price's views were expressed in his *Observations on the Nature of Civil Liberty* and his *Additional Observations*, published in 1776 and 1777 respectively. He followed Rousseau more closely than did Priestley and acknowledged that, ideally, citizens should give their consent in person. Since this was impossible in any sizeable state, representative institutions would have to be relied upon. But the legislature could not claim to be sovereign for political authority belonged to the people and could not rightly be taken from them.[3]

Tom Paine was less of a scholar than Priestley or Price but a much more effective propagandist. It is unnecessary to try to summarize his attacks on the Monarchy, on the Church, and on the British Parliamentary system, many of which are couched in the style of the pamphleteer rather than that of the theorist. But Leslie Stephen was somewhat unfair in his remark that Paine 'represents the revolutionary sentiment, and does nothing to develop its theories'.[4] In the first

[1] An interesting account of the ideas and the role of dissenters in this period is to be found in A. H. Lincoln, *Some Political and Social Ideas of English Dissent: 1763–1800* (Cambridge, 1938).

[2] There are useful short summaries of Priestley's ideas in Stephen, op. cit., Chapter X, and Robbins, op. cit., Chapter IX.

[3] For Price's ideas see Lincoln, op. cit., Stephen, loc. cit., and Robbins, loc. cit.

[4] Op. cit., p. 264.

few pages of *Common Sense*, written in America and published in 1776, Paine justified his belief in the doctrine of popular sovereignty by giving a hypothetical account of the origin of government which had the advantage, as compared with Rousseau's doctrines, of leading directly to a theory of representation.

Paine envisaged the origin of government in a small colony, whose members come together to make regulations for their common good, so that members of the colony who lapse from the path of duty may be punished—at first by no more than 'public disesteem'. In this first Parliament 'every man by natural right will have a seat'. As the colony increases in number, it becomes inconvenient for all to confer together, so representatives are needed. They

'are supposed to have the same concerns at stake which those have who appointed them, and who will act in the same manner as the whole body would act were they present. . . . And that the *elected* might never form to themselves an interest separate from the electors, prudence will point out the propriety of having elections often; because as the *elected* might by that means return and mix again with the general body of the *electors* in a few months, their fidelity to the public will be secured by the prudent reflection of not making a rod for themselves. And as this frequent interchange will establish a common interest with every part of the community, they will mutually and naturally support each other, and in this (not on the unmeaning name of king) depends the *strength of government, and the happiness of the governed.*'[1]

In a classification of political theories Paine's views could be placed somewhere between the theories of Rousseau and those expressed in the later writings of Bentham. As a thinker Paine was not in the same class as either. But he is important because his direct style appealed to the workers of the growing industrial towns, among whom his writings had a wide circulation. Over 50,000 copies of *The Rights of Man* were sold within three months of its publication in 1792,[2] and it has been estimated that about 200,000 copies were sold within two years.[3] Cheap editions were read all over the country, and Paine's telling phrases were repeated whenever working men met to discuss the need for political reform. In this way Tom Paine made a significant contribution to the development of political organizations in the industrial areas.

[1] *The Writings of Thomas Paine*, ed. M. D. Conway (New York, 1894–5), vol. I, pp. 70–1.
[2] H. Pearson, *Tom Paine: Friend of Mankind* (London, 1937), p. 147.
[3] P. A. Brown, *The French Revolution in English History* (London, 1918), p. 84.

The story of these organizations is well known.[1] They were created and achieved immediate success in the years following the French Revolution: in 1795 the London Corresponding Society claimed that over two hundred thousand people attended one of its demonstrations.[2] The government, so alarmed by events in France that they were more hostile to change than they would otherwise have been, subjected workers' organizations to intermittent repression, and their influence waxed and waned as conditions changed. But after 1806 they burgeoned in all the industrial areas, and eventually they came to constitute a force which the ruling classes could not afford to ignore. In almost every town there were small groups of men who studied the writings of Paine and the subsequent pamphleteers, and constantly advocated the need for radical reforms in government and the social order. Low wages became a source of increasing discontent among industrial workers, and political organizers were able to turn the ensuing protests into demands for political change. Large numbers of men took part in clandestine drills and turned out to attend demonstrations and mass meetings. As the movement for Parliamentary reform grew in strength, the fear of direct action by the labouring classes led more and more of the Whig politicians to feel that a moderate measure of reform would be the lesser evil; that it would be better to make a limited concession voluntarily than to be forced to make major changes a few years later.[3] And in the seventeen months between the introduction of the first Reform Bill in March 1831 and the eventual passage of the Act, the riots in Bristol and the threats of the Political Unions in Birmingham and other large towns played a considerable part in persuading the Whig leaders that they must at all costs get the measure passed.[4]

In this way the political writers who accepted the doctrines of the American and French Revolutions had a significant influence on the development of British representative institutions. However, the impact of their ideas on the governing aristocracy was negligible. Of the Members of the unreformed House who supported reform only two based their arguments on a belief in the natural rights of man,[5] and neither of these commanded much respect in the House. The belief in natural rights, and with it the belief in popular sovereignty,

[1] See P. A. Brown, op. cit., and E. Halevy, *History of the English People in the Nineteenth Century* (London, 1949), vols. I and II.

[2] MacCoby, op. cit., p. 66.

[3] We are speaking here of the more conservative Whigs; the Foxite Whigs were always in favour of reform.

[4] See J. R. M. Butler, *The Passing of the Great Reform Bill* (London, 1914), pp. 423–5, for an assessment of the importance of the Political Unions.

[5] Sir Francis Burdett, M.P. for Westminster, 1807–34, and Henry Hunt, M.P. for Preston, 1830–2.

secured acceptance only in the lower ranks of society, and only for a limited period. It had some influence in the Chartist Movement, but this was based on economic discontent rather than political aspiration, and its political achievements were slight. After 1848 reformers ceased to speak in terms of the rights of men (though some continued to speak of the rights of women). By the middle years of the century most working-class leaders had followed the example of middle-class reformers and were phrasing their claims in Utilitarian language.

## THE UTILITARIANS[1]

Utilitarianism is both an ethical and a political doctrine. As an ethical doctrine, it was gradually built up by a number of writers during the eighteenth century. As a political doctrine, it was formulated by Jeremy Bentham, encouraged by James Mill, in the early years of the nineteenth century. Bentham was essentially a legal theorist, and it was not until he reached his late fifties that he turned his attention to the question of Parliamentary reform. But when he did so, he provided the reformers with a completely new set of arguments.

Bentham's approach to the problems of politics was fundamentally different from that of any of the theorists we have so far discussed. On the one hand, he was indifferent to the appeal to English traditions made by Tory writers and to the emphasis placed by the Whigs on the importance of continuity in the social and political system. He regarded Burke's repeated warnings of the dangers of tampering with established institutions as no more than an appeal to prejudice. He was prepared to advocate sweeping changes in the system of government if the principles of social action indicated that these were necessary. On the other hand, he regarded appeals to the natural rights of man as misleading and nonsensical. He had no higher an opinion of Rousseau than of Burke: neither of them understood the principle which was the key to the solution of all moral and political problems.

This principle was that actions were good if they increased the sum total of human happiness and bad if they reduced it. The test of all institutions and laws was whether they were likely to promote the greatest happiness of the greatest number, and other considerations were irrelevant. Clearly this view of politics had explosive possibilities, but it was not until about 1808 that Bentham, who had been writing on legal problems since 1776, espoused the cause of

[1] The best guides to the political ideas of the English Utilitarians are Leslie Stephen, *The English Utilitarians* (3 vols., London, 1900) and E. Halevy, *The Growth of Philosophic Radicalism* (London, 1928).

the Parliamentary reformers. The immediate causes of this development were Bentham's friendship with the political reformer, James
Mill, and (as a precipitating factor) Bentham's resentment at the
way the government had treated his scheme for the construction of a
model prison in London. He felt that there must be something wrong
with a set of rulers who could so wantonly refuse to adopt a plan
which would so clearly contribute to the public welfare. What was
wrong, he concluded, was that the rulers did not really want to
promote the greatest happiness of the greatest number, but were
concerned only with the selfish interests of the class from which they
were drawn. To remedy this state of affairs, the representative system
must be reformed.

Bentham set out his arguments for reform in his *Plan for Parliamentary Reform in the Form of a Catechism*, written in 1809 but not
published until 1817, and the *Constitutional Code*, written between
1818 and 1832, published in part in 1830 and in full in 1841. Similar
arguments were adduced in James Mill's *Essay on Government*,
published in 1820. Two propositions, or principles, are of central
importance in each of these works. The first is the principle of 'self-
preference', by which it is affirmed that all men, including governors,
desire to maximize their own happiness. The second is the principle
of 'greatest happiness', by which it is claimed that 'the right and
proper end' of government is the 'greatest happiness of the greatest
number' of citizens.[1]

If these principles are accepted, the problem becomes clear: it is
to ensure that governors and legislators, in pursuing their own
happiness, will also maximize the happiness of the citizens as a
whole. The Tory view of government provided no answer to this
problem, for a monarch, charged with the duty of governing in
accord with the interests of the whole nation, would merely follow
his own personal desires. The Whig view was equally useless, for
Members of Parliament who were drawn from such a small class as
was general in the eighteenth century, and who were given so much
independence of action, would promote the interests of only that
section of the nation from which they were drawn. Rousseau's theory
of popular sovereignty was likewise condemned, for it rested on a
distinction between men's actual, selfish wills and the general will
they would share as members of a united community, and this was a
distinction that Bentham and Mill would not accept. Indeed, these
writers denied the existence of the contrast implied by many political
theorists between the aggregate of individual interests and the
national interest of the whole. In their view the national interest *was*

[1] See *Constitutional Code*, in *Works*, ed. J. Bowring (London, 1838–43), vol.
IX, p. 8.

the aggregate of individual interests, properly calculated by adding potential pleasures and subtracting potential pains. 'Take for the description of the ultimate end', wrote Bentham, 'the advancement of the universal interest. In the description of this end is included comprehension of all distinguishable particular interests: viz. in such sort, that such of them between which no repugnancy has place may be provided for in conjunction, and without defalcation: while in regard to such of them between which any such repugnancy has place, such defalcations, and such alone, shall be made as, when taken all together, shall leave in the state of a maximum whatsoever residuum of comfort and security may be the result.'[1]

The problem could be solved by what Mill called 'the grand discovery of modern times, the system of representation'.[2] Government should be directed by an elected assembly which 'must have an identity of interest with the community'.[3] The members of this assembly should have no more independence than would be necessary to enable them to carry out their duties, and they should therefore be subject to annual election. The shortness of their term of office would not give them time to develop many interests of their own, as politicians, and would ensure that they represented the true interests of their electors. The suffrage would be universal, not because people had a natural right to vote, but because only in this way could the interests of the whole population be reflected in the legislature.

Bentham advocated the abolition of the Lords and the monarchy, while Mill thought that both could be retained, provided they did not interfere with the course of good government. This difference is unimportant, for both writers agreed that the ultimate power of decision, between elections, should rest with the assembly which would reflect the interests of the whole community. If the majority in this assembly were to support a proposed action, it could be assumed that a majority in the nation would also favour it and that it would increase the sum total of human happiness.

It is evident that this was a comprehensive theory of the proper relationship between public and government. In its comprehensiveness and apparent logic it was far superior to the theories of the other British Radicals and could reasonably be set up in opposition to the conservative view of the constitution of which Burke was the most distinguished exponent.

Whether the theory is valid is another question. The assumption

[1] *Plan of Parliamentary Reform in the Form of Catechism*, in *Works*, op. cit. vol. III, p. 452. The italics of the original have been omitted.
[2] *An Essay on Government* (1820, reprinted Cambridge, 1937), p. 34.
[3] Ibid., p. 35.

about human nature on which the theory is based—that man may be likened to a hedonistic calculating machine—has been thought one-sided by most subsequent students of human affairs. The view of the good life which is implied by Bentham and Mill has proved unacceptable to most subsequent philosophers. In the nineteenth century the fundamental beliefs of the Utilitarians were subject to almost constant attack in academic and literary circles.

At a more practical level, the theory is not without ambiguities and difficulties. For one thing, it is not easy to see why a process of free election in geographical constituencies should automatically produce a House of Commons which is a microcosm of the interests of the nation. Some interests, being those of a minority in each constituency, might never be represented at all. Beyond this, there is the problem presented by the differences in the intensity with which pains and pleasures are felt. Bentham was well aware of this, for in the *Principles of Morals and Legislation* (printed in 1780) he had discussed it at some length. His conclusion about such differences was that either their 'existence cannot be ascertained, or the degree cannot be measured. These, therefore, cannot be taken into account, either by the legislator or the executive magistrate'.[1] This admission has alarming implications for the theory of representation Bentham put forward later in his life: if his ideal legislators were to take no account of differences in intensity, the interests of the majority would always be put first, even if the majority were only mildly in favour of a proposal while the minority felt that it threatened their wellbeing and even their lives.

Despite these difficulties, the Utilitarian theory acquired a great deal of influence in the first half of the nineteenth century. It did so largely because it met the needs of influential groups. The manufacturers of the northern industrial towns and the traders and craftsmen of Greater London were alike in wanting fairly radical reforms in the system of Parliamentary representation. The Whig theory, though it could be used to support reform, was too moderate and too aristocratic in tone for them; the views advanced by Tom Paine and his followers were unacceptable because they insisted on the dangerous doctrine of the natural rights of man. The Utilitarian theory had the advantage of being radical without seeming revolutionary; it was apparently logical and apparently hard-headed; it was admirably suited to be a vehicle for the claims of the new middle classes.

[1] *Works*, op. cit., vol. I, p. 31.

# CHAPTER 4

# Parliamentary Reform and Victorian Liberalism

## THE REFORM OF PARLIAMENT

The controversy that preceded the passage of the 1832 Reform Act was the culmination of a long movement for the reform of the representative system. The Parliamentary debates themselves were extensive and repetitious, taking up no less than sixty-two days in the Committee of the Commons alone.[1] The prolonged controversy gave ample opportunity for all attitudes to the constitution to be expressed, and each of the theories and attitudes mentioned in the preceding pages was reflected in the discussions.

What we have described as the Tory attitude was represented by the Duke of Wellington and his immediate supporters, who assessed the proposals for reform, in their constitutional aspect, almost entirely in terms of the effect they would be likely to have on the executive. These speakers maintained that reform would deprive the Crown of the services of many ministers and potential ministers, who would not be able to secure seats if the corrupt and rotten boroughs were abolished; that it would mean that the executive would no longer be able to rely on the support of Parliament for its measures; and that in consequence the government would become both weak and unstable.

Not all Tories took this view, however. In 1831 and 1832 most of the Tory M.P.'s, while opposing the Bill, did so in terms of the Whig theory of representation, using arguments that owed much to Blackstone and Burke and that were accepted by many members of the Whig Party. The first of these arguments was that any proposal for radical change was dangerous in that it was based on the false assumption that the products of human reason could be superior to the experience and wisdom of past generations. Burke had put this point of view almost fifty years earlier (in May 1782) in his speech on Pitt's motion for a committee to inquire into the state of the representation of the Commons in Parliament. At that time Burke declared that 'it is a presumption of any settled scheme of govern-

---

[1] See J. R. M. Butler, *The Passing of the Great Reform Bill*, p. 235. This book gives a thorough account of the whole sequence of events that culminated in the passage of the Bill.

ment against any untried project, that a nation has long existed and flourished under it'. The British constitution, he continued, is 'made by what is ten thousand times better than choice, it is made by the peculiar circumstances, occasions, tempers, dispositions, and moral, civil and social habitudes of the people, which disclose themselves only in a long space of time'. The representative system must be assumed to be 'as nearly perfect as the necessary imperfection of human affairs and of human creatures will suffer it to be; . . . it is a subject of prudent and honest use and thankful enjoyment, and not of captious criticisms and rash experiment'.[1] Canning put the same view in personal terms, and rather bluntly, when he said that he 'trusted the wisdom of six centuries rather than that of Lord John Russell and Henry Hunt'.[2] And in the debates of 1831 and 1832 a number of speakers developed variations on the same theme.

Another line of argument, which followed from the first, was that a move towards democracy would upset the delicate balance of the constitution, in which King, Lords, and Commons all had a part to play. Peel expressed this view in the following words:

'Without imputing disaffection to the people, or a deliberate intention on their part to undermine the Monarchy or destroy the Peerage, my belief is that neither the Monarchy nor the Peerage can resist with effect the decrees of a House of Commons that is immediately obedient to every popular impulse, and that professes to speak the popular will; and that all the tendencies of such an assembly are towards the increase of its own power, and the intolerance of any extrinsic control.'[3]

Many Members felt, in addition, that a House of Commons which mirrored the people's interests too faithfully 'would also reflect their prejudices and moods of transitory passion'.[4] Peel insisted that 'we are here to consult the interests, not to obey the will of the people, if we honestly believe that that will conflicts with those interests'.[5]

Yet another argument used by those who opposed reform was that changes in the distribution of population, on which the reformers based so much of their case, were actually irrelevant to the issue. It was true that a number of large cities had developed which had no direct representation in Parliament, including Manchester, Birmingham, Leeds and Sheffield. But Parliament included representatives of other industrial cities with similar interests, and places like Manchester and Birmingham were virtually represented by the

[1] See Burke's *Works*, vol. VI, pp. 144–7.    [2] See Butler, op. cit., p. 239.
[3] Quoted in ibid., p. 241.    [4] Ibid.
[5] Speaking on September 21, 1831. See *House of Commons Debates*, 3rd s., v. 7, c. 436.

Members for Liverpool and Leicester. So long as the House contained some Members from industrial cities, so that their interests would be taken into account in Parliamentary deliberations, there was no need for them all to be accorded direct representation.

The Parliamentary proponents of reform can be divided into three groups. The most moderate group denied that the proposed measure was revolutionary either in intention or in its probable consequences. It was rather a matter of modifying existing institutions to meet changed circumstances, and at the same time remedying one or two obvious abuses. While accepting the concept of virtual representation, these moderate reformers did not feel that it could be stretched far enough to cover the disparities of the representative system in 1831. They agreed that population was not a suitable basis for representation, and that the Members for Preston, for instance, could be regarded as virtual representatives of all the cotton towns. But they thought it reasonable that some of the other cotton towns should also be given direct representation,[1] at the expense of some of the tiny boroughs in the southern counties. Sir George Cornewall Lewis supported this in terms of the Whig theory at its purest when he argued that 'it is not more expedient that a large town should be represented rather than a small town because its interests will be watched by its own delegate; but because it is more likely to send a good representative to the national councils'.[2]

The more progressive reformers based their case on a partial acceptance of Utilitarian arguments. The idea that men had natural rights, which formed the basis of so many Radical claims, was anathema to the Whigs, but nobody had dealt with this idea more effectively than Bentham—he called it 'nonsense on stilts'—and his own views, although extreme, were couched in terms of self-interest which they could understand and appreciate. The argument that Parliamentary decisions would be biassed unless the House of Commons directly represented all the interests in the nation seemed sensible, and had obvious attractions for spokesmen from the expanding urban areas who felt that the existing representation of industrial and commercial interests was grossly inadequate.

To the left of these Whigs were the handful of Radicals in the House, not very effective in themselves, but supported offstage by the

---

[1] In Lancashire the boroughs of Liverpool, Wigan, Newton, Preston, Clitheroe and Lancaster enjoyed direct representation. The other urban areas were all represented by the two 'knights of the shire' whom Lancashire as a whole returned. For details of the electoral system at that time, see E. and A. G. Porritt, *The Unreformed House of Commons* (Cambridge, 1909).

[2] *Remarks on the Use and Abuse of Some Political Terms* (first published 1832, new edn., Oxford, 1877), p. 105.

vociferous demands of the Political Unions and the tens of thousands of workers who gathered in mass demonstrations and were reported to be preparing for revolution. This ill-assorted combination eventually secured the passage of the Act.

There is a sense in which the process of passing the Act was more important than the changes it introduced. In the election of 1831 the proposed reform was the only important issue, and in constituencies up and down the country reformers demanded that the candidates pledge themselves to support it if they were returned. The result was a sweeping victory for the reformers, and the subsequent Parliament was the first one in which a large number of Members could claim that they had been instructed by the electors to pursue a specific policy. The other new development was that the Prime Minister persuaded the King to agree to create sufficient new peers to secure the passage of the Bill through the House of Lords. The threat proved sufficient and the Lords eventually let the Bill go through. The potential supremacy of the people over the Commons was thus made clear for the first time in the election of 1831, and the supremacy of the Commons over the Lords was asserted for the first time just twelve months later. It was this that led Disraeli to remark that 'the aristocratic principle has been destroyed in this country, not by the Reform Act, but by the means by which the Reform Act was passed'.[1]

The opponents of reform had argued that the passage of the Bill would transform the constitution and undermine the position of the peerage and the monarchy; and some of the more extreme Radicals took the same view.[2] The events of the next few decades suggested that these expectations had been unfounded: the peerage and the monarchy retained much of their influence, and there was no further reform of the representative system until 1867. But if we take a wider and longer view we can see that the Tories and the Radicals were more accurate in their estimation of the consequences of reform than were most of the Parliamentary supporters of the Bill. On the one hand, reform of Parliament was followed by a series of reforms in other spheres. Municipal government was reformed; justices of the peace lost some of their powers; the administrative system of the state was centralized; the Corn Laws were repealed; sinecures in the civil service were abolished and a system of competitive entry was established; the universities of Oxford and Cambridge were opened to non-Anglicans; the system whereby army commissions could be purchased was modified and eventually abolished. All these reforms, and others, were blows to the landed families whose interests had

[1] What is He?' (1833) reprinted in *Whigs and Whiggism*, p. 19.
[2] For instance, Francis Place. See Butler, op. cit., p. 257.

been secure under the eighteenth-century system: the measures can all be regarded as part of a general movement for political reform which won its first and most important victory with the passing of the 1832 Reform Act.

On the other hand, the passing of the Act made further reforms of the representative system inevitable. The immediate effects of the Act were relatively small: in summary, it abolished or reduced the representation of the smallest boroughs; gave representation to the new industrial towns; gave the larger counties more Members than the smaller, instead of two each, as hitherto; and imposed on the whole of England and Wales a franchise which was uniform except for the distinction between counties and boroughs. But the first three of these changes amounted to an implicit acceptance of the principle of representation by population; and the fourth, while it increased the total electorate by less than 50 per cent,[1] implied that henceforth representation was to be accorded to individuals rather than communities. In this way the old principles of representation were abandoned, and the gates were opened to further instalments of reform. Burke's powerful arguments in favour of the eighteenth-century system could no longer be successfully invoked, and the opponents of further reforms had no firm ground on which to take their stand. Partly because of this, Victorian debates on Parliamentary reform were never so clear-cut or intellectually coherent as those before the Act of 1832.

## VICTORIAN LIBERALISM

It is fair to say that Victorian discussions about representative government were dominated by Liberal ideas, and that these ideas, at first held by only a minority of politicians and writers, gradually won widespread acceptance until by the end of the century they had come to constitute the prevailing constitutional doctrine. These Liberal ideas were by no means entirely novel, but developed, with a new emphasis of their own, from the Whig and Radical ideas that had moulded progressive opinion at the time of the Reform Act. Before discussing their development it must be emphasized that in this and the following chapter we shall use the word Liberal to refer to the ideas and the men who espoused them, rather than to members of the Liberal Party as such.

The new emphasis of the Victorian period was that after the 1830's Liberals came to discuss politics less and less in terms of a conflict of interests and more and more in terms of a conflict of opinions.

[1] The electorate was increased from 510,000 to 720,000; i.e. from 5 per cent to 7 per cent of the adult population.

The Societies for the Abolition of the Slave Trade and the Abolition of Slavery were the first examples of a new kind of political movement, devoted to the furtherance of a moral cause rather than to the advancement of an interest. Their success presaged the moralization of politics that took place during the Victorian era. This was seen, on the one hand, in the proliferation of reform movements devoted to moral causes, and in the growing tendency to discuss even economic matters, such as the repeal of the corn laws, in moral as well as in economic terms. On the other hand, it was reflected in the tendency to emphasize Parliament's role as a debating chamber in which issues of principle could be resolved. Whigs, Radicals, and Conservatives alike shared in this tendency, which later became one of the central features of Victorian Liberalism. On the Radical side, John Stuart Mill asserted that Parliament should be a 'Congress of Opinions: an arena in which not only the general opinion of the nation, but that of every section of it . . . can produce itself in full flight and challenge discussion'.[1] On the Conservative side, Disraeli claimed that Parliament should be a 'mirror of the mind as well as the material interests of England'.[2]

This change in emphasis tended to undermine some of the principles of the Whig theory of representation. If Members represented bodies of opinion rather than communities, it no longer made sense to defend the idea of virtual representation. It was one thing to argue that the material interests of citizens would be adequately represented so long as Parliament contained Members from all the areas, industries and professions of the country. Given the tacit assumption that all people engaged in the same industry shared the same interests, it was plausible to maintain that, for instance, the unenfranchised citizens of a cotton town were virtually represented by an M.P. for another cotton town. This kind of argument for virtual representation could not reasonably be advanced by Liberals who said, first, that the main function of M.P.'s was to represent individual opinions and, second, that there was no necessary connection between opinions and occupations. The logical implication of this new emphasis on opinions was that everyone capable of holding an opinion should have the vote.

After 1832 the followers of Bentham, known variously as Benthamites, Utilitarians, and Philosophic Radicals, continued to propagate the doctrine of manhood suffrage. They formed a group of great intellectual power and considerable organizing ability, and their

[1] *Considerations on Representative Government* (first pub. 1861, new edn. ed. R. B. McCallum, Oxford, 1946), p. 172.
[2] Speech in the House of Commons, February 28, 1859, quoted in R. J. White (ed.) *The Conservative Tradition* (London, 1950), p. 167.

influence on the course of British politics was greater than any other group of reformers has ever enjoyed. Until his death in 1836 the leader of the group was James Mill, who has been described as 'the indispensable intermediary between Bentham and the external world'.[1] Mill propagated Utilitarian ideas in a more concise and direct form than Bentham himself was capable of, and he had a passionate belief in the need for political and administrative reform. His associates included such influential persons as Francis Place, the tailor of Charing Cross whose activities as a political and electoral organizer had been crowned with striking success, John Black, owner of the *Morning Chronicle*, J. R. McCulloch, the Scottish economist, and Joseph Hume and George Grote, Members of Parliament and founders of the Anti-Corn-Law Association.[2] The group also had the support of a younger generation of writers gathered around John Stuart Mill, who had founded the Utilitarian Society as early as 1823, when he was only 17.

The group believed that politics, like economics, could become a science. The aims and nature of legislation should be determined by applying the principle of utility; the representative system should be reconstructed so that the House of Commons would be capable of assessing the greatest happiness of the greatest number of citizens; and the penal system should be reformed according to the principles Bentham had discovered. In all this the Utilitarians followed the lead given by their master, but in one important respect they diverged from his teachings. Bentham had believed that the merits of legislation in economic affairs, as in any other field, could be tested only by assessing the pleasure and pain it would be likely to cause. On this view there was no general ground for objecting to measures of economic planning and control, for each measure had to be considered on its merits. Bentham himself suggested a number of economic and social measures which it might be appropriate for the government to undertake, including nationalization of the Bank of England, general control of other banking, public works to deal with unemployment, responsibility for health services and public transport, and the conduct of life insurance and the activities of friendly societies.

The Utilitarians of the 1830's, however, accepted the full implications of the teachings of Adam Smith and Ricardo. They believed that the natural harmony of economic interests was such that any kind of government intervention in economic affairs would be certain

---

[1] E. Halevy, *The Growth of Philosophic Radicalism* (London, 1928), p. 308. Bentham himself died in 1832, two days after the third reading of the Reform Bill which his ideas had helped to promote.

[2] Later known as the Anti-Corn-Law League.

to diminish the total sum of human wealth, and was thus undesirable. They therefore propagated the gospel of *laissez-faire*, and were individualists not only in the sense that they believed each individual to be the best judge of his own interests but also in the sense that they thought individual freedom, by which they meant freedom from government intervention, was necessary in the interests of all.

Utilitarian ideas on the aims of legislation were accepted more quickly than their ideas on the suffrage. The Poor Law Amendment Act of 1834 put an end to the system whereby poor people were cared for by their communities, and had the effect of forcing unemployed persons to migrate in search of work. Freedom to deal in land and other property was established by a series of Acts between 1832 and 1845, and freedom to lend money for interest was established by the repeal of the usury laws. The cause of civil and religious freedom was advanced by the extension of the Toleration Act to Unitarians in 1813, the Roman Catholic Relief Act of 1829, the Nonconformist's Chapels Act of 1844, and a number of other measures. These were only the most notable of a series of legislative reforms based on the individualist philosophy which were passed between 1820 and 1850 and which made it possible to refer to the middle decades of the century as the age of individualism.[1]

Utilitarian ideas on the suffrage met with greater resistance because the social groups represented in Parliament were genuinely afraid of the consequences of giving the vote to illiterate labourers. Even though many Whig and Liberal leaders could appreciate the logical force of the arguments for a further and much more radical extension of the franchise, they felt that the ignorance of the multitude was an unsurmountable barrier to such a reform. In this situation it was natural for Parliamentarians to argue that only informed opinions were worth consideration, and to insist that education was a necessary qualification for the right to vote.

James Mill had anticipated this reaction in his *Essay on Government*, written in 1820. This essay was published anonymously in a supplement to the *Encyclopaedia Britannica*, and Mill clearly felt it appropriate to couch his views in moderate terms that would appeal to, or at least would not greatly shock, his publisher and readers. After a crisp outline of Benthamite theories which implied that universal suffrage was desirable, he suggested that in practice the

[1] The period is also commonly referred to as 'the age of *laissez-faire*', but this is misleading. Certainly the mercantilist policies of an earlier period were abandoned, and, as noted, some restrictions on business activities were abolished. But some controls on industrial conditions were imposed and manufacturers, as a group, were subject to more legislative regulation in this period than in the eighteenth century.

vote need only be given to male citizens over the age of 40. In terms similar to those used by advocates of the Whig theory of virtual representation, he argued that the opinions of women and of younger men would be adequately represented if the older men in each family were enfranchised. Although the Benthamite theory demanded that people from all levels of society should be given the vote so that their interests could be represented, Mill proceeded to reassure his educated readers by asserting that the ignorant multitude 'would be sure to be guided by their advice and example'. 'There can be no doubt', he wrote, 'that the middle rank, which gives to science, to art, and to legislation itself, their most distinguished ornaments, the chief source of all that has exalted and refined human nature, is that portion of the community of which, if the basis of representation were ever so far extended, the opinion would ultimately decide.'[1]

This argument, though frequently quoted, did not convince many people. By the 1850's a considerable section of public and Parliamentary opinion had been won over to the cause of radical reform, but few of the reformers felt it safe to assume that ignorant people would seek the advice of their betters before casting their votes. Instead, they placed their hopes on another suggestion Mill had made, and which was developed by his son until it became one of the main articles of faith in the latter's philosophy. This was the belief that political reform would itself lead to the education of the masses: that granting men the right to vote would develop their sense of social responsibility and would stimulate them to understand and prepare themselves to take part in political life.

After Liberal reform bills had been introduced and defeated in 1852, 1854, and 1860, and a Conservative bill had met the same fate in 1859, it became clear that further reform could not be long delayed. In 1865 Gladstone defined the Liberal attitude as 'trust in the people, only qualified by prudence' and the Conservative attitude as 'mistrust of the people, only qualified by fear'[2] and this was only a somewhat tendentious way of saying that the parties were not deeply divided on the question. Lord Grey had already warned the Conservatives that they would lose public support unless they agreed to reform,[3] and in 1867 it was Disraeli, not the Liberals, who introduced the bill that was enacted.

The passage of this Act was a triumph for the Liberal view of politics This view found no more eloquent spokesmen than John

[1] *An Essay on Government* (reprinted Cambridge, 1937), p. 72.

[2] In a speech at Chester, May 31, 1865, quoted in A. Bullock and M. Shock (eds.), *The Liberal Tradition* (London, 1956), p. 143.

[3] See *Parliamentary Government Considered With Reference to a Reform of Parliament* (London, 1858), p. 149.

Stuart Mill, who developed and revised the Utilitarian ideas of his father in ways that reflected not only the faith but also the anxieties and inconsistencies of Victorian Liberalism. Rather than follow the manoeuvres and counter-manoeuvres which led up to the passage of the second Reform Act, it will be more rewarding to examine the Liberal doctrine as it is expressed in Mill's writings.

## JOHN STUART MILL'S VIEWS ON REPRESENTATION

Mill's *Considerations on Representative Government* is the most systematic attempt ever made in Britain to set out a theory of the purpose and proper organization of representative institutions. Mill had been discussing and reflecting on the problems of representative government for over thirty years before he wrote the book, and he was influenced by a number of writers, of whom the most important were Bentham, James Mill, Coleridge and Tocqueville. His early training was in the principles of the Benthamite school, and he has described in his *Autobiography* both the way in which his father inculcated this doctrine and the way in which his reservations grew until he was forced to reject, one by one, the fundamental tenets of Bentham's social and political philosophy.

In 1829, when Macaulay attacked James Mill's *Essay on Government* in an article in the *Edinburgh Review*, the younger Mill 'could not help feeling . . . that there was truth in several of his strictures on my father's treatment of the subject'. In particular, he noted that: 'Identity of interest between the governing body and the community at large is not, in any practical sense which can be attached to it, the only thing on which good government depends; neither can this identity of interest be secured by the mere conditions of election.'[1] This admission, if true, destroyed the basis of Bentham's and James Mill's theory of representation, though at this time J. S. Mill was apparently unwilling to draw this implication.

In 1835 he returned to the question of the popular interest in two articles in the *London Review*, in which he argued that the real interest of the people was not to decide every question for themselves, but to elect to the legislature the most educated and able persons who would take decisions on their behalf and should be left free, as far as possible, to decide where the people's best interests lie.[2] This was an unsatisfactory argument because of its ambiguous use of the term 'interests', but it was perhaps a stepping stone to his analysis of the term in his essay on Coleridge. In this Mill distin-

[1] *Autobiography* (first published 1873, reprinted Oxford, 1935), pp. 133–4.
[2] See *Dissertations and Discussions* (London, 1859), vol. I, Appendix, pp. 468 and 472.

guishes between men's objective and ultimate interests, as they would appear to 'a calculating bystander', and the immediate interests and gratifications which men habitually seek. He suggests that Bentham's failure to draw such a distinction is an example of his shallowness as a political philosopher. Of Bentham's political theory, he says, 'it would be difficult to find among theories proceeding from philosophers one less like a philosophical theory, or, in the works of analytical minds, anything more entirely unanalytical'.[1]

Although Mill had thus, by 1840, rejected the basic assumptions and arguments of the theory of which he had been a youthful exponent, and with which he was still generally identified in the public mind, he had not rejected the practical conclusions which Bentham and the elder Mill drew from this theory. He believed that they were essentially right in their criticisms of the British political system and in their advocacy of universal or manhood suffrage, though he based these conclusions on somewhat different arguments.

In a pamphlet published in 1859 Mill gave two reasons for extending the franchise without delay. One was that the interests of the unenfranchised were apt to be put second to those of the enfranchised. The other, which Mill regarded as 'still more important', was that the franchise was 'one of the means of national education'.[2] This insistence on the importance of education arose from Mill's fear that democracy might lead to the tyranny of an ignorant multitude. Whereas Bentham and the elder Mill were concerned about the dangers of rule by the minority, the younger Mill and his contemporary, Alexis de Tocqueville, were almost equally concerned about the dangers of rule by the majority. In his essay *On Liberty* Mill insisted that majority views could be just as fallacious as minority views, and drew attention to the tyranny that the majority might exercise over public opinion. In his reports on American society Tocqueville provided evidence for Mill's arguments from the one country which, in its progress towards popular government, was ahead of Great Britain. However, on balance the lessons to be drawn from *Democracy in America* were encouraging rather than depressing, for it appeared that the wide franchise in that country had had a beneficial effect on the general education and attitudes of the people which outweighed the dangers of giving the vote to poorly educated classes. Mill regarded this book as the most masterly analysis of the virtues and limitations of popular government that had ever been published,[3] and the views which he advanced in his later writings clearly owed a great deal to Tocqueville's work.

[1] See *Dissertations and Discussions* (London, 1859), vol. I, pp. 449–50.
[2] *Thoughts on Parliamentary Reform* (London, 1859), p. 17.
[3] See *Autobiography*, p. 162.

In his second review of this work, Mill quoted with approval a long passage from Tocqueville's chapter on 'The real advantages that American society derives from democratic government', which can best be summarized in a few extracts. 'It is incontestable', said Tocqueville, 'that the people frequently conduct public business very ill; but it is impossible that the people should take a part in public business without extending the circle of their ideas, and without quitting the ordinary routine of their mental occupations. The humblest individual who is called upon to co-operate in the government of society acquires a certain degree of self-respect; and, as he possesses power, minds more enlightened than his own offer him their services. . . . He takes a part in political undertakings which did not originate in his own conception, but which give him a taste for such undertakings. New ameliorations are daily suggested to him in the property which he holds in common with others, and this gives him the desire of improving that property which is peculiarly his own. He is, perhaps, neither happier nor better than those who came before him; but he is better informed and more active. . . . Not what is done by a democratic government, but what is done under a democratic government by private agency, is really great. Democracy does not confer the most skilful kind of government upon the people, but it produces that which the most skilful governments are frequently unable to awaken, namely, an all-pervading and restless activity—a superabundant force—an energy which is never seen elsewhere, and which may, under favourable circumstances, beget the most amazing benefits. These are the true advantages of democracy.'[1]

Tocqueville did not ignore the other arguments for democracy; indeed, he elaborated what were essentially the Utilitarian arguments about the representation of interests, though in a more subtle form than the Utilitarians had ever given them; but he appeared to think that the social benefits of democracy were more certain, and could be stated with less need for qualification, than the purely political benefits.

Mill adopted this view as his own. He tells us that before he read Tocqueville he had already come to regard the choice of political institutions 'as a moral and educational question more than one of material interests, thinking that it ought to be decided mainly by the consideration, what great improvement in life and culture stands next in order for the people concerned, as the conditions of their further progress, and what institutions are most likely to promote that'.[2] Tocqueville's argument that in America the existence of

[1] Quoted by Mill in *Dissertations and Discussions*, vol. II, pp. 28–9.
[2] *Autobiography*, pp. 144–5.

democratic institutions was largely responsible for the enterprise and social advancement of the people convinced Mill that representative democracy could best be justified in these terms. In *Representative Government* he asserts that the merit of any set of political institutions 'consists partly of the degree in which they promote the general advancement of the community, including under that phrase advancement in intellect, in virtue, and in practical activity and efficiency; and partly of the degree of perfection with which they organize the moral, intellectual, and active worth already existing, so as to operate with the greatest effect on public affairs'.[1] In subsequent chapters he claims that representative government is, by these criteria, superior to all other forms; that the best kind of representative government is one in which public participation is 'as great as the general degree of improvement of the community will allow'; and that 'nothing less can be ultimately desirable than the admission of all to a share in the sovereign power of the State'.[2] A certain benefit of such a reform, he insists, would be 'that education of the intelligence and of the sentiments which is carried down to the very lowest ranks of the people when they are called to take part in acts which directly affect the great interests of their country'.[3]

These arguments for Parliamentary reform are on a different plane from those advanced by Bentham and James Mill. The ideal of promoting the intellectual and moral advancement of the community is not the same as that of promoting the greatest happiness of the greatest number. The argument that extending the franchise is one of the best ways of encouraging citizens to take an active interest in public affairs is very different from the argument that it is the only way to increase the efficiency of the government. These new arguments, if logically less rigorous than those of the older Utilitarianism, were psychologically more plausible, and they were accepted by an ever-increasing number of people.

It is clear that in the period between 1820 and 1860 the ideas of the radical reformers underwent two kinds of change. From being the rigorous doctrine of a small minority, they gradually became part of a much more diffuse body of thought that was accepted by the Liberals in Parliament and, eventually, by the majority of the nation. At the same time they were affected by the concern with moral progress and personal improvement that characterized the mid-nineteenth century. In the early days the reformers advocated an extension of the suffrage irrespective of education; later they decried the dangers of granting the vote to the masses on the ground that the franchise would stimulate education, in the widest sense of the

---

[1] *Considerations on Representative Government*, p. 129.
[2] Ibid., p. 151.　　　　　　　　　　[3] Ibid., pp. 209–10.

term; and later still J. S. Mill was claiming that the spread of moral and intellectual virtues that would follow the extension of the franchise was in fact the main reason why the electoral system should be reformed.

This was no longer a Utilitarian viewpoint, in the strict sense of the term, but it was of the essence of Victorian Liberalism. Gladstone's statement that all men are 'morally entitled to come within the pale of the constitution' showed his acceptance of Mill's argument. Lowe's comment that 'we must at least persuade our future masters to learn their letters' was testimony from an opponent of reform to that argument's relevance. And when W. E. Forster introduced the 1870 Education Bill he told Parliament that 'now that we have given them (the people) political power, we must not wait any longer to give them education'.

Developments after the Reform Acts of 1867 and 1885 did much to justify the Liberals' hopes. The extensions of the franchise did not, it is true, bring about quite that diffusion of the spirit of commercial enterprise, that emulation of the American way of life, for which Mill apparently hoped. But they certainly stimulated the growth of popular education; they enabled working men to feel that they were not excluded from the political community; they encouraged the growth of political clubs and associations in all parts of the country, with Parliamentary affairs as the focus of their attention; and they made possible the subsequent decision of the trade unions to seek their political ends by Parliamentary representation rather than by strikes and threats of violence.

Mill's other views on representative government can be dealt with more briefly. They consist partly of an argument in favour of votes for women and partly of a number of practical suggestions regarding the representative system of his time. The argument in favour of votes for women was not so much a part of Mill's general case for the extension of the franchise as a part of his general case for the removal of the legal, social, and political disabilities from which women then suffered. He believed that as women were equal to men save for 'the accident of sex', it was a matter of simple justice that they should be treated equally.[1] In a speech on the subject during the debates on the 1867 Reform Bill, he claimed that justice requires 'that we should not, capriciously and without cause, withhold from one what we give to another'.[2]

This was a different kind of argument from those Mill put forward in favour of extending the male franchise in his book on *Representative Government*. The practical suggestions about the representative

[1] This is argued at length in *The Subjection of Women* (London, 1869).
[2] See *The Admission of Women to the Electoral Franchise* (London, 1867), p. 4.

system were more in line with the argument of the book, though the logical connection is not strong and acceptance of Mill's general case does not necessarily involve acceptance of all his particular recommendations.

The most important of these recommendations were qualifications to the principle of universal suffrage which Mill added because of the fear that otherwise the opinions of the educated classes would be submerged in the prejudices of the ill-informed majority. Mill hoped this would be only a temporary problem, to which the spread of education would eventually provide an answer. But in the meantime he recommended that the vote should be withheld from those who could not read, write, and do simple arithmetic. At the other end of the scale, he suggested that people of superior intelligence and accomplishments should have more than one vote, so as to give their opinions the weight which they deserved. Persons in skilled and managerial occupations should have two or three extra votes; persons holding diplomas and degrees should be similarly privileged; and open examinations should be held at which all but the very poorest persons would be able to qualify for an additional vote or two if they could show the required degree of intelligence. The qualification is necessary because people who were so poor that they paid no taxes would not be enfranchised at all, on the ground that they would have no personal interest in the economic management of public funds.

The difficulty about these suggestions was that, however many theoretical arguments might be adduced in their favour, they would inevitably have been regarded by the voters as no more and no less than a way of benefiting the wealthier classes and penalizing the poorer. In Victorian Britain there were practical reasons for caution in extending the franchise, but the simple method of relaxing the property qualification step by step was easier and less controversial than Mill's complicated proposals, and had the additional advantage of having as its logical conclusion the straightforward system of 'one man, one vote'. It is not surprising that, although there was a good deal of discussion of plural voting, the simpler method was preferred.

Another chapter of *Representative Government* was devoted to the problem of securing adequate representation of all shades of opinion in society. In this chapter Mill adduced the proposition that 'real equality of representation is not obtained unless any set of electors amounting to the average number of a constituency, wherever in the country they happen to reside, have the power of combining with one another to return a representative'.[1] He proposed that electors might be given this power by the adoption of an ingenious

[1] *Considerations on Representative Government*, p. 194.

electoral system, which had been suggested in 1859 by Thomas Hare, in which 'any elector would be at liberty to vote for any candidate in whatever part of the country he might offer himself'.[1] In this way any minority opinion having the minimum quota of adherents would be represented by at least one Member of Parliament and every voter (except those few belonging to minorities too tiny to qualify) would be represented by the man of his choice, instead of by, at best, the better of two or three available candidates and, at worst, a man against whom the elector had voted.

The advocacy of this scheme reflected both Mill's faith in the rationality of electors and his view of the functions of M.P.'s. He visualized voting decisions as purely intellectual decisions, made by people whose sole concern would be to ensure that their individual opinions about politics were reflected as closely as possible by their representatives. Since opinions were not necessarily related to place of residence, geographical constituencies had no special merit and self-elected constituencies would be better. The fact that Hare's electoral system would probably result in a Parliament in which no one opinion could command a majority was not seen by Mill as a drawback, for he was in any case fearful of the possible tyranny of the majority that might follow the democratization of the franchise.

Other Liberals, although arguing from the same premises, were unwilling to draw such radical conclusions. Many of them felt that the electoral system he proposed would lead to the election of dogmatic and doctrinaire Members who could not join in the normal process of bargaining and compromise without sacrificing their chances of re-election, and that this would weaken the whole system of Parliamentary government. The proposal met with no more practical success than the idea of plural voting or Mill's suggestions about the open ballot and the reform of the House of Lords.

Nevertheless, Mill's book illustrates a number of Liberal attitudes that came to be very widely accepted in the last few decades of the nineteenth century, and the illustration is all the clearer because Mill was more willing than most politicians to push his arguments to their logical conclusions. The following beliefs, all held by Mill, were at the heart of the Liberal view of politics. First, men behave in politics as rational individuals, each forming his own opinions and considering his own interests. Second, although a wide variety of opinions is to be expected, and indeed is to be encouraged, there is no fundamental conflict between men's interests. Third, only men with a certain degree of education can form worthwhile opinions about politics. Fourth, the extension of the franchise should march hand in

[1] *Considerations on Representative Government*, p. 94.

hand with the spread of popular education, and both should en-compass the whole body of citizens as soon as possible.

These beliefs formed the basis of the Liberal theory of representation, and this theory was itself an integral part of a much wider theory of constitutional government. This wider theory will be discussed in the next chapter.

# CHAPTER 5

# The Liberal View of the Constitution

Controversies about the organization of government in Victorian times were not confined to the question of representation, and the Liberal theory of representation was only one aspect of the Liberal view of the constitution.[1] This view, as it emerged in the second half of the last century, comprised four distinct but inter-related doctrines. First, there was the theory of representation we have just discussed, the eventual aims of which were crudely expressed in the popular slogan 'one man, one vote; one vote, one value'. Second, there was the doctrine of Parliamentary sovereignty, combined with the belief that in any conflict between the two Houses the views of the Commons ought to prevail. It was asserted that supreme power in the state resided in Parliament, and did so rightfully because the Members of Parliament represented the opinions and interests of the whole body of citizens. On this view the House of Lords could have no more than a subsidiary role. Third, Liberals insisted that ministers of the Crown were accountable to Parliament for their actions, and not, except in a formal sense, to the monarch. Only in this way, they maintained, could the political system provide for responsible as well as representative government, in the sense in which the term 'responsible government' was generally used in the nineteenth century.[2] Fourth, Liberals attached great importance to certain legal principles that came to be known as 'the Rule of Law'. The relevant parts of this doctrine were, first, that no man could be deprived of liberty or property unless he had been found guilty, after a fair trial, of breaking the established law of the land; and second, that all men were equal before the law, officers of the Crown having no privileges that were not accorded to other citizens.

Much could be written about each of these doctrines, for they have numerous and controversial implications. At this point, however, it will suffice to make two general comments on their nature. The first is that, taken as a whole, this view of the constitution amounted to a theory of legitimate power. As such, it had the great advantage

[1] In this chapter, as in the last, the word Liberal is used to refer to the theory and its exponents, and not, except where indicated, to the policies and the members of the Liberal Party as such.

[2] The development and nature of ministerial responsibility is discussed in Part IV of this book.

over the other two theories that have inspired democratic reformers, those associated with the names of Locke and Rousseau, that it did not depend upon the notion of a mythical social contract. Moreover, it was clear and precise where the theories of Locke and Rousseau were, in their different ways, vague and ambiguous. As an ideology of reform it had all the virtues, not least among which was the fact that it was tied so closely to existing institutions in Britain. Partly because it was a local rather than a universal theory, it could readily be accepted by the man-in-the-street. It was not necessary to be a philosopher to understand the proposition that Britain was, or soon would be, a free country because its citizens had only to obey what their freely-elected representatives decreed, and could only be punished if their disobedience were established in a fair trial to the satisfaction of twelve fellow-citizens. It was largely because of the popularity of the Liberal theory in the country that Disraeli introduced the second Reform Bill and later Conservative leaders accepted, somewhat reluctantly, that sooner or later everyone must have the vote.

The second general comment that is worth making is that in the past 130 years the Liberal theory of the constitution has passed through three phases. It has been successively the basis of a programme of reform, a slightly idealized version of an existing situation, and a set of traditional principles to which practice no longer corresponds. These phases have overlapped in time. As an ideology of reform the Liberal theory was propagated in the 1830's, had attained widespread popularity by the 1860's, but was not fully translated into practice until the Representation of the People Act of 1948. But by the 1880's some parts of the Liberal theory had become the accepted doctrine of the constitution and by 1930 some critics were already asserting that political developments had created a gulf between Liberal principles and current practice. These three phases of the Liberal theory of the constitution will be outlined more fully in the remaining sections of this chapter.

## LIBERALISM AS AN IDEOLOGY OF REFORM

The passage of the 1867 Reform Act was, in quantitative terms, the greatest single achievement of the movement to liberalize the representative system.[1] At one stroke the electorate was almost doubled, and in the towns the effect of the Act was to ensure that at least one member of virtually every household had the vote. The Act also deprived the House of Commons of the right to decide on the

[1] The 1832 Act was more important in terms of the principles involved but it did not make so much difference to the size of the electorate.

validity of elections in cases of protest, and put questions of this kind within the jurisdiction of the courts. It has been said that this, 'in conjunction with much more rigid limits on expenses, started a real move towards electoral purity'.[1] This move was carried further by the adoption of the secret ballot in 1872 and the establishment of effective sanctions against bribery by the Corrupt Practices Act of 1883.

The further extension of the franchise in 1884 gave the vote to nearly all adult men, and increased the electorate by 67 per cent. Perhaps equally important, the Redistribution Act of the following year was the first important step towards the equalization of territorial constituencies. Before this Act the electorates in the most populous constituencies in England were over forty times as big as those in the smallest constituencies; after the Act the ratio was only seven to one.

These two Acts did not satisfy the Radical wing of the Liberal Party, led by Joseph Chamberlain. Indeed, the Acts represented a compromise by Gladstone between the demands of the Radicals (some of whom were in his cabinet) and the conservatism of the House of Lords. The prolonged debates on reform between 1883 and 1885 included discussion of a number of Radical proposals which had never before received substantial support in Parliament. One was the proposal that women should be enfranchised, which was rejected by only 130 votes to 114 in 1883. Another was the demand for the abolition of the right of business proprietors to qualify for a vote in respect of their business premises as well as in respect of their residences. Several attempts were made by Radicals to change this state of affairs, but they were all successfully opposed by Gladstone, who would otherwise have lost the support of Members with Whig sympathies. Yet another Radical proposal was to abolish the university constituencies. This was supported quite widely and seemed at one time to have a good chance of success, but by the time the vote was taken the government had given pledges to the opposition which made acceptance of the proposal impossible. Finally, a number of Radicals demanded that the powers of the Lords should be curtailed, so that the permanent Conservative majority there should no longer be able to veto measures passed by the Commons. The feelings of the Radicals on this issue can be gauged by the following passage from a speech by Chamberlain, then President of the Board of Trade, at a public meeting at Bristol on November 26, 1883.

'What we have to deal with, the evil against which we are protesting, is the inordinate influence and power which minorities have obtained in our system. . . . A minority of the population, and only a minority,

[1] D. E. Butler, *The Electoral System in Britain: 1918–1951* (Oxford, 1953), p. 5.

have any votes at all at the present time; of that minority another minority, not more than one-fifth, returns a majority of the House of Commons; and when this minority of a minority has succeeded in passing anything . . . then we allow another minority, an infinitesimal fraction of the people, without any representative authority whatsoever, whom we call a House of Lords, to exercise an absolute veto.'[1]

When the Lords held up the Franchise Bill in the following year their action caused bitter criticism from the Radicals. Chamberlain coined the phrase 'the Peers against the People'; John Morley made speeches and wrote articles on the theme 'Mend them or end them'; John Bright insisted that the Lords' power of veto should be replaced by a limited power of delay; and mass meetings of protest were held in Hyde Park and elsewhere. The agitation did not affect the position of the Lords, for Gladstone made an agreement with Salisbury whereby the Tory peers accepted the Franchise Bill in return for a scheme of redistribution which would have the practical effect of increasing Conservative representation in the Commons for any given proportion of votes which the party secured. However, the agitation was a prelude to the successful campaign against the Lords which the Liberals were to wage twenty-seven years later.

This later campaign was the one which carried the liberalization of the Parliamentary system its next stage forward. It was probably inevitable that sooner or later the Lords' powers would be reduced, and the behaviour of the Conservative peers from 1905 to 1910 precipitated this development. By rejecting the Liberal Government's bills one after another, they were thwarting the wishes of the electorate and 'breaking the spirit, though not yet the letter, of the constitution'.[2] The rejection of the 1909 budget played into the reformers' hands: it was a breach of what many people regarded as one of the most fundamental unwritten rules of the constitution, that the power of the purse belonged to the Commons alone, and it led inexorably to the passage of the Parliament Act in 1911. By this Act the power of the second chamber was broken and its influence was greatly reduced. Controversies about its composition and value have continued to this day, but after 1911 the supremacy of the Commons was an established fact of the British political system.

With this reform the most important of the Liberal objectives had been attained. The great majority of adult male citizens were enfranchised; the electoral laws prevented bribery and intimidation; the supremacy of the Commons over the Lords was firmly established

[1] Quoted in S. MacCoby, *English Radicalism: 1853–1886* (London, 1938), p. 282.    [2] R. C. K. Ensor, *England: 1870–1914* (Oxford, 1936), p. 409.

in law; and the conventions relating to the Crown had developed so that it was now improbable that any monarch would try to exert the kind of influence over his ministers that Queen Victoria had sometimes tried to exert over hers. The remainder of the agenda of Liberal reforms comprised complete manhood suffrage, which was attained by general agreement in 1918; votes for women; the abolition of plural voting by business proprietors and university graduates;[1] equal electoral districts; and, much less certainly, the establishment of proportional representation.

The campaign for female suffrage was violent and prolonged, the unhappiest page in the whole history of electoral reform. The Liberal Party was divided on the issue, and the Prime Minister and his colleagues could invoke no clear principle in support of their opposition to the reform. The agitation was led partly by extremists, and in retrospect it seems as if the entire episode was characterized by unnecessary obstinacy on both sides. It is likely that the violence of the suffragettes' campaign actually delayed the achievement of their object, for the Government was determined not to yield to intimidation, and did not support the reform until after the war had brought the militant campaign to an end.[2]

The abolition of plural voting by business proprietors was not of great practical importance, for the number of votes involved was never large. The Liberal Government attempted to carry out this reform first in 1906, when the measure was rejected by the Lords, and then in 1912, when the bill was withdrawn because of a procedural complication. In 1930 the Labour Government, supported by the Liberal Party, included the abolition of this kind of plural voting in its Electoral Reform Bill, but the Bill was amended out of all recognition by the House of Lords and it never reached the Statute Book.[3] It was not until the Labour Party came to power with a clear majority in 1945 that both kinds of plural voting (and therefore the university seats) were abolished. It was a coincidence that the election immediately following this reform was the first general election in the twentieth century in which the result was so close that plural voting would have affected the composition of the government.

Although the scale of plural voting was never great enough (with this one exception) to have made much practical difference, its survival for so long after the general principle of 'one man, one vote' had been accepted is in itself an interesting phenomenon. The

[1] These forms of plural voting are to be distinguished from the kind advocated by J. S. Mill, which was never adopted.
[2] See below, p. 101, for Asquith's remarks on the subject.
[3] See D. E. Butler, op. cit., Chapter 3 for details of this Bill and its progress through Parliament.

arguments about the business vote show that the eighteenth-century belief in the representation of communities was not entirely dead, even in the mid-twentieth century. One argument frequently used in favour of the business vote was that without it there would be no basis for the survival of the City of London as a separate constituency. Some people were apparently so reluctant to see the disappearance of the separate representation of the City in Parliament that they thought the business vote was worth preserving on this ground alone.

The discussion of university representation also produced a number of arguments drawn from earlier modes of thought. Many Members defended the university seats in a manner reminiscent of the defence of rotten boroughs before 1832: whatever their merits as constituencies, they returned distinguished M.P.'s who might not otherwise be able to secure election. Another argument was reminiscent of John Stuart Mill: the second vote for graduates was a way of giving political recognition to the claims of intelligence. Yet another argument was that, irrespective of the merits of either the constituencies or the electors, university representation served the valuable function of ensuring the return of Members who were independent of the parties. The factual basis of this assertion was dubious, since between 1935 and 1948 eleven of the twelve university representatives had consistently supported the Conservative cause. But it was an interesting example of a Liberal argument being used to defend a pre-Liberal institution in a post-Liberal period.

The advocacy of equal electoral districts was an important part of the Radical programme in the 1830's, but by the turn of the century most of the steam had gone out of this argument. As noted, the redistribution of 1885 had greatly reduced the inequality of constituencies, and Liberals were prepared to accept that, up to a point, the principle of equality had to give way to the claims of local interests and administrative convenience. There was a further redistribution of seats in 1918, but after that nothing was done until 1944, when four permanent Electoral Boundary Commissions[1] were established. Their instructions were to undertake a more or less continuous review of constituency boundaries with the object of securing something approaching equality in the population of constituencies. The Commissions were told to take account of the boundaries of local authorities when carrying out this task, and this, together with a variety of other factors, has meant that the ratio between the biggest and smallest constituencies is still of the order of two to one. However, the appointment of the Commissions has gone some way towards taking the matter out of politics, and though the need to

[1] One each for England, Wales, Scotland, and Northern Ireland.

change constituency boundaries still poses delicate and sometimes embarrassing problems it is not easy to see how the present arrangements could be improved upon.[1]

The other Liberal objective in electoral reform, the establishment of proportional representation, has not been attained and is now unlikely to be attained. One reason for this is that it is a question on which Liberals have always been divided. John Stuart Mill was logically correct in asserting that proportional representation (henceforth referred to as P.R.) was essential if all major currents of opinion among the electorate were to be fairly represented in Parliament, but many Liberals saw practical disadvantages in the scheme which they thought would outweigh its merits. P.R. was and remains a difficult cause to promote, partly because there are several different systems of P.R. each having different effects, partly because all the systems are much more complicated than the existing British electoral system, and partly because it is not easy to persuade politicians commanding a Parliamentary majority that there are virtues in a reform which is calculated to reduce the size of that majority.

Certainly no Liberal government ever attempted to introduce P.R., though in 1909 Asquith appointed a Royal Commission on Systems of Election which heard extensive evidence in its favour from members of the Proportional Representational Society. However, the Conservative Chief Whip, the Secretary of the Liberal Unionist Association, and the Secretary of the Registration Department of the Liberal Central Association all expressed their opposition to P.R. The last-mentioned said that he thought the two great parties covered practically every shade of opinion in the country, except Socialist opinion, and he saw no advantage in a scheme which would facilitate the return of independent members and lead to instability in government. He asserted that Liberal Party agents throughout the country shared his view.[2] In face of this opposition from the three main parties, the Commission decided not to recommend the introduction of P.R.

In 1916 the coalition government appointed a Speaker's Conference on Electoral Reform which recommended the establishment of P.R. in the larger towns as part of an elaborate compromise designed to secure agreement between all parties, but in the subsequent Parliamentary debates and negotiations this proposal was dropped.

Since the Liberal Party has become the smallest of the three main parties it has committed itself officially to the advocacy of P.R.,

[1] The best analysis of the problems of constituency delimitation is to be found in W. J. M. Mackenzie, *Free Elections* (London, 1958), Chapter XII.
[2] *Minutes of Evidence to the Royal Commission on Systems of Election*, Cd. 5352 of 1910, pp. 59–61.

which is indeed one of the central features of its programme. Its conversion was too late, however. In the present state of British politics neither of the two main parties is likely to promote P.R., both because it would be contrary to their electoral interests to do so and because neither of them accepts the individualistic philosophy of Victorian Liberalism of which a belief in P.R. is one expression. The ideas which have replaced this philosophy will be discussed in Part III of this book: here it need only be noted that the Conservative Party has never viewed P.R. with any sympathy and the Labour Party has been officially opposed to it since 1914.[1]

## LIBERALISM AS AN IDEALIZED VERSION OF THE CONSTITUTION

By the 1880's many politicians and writers had come to regard the British constitution as the embodiment of Liberal ideals. The sovereignty of Parliament, the dominance of the Commons within Parliament, and the responsibility of the executive to Parliament were said to be the central features of the system, and to ensure that it was truly a system of representative and responsible government.

Gladstone regarded the supremacy of the Commons over the ministers and other authorities as 'the cardinal axiom' of the constitution,[2] and described the Commons as the centre of the political system. John Morley, who was a member of each Liberal cabinet between 1886 and 1914, described the first feature of the British cabinet system as 'the doctrine of collective responsibility' and continued: 'The second mark is that the cabinet is answerable immediately to the majority of the House of Commons, and ultimately to the electors whose will creates that majority. Responsibility to the Crown is slowly ceasing to be more than a constitutional fiction. . . . Responsibility to the House of Lords means no more than that that House may temporarily resist bills of which it disapproves, until the sense of the electors of the House of Commons has been taken upon them. . . . The only real responsibility is to the House of Commons.'[3]

An even more comprehensive summary of the situation as it then appeared was given by the 8th Duke of Devonshire, who as Lord Hartington had been successively leader of the Liberal Party in the Commons and leader of the Liberal Unionists, and who subsequently became Lord President of the Council in Salisbury's third cabinet.

[1] See *Report of the 14th Annual Conference of the Labour Party* (1914), pp. 104–13, for the debate which resulted in this decision.

[2] *Gleanings from Past Years* (London, 1879), vol. 1, p. 236.

[3] J. Morley, *Walpole* (London, 1889), p. 156.

Speaking in the Lords on September 5, 1893, he said: 'Parliament makes or unmakes our ministries, it revises their actions. Ministries may make peace and war, but they do so at pain of instant dismissal by Parliament from office; and in affairs of internal administration the power of Parliament is equally direct. It can dismiss a Ministry if it is too extravagant or too economical; it can dismiss a Ministry because its government is too stringent or too lax. It does actually and practically in every way directly govern England, Scotland and Ireland.'[1]

Political leaders were supported in these views by academic commentators, of whom the most famous was A. V. Dicey. In the *Law of Constitution*, first published in 1885 and used as an academic text-book ever since, he claimed that 'the sovereignty of Parliament is (from a legal point of view) the dominant characteristic of our political institutions'.[2] Behind this legal sovereignty of Parliament, he continued, stands the power of the electors. 'The essence of representative government is, that the legislature should represent or give effect to the will of the political sovereign, i.e. of the electoral body, or of the nation.'[3] And 'we may assert that the arrangements of the constitution are now such as to ensure that the will of the electors shall by regular and constitutional means always in the end assert itself as the predominant influence in the country'.[4] This influence was said to extend to the executive as well as to the legislature because the conventions of the constitution, which Dicey thought were ultimately backed by legal sanctions, included ministerial responsibility to Parliament for all the actions of the executive.

This book, which is written in an exceptionally clear and attractive style, has probably had more influence than any other on the teaching of British government in the twentieth century, and many other texts have echoed Dicey's analysis. A good early example is Leonard Courtney's *The Working Constitution of the United Kingdom*, published in 1901. This work begins by declaring that 'the fundamental fact of our constitution is the absolutely unqualified supremacy of Parliament'.[5] The possibility of conflict between the two Houses is acknowledged, but this could always be settled by a general election: 'the will of the nation finds its most absolute expression in the judgement of the House of Commons elected for the purpose of ascertaining its will upon some definite issue; and this principle is, in fact, now admitted by all parties as beyond controversy'. Courtney

[1] *House of Lords Debates*, 4th s., v. 17, cc. 33–4.
[2] *Law of the Constitution* (8th edn., London, 1931), p. 37.
[3] Ibid., p. 425.        [4] Ibid., p. 71.
[5] This and the following quotations are taken from pp. 4–6.

73

goes on to define the generally accepted view of the constitution in the following terms:

'first, that the country must be ruled in accordance with the will of the nation; next, that that will is most faithfully expressed in the result of any general election; and thirdly, that the House of Commons as the embodiment of that will has a claim to predominance, at least until circumstances change so as to qualify its title as a faithful reflex of the national judgement. This principle thus recognized, that a House of Commons issuing from a general election is the most authoritative expression of the will of the nation, involves as an inevitable consequence the further principle that the administration of public affairs and the guidance of legislation should be entrusted to persons approved by a majority of the House.'

It might be thought that a view of the constitution advanced by such eminent authorities as Gladstone, Morley, Devonshire, and Dicey, as well as many others, would almost certainly be an accurate view. Looking back on the situation, however, it is only too clear that it was in fact an idealized view. It assumed that political power flowed exclusively in one direction, from the electors to Parliament and from Parliament to the government, and never in the opposite way. It took no account of the growth of party management and the extent to which the cabinet could influence, if not control, Parliament. Its description of Parliamentary control of the executive was appropriate to, and was based on the experience of, the situation between the Reform Acts of 1832 and 1867, but it rapidly ceased to be appropriate to the situation which developed after 1867.

Liberals had always assumed that the extension of the franchise would extend the popular basis of Parliament without otherwise changing its nature, and it was perhaps natural for them to be slow to realize that this was not to be the case. In practice the second Reform Act led to a growth of party organizations in the country and the development of the means by which party leaders could discipline their back-bench supporters. Members had to secure the votes of an electorate too numerous to be canvassed personally by the candidates, who therefore became dependent on the endorsement and support of a party organization. This might have led to the growth of local party machines and bosses, as in the United States. In fact, for a number of reasons which need not be discussed here, it was the national party leaders rather than the local party branches who gained most from this development in Britain. The consequence was that the members of the government were able to put pressure on their own back-benchers by threatening that if the latter voted against the government in Parliament they might find themselves in the uncomfortable position of having to fight the next election without the support of the party. The sanction was rarely imposed, but the threat of it diminished the independence of Parliament both as a legislature and as a body that made and unmade ministries.

As it happened, the strength of the government in relation to the House of Commons was also increased by the procedural reforms of the early 1880's, which considerably restricted the opportunities of back-benchers. These two developments, taken together, transformed the relationship between Parliament and the cabinet in the twenty-five years following the second Reform Act: the nature of the change is indicated by the figures in the following table. These show, first, the total number of divisions in which governments were defeated in the years 1851–1903, and second, the number of amendments to government bills (excluding estimates) carried against government whips in the same years. The figures in the first line are for five Parliamentary sessions and those in each subsequent line are for six sessions.[1]

| Parliamentary Sessions | Number of government defeats | Number of amendments to government bills |
|---|---|---|
| 1851–5 | 59 | 29 |
| 1856–61 | 52 | 24 |
| 1862–7 | 60 | 26 |
| 1868–73 | 50 | 27 |
| 1874–9 | 8 | 1 |
| 1880–5 | 26 | 11 |
| 1886–91 | 13 | 5 |
| 1892–7 | 9 | 2 |
| 1898–1903 | 2 | 1 |

Although this development may have been more difficult to appreciate at the time than it is in retrospect, there were a number of contemporary observers who noticed what was happening. Probably the most distinguished of these was Sir Henry Maine, whose *Popular Government*, written in 1885, predicted that the extension of the franchise would radically change the nature of British politics. In the first place, he said, it would lead to a system of party government in which party policies 'will less and less reflect the individual mind of any leader, but only the ideas which seem to that mind to be most likely to win favour with the greatest number of supporters'.[2]

[1] These figures are taken from A. L. Lowell, *The Government of England* (New York, 1919), vol. 1, p. 317, and vol. 2, pp. 79–80.

[2] *Popular Government* (2nd edn., London, 1886), p. 33.

Secondly, it would undermine the independence of M.P.'s and convert 'the unfettered representative into the instructed delegate',[1] as the result of the inevitable growth of party caucuses. In the third place, Maine alleged, party government was inseparable from corruption, and if Britain rejected the American system of patronage we should be only too likely to find ourselves accepting another kind of corruption. He called this 'the directer process of legislating away the property of one class and transferring it to another. It is this last which is likely to be the corruption of these latter days.'[2]

There was an element of political bias in this last prediction, but Maine proceeded to an account of the British constitution as it then was which cannot be criticized on this ground. The constitution, he asserted, did not correspond to the Liberal view of a system dominated by the power of the people's representatives in the Commons. The Crown had not lost all its powers, and neither had the House of Lords. More important still, the cabinet had acquired great power: it was 'manifestly the English institution which is ever more and more gaining in authority and influence', and it had 'taken to itself nearly all the legislative powers of Parliament, depriving it in particular of the whole right of initiation'.[3]

Some of Maine's assertions were repeated and documented by the continental writer, M. Ostrogorski. In his monumental study of *Democracy and the Organization of Political Parties*, Ostrogorski painted an alarming picture of the consequences of the growth of caucuses. They were beginning to dominate Parliament, destroy the independence of back-benchers, convert Parliamentary leaders into party dictators, and act as an arbiter 'between Parliament and outside opinion'.[4] As a result, the delicate equilibrium of cabinet government was being 'destroyed in favour of the leaders. Formerly . . . the leader of the party was only *primus inter pares*; now he is a general in command of an army. . . . Raised above the levelled crowd of M.P.'s, the leaders now lean directly on the great mass of voters, whose feelings of loyalty go straight to the leaders over the heads of the Members. . . . This being so, the elections have assumed the character of personal plebiscites, each constituency voting not so much for this or that candidate as for Mr Gladstone or against Lord Beaconsfield or Lord Salisbury.'[5]

Similar views were expressed by Goldwin Smith, the Liberal writer who emigrated to Canada, Sidney Low, the English historian, and A. L. Lowell, the President of Harvard University. Goldwin

---

[1]*Popular Government* (2nd edn., London, 1886), p. 94.
[2]Ibid., p. 106.    [3]Ibid., p. 115.
[4]*Democracy and the Organization of Political Parties* (London, 1902), vol. 1, pp. 215-6.    [5]Ibid., pp. 607-8.

Smith went so far as to say that 'the caucus is enthroned on the ruins of the old British constitution'.[1] Low observed that in recent years the cabinet had grown in power, and tended to be 'amenable to the control of the constituent bodies themselves rather than to that of their elected representatives'.[2] Criticizing the speech made by the Duke of Devonshire which is quoted above, Low pointed out that the real power of the House of Commons was declining. 'Much of its efficiency has passed to other agents. Its supremacy is qualified by the growth of rival jurisdictions. Its own servants have become for some purposes, its masters. The cabinet is more powerful, and has drawn to itself many attributes which the Commons are still imagined to possess. The electorate, more conscious of its own existence under an extended franchise, wields a direct instead of a delegated authority.'[3] A. L. Lowell began his study of *The Government of England*, first published in 1908, with an account of the Crown and the cabinet. In his subsequent discussion of the House of Commons he pointed out that the House had lost the initiative to the cabinet, and defined the legislative process as one in which 'the cabinet legislates with the advice and consent of Parliament'.[4]

It now seems clear that the view of the political system given by Maine, Low and Lowell was nearer to the truth than the Liberal view. In spite of this, most commentators continued to write of the constitution in Liberal terms until well into the present century, and many still do so. Until the 1930's most exponents of the constitution regarded Parliamentary sovereignty as its central principle, and most critics of the constitution regarded the power of the House of Lords to check the popular will as the constitution's most serious defect. It is noteworthy that in 1929 the Committee on Ministers' Powers were instructed by their terms of reference 'to report what safeguards are desirable or necessary to secure the constitutional principles of the sovereignty of Parliament and the supremacy of the Law',[5] and that in 1934 another government committee stated as a 'familiar British conception' that 'the only form of self-government worthy of the name is government through Ministers responsible to an elected legislature'.[6] In 1933 C. S. Emden argued at length that a ministry was bound by the people's mandate, transmitted through the House of Commons, and suggested that if a ministry adopted an

---

[1] See *A Trip to England* (London, 1892), p. 120. Quoted in Ostrogorski, op. cit., p. 618.

[2] *The Governance of England* (London, 1904), p. 54.   [3] Ibid., pp. 58–9.

[4] *The Government of England* (new edn. New York, 1919), vol. 1, p. 326.

[5] Cmd. 4060, p. v.

[6] *Report of the Joint Committee on Indian Constitutional Reform*, vol. 1, part 1, p. 5.

entirely new policy which had not been in issue at a general election, a supporter who disagreed with the policy should stand by his principles and would have 'some justification for arguing that the ministry should go to the country'.[1]

## LOOKING BACK TO LIBERALISM

During the 1930's this kind of discussion became somewhat out-moded, even though it continued in many circles. In 1929 the Lord Chief Justice, Lord Hewart, published a book entitled *The New Despotism*, in which he alleged that the principles of Parliamentary sovereignty and the rule of law had been undermined by the growth of executive powers. His direct concern was with the legal sovereignty of Parliament but, as a good Liberal, he maintained that this was an essential feature of the country's representative system. 'The citizens of a state may indeed believe or boast that . . . they enjoy . . . a system of representative institutions. . . . But their belief will stand in need of revision if, in truth and in fact, an organized and diligent minority, equipped with convenient drafts, and employing after a fashion part of the machinery of representative institutions, is steadily increasing the range and the power of departmental authority.'[2]

Hewart's book started a good deal of general controversy about the powers of the executive. In the following year Ramsay Muir, a Liberal historian, published a forceful indictment of recent constitutional developments which considerably broadened the attack. 'During the last half-century,' he wrote, 'a series of changes have come about, almost unnoticed, in the working of our institutions which have completely transformed their character.'[3] He summarized the most important of these changes, as, first 'an enormous increase in the range and power of bureaucracy'; second, 'the growth of cabinet dictatorship'; and third, 'an increased rigidity of party organization which has provided the foundation for cabinet dictatorship, while it has almost reduced the House of Commons to a mere registering machine'. One result of these changes, he said, 'is the increasing incapacity of the House of Commons to perform its work'; another is that 'organized interests not recognized by the constitution are beginning to exercise direct pressure upon, or even control over, the government, which often pays greater deference to them than to Parliament'.

Ramsay Muir's prescription was that proportional representation

---

[1] *The People and the Constitution* (Oxford, 1933), p. 31.

[2] *The New Despotism* (London, 1929), p. 12.

[3] This and the succeeding quotations are taken from *How Britain is Governed* (London, 1930), pp. 320–2.

should be adopted and Parliamentary procedure should be reformed, with the object of increasing the independence of Members and the effectiveness of their control over the government. In the following years a procession of other writers discovered that political practice no longer corresponded to Liberal principles, and suggested a variety of reforms designed to remedy this defect, as it was commonly regarded.

In 1932, for instance, Gilbert Murray advocated proportional representation on the ground that the decline of Parliamentary government could only be halted if the voting system were made to be and to appear more fair.[1] In 1934 W. Ivor Jennings published a book on *Parliamentary Reform* in which he observed that 'during the past fifty years the British Parliament has become progressively less efficient'[2] and noted that 'the back-bench Member is almost entirely impotent in the House'.[3] He proposed a series of reforms, including the establishment of a drafting committee and the replacement of the standing committees by specialized committees which would not only consider legislation but also act as a constant check on the activities of the departments with which they were concerned.

In 1935 Sir Bryan Fell regretted that the spirit of independence among M.P.'s was 'nearly dead' and that the executive was becoming more and more impatient of criticism. He thought that the government's control over the time of the House was 'not without dangers which might even threaten the very existence of our Parliamentary institutions'.[4] In 1943 J. F. S. Ross wrote of 'the failure of Parliament to conform to our ideals and fulfil our expectations'[5] and recommended the adoption of proportional representation, an increase in M.P.'s salaries, and the payment by the state of a proportion of all candidates' electoral expenses, so as to encourage a wider variety of candidates to stand than could then afford to do so.

After the war the lament continued. In 1949 Christopher Hollis pointed out that M.P.'s had become servants of the party machines, and observed that: 'It would be simpler and certainly more economical if a flock of tame sheep, kept conveniently at hand, were driven through the division lobbies in the appropriate numbers at agreed times.'[6] He suggested that some of the lost vigour of the Parliamentary system might be restored if the electoral system were reformed so that Members could no longer be elected by a mere plurality of votes, if the size of the House of Commons were reduced, if a new House of

---

[1] See the *Contemporary Review*, vol. 141 (March 1932), p. 296.
[2] *Parliamentary Reform* (London, 1934), p. 7.    [3] Ibid., p. 9.
[4] *The Nineteenth Century and After*, vol. 118 (August 1935), p. 131.
[5] *Parliamentary Representation* (London, 2nd edn. 1948), p. 7.
[6] *Can Parliament Survive?* (London, 1949), pp. 64–5.

Industry were created to take over some of the more detailed and technical work now done by the Commons, and if the Parliamentary committee system were extended.[1]

The virtual extinction of independent M.P.'s in the general election of 1950 was widely regretted by leader-writers and other commentators. Later that year Lord Cecil of Chelwood moved a resolution in the House of Lords that 'the growing power of the cabinet is a danger to the democratic constitution of the country',[2] and Sir Arthur Salter said in a public lecture that 'the British Parliament has a past of glory, a present of frustration, a future of uncertainty. Our destiny turns largely, I think, upon our ability . . . to restore the traditions and the authority of Parliament so that it can be once more the effective guardian of our liberties'.[3]

In 1952 the most sweeping of all attacks on modern developments in British politics was published. In *The Passing of Parliament* Professor G. W. Keeton criticized the growth of party discipline, the decline in the independence of Parliament, the extension of delegated legislation, the erosion of the rule of law, and the general lack of effective checks on the power of the administration. He observed that the nineteenth-century assumption that Parliament, strengthened by successive extensions of the franchise, could effectively control the executive had 'proved completely fallacious',[4] and he described twentieth-century developments as involving 'the relentless advance of administrative tyranny'.[5] However, unlike most other writers who looked back to Liberalism with nostalgia, he did not suggest any reforms which would enable the clock to be put back. So long as Parliament was willing to delegate its powers and citizens were willing to live in a planned society, he saw no prospect that institutional changes would stem the tide.

This catalogue could be greatly extended, but enough examples have been cited to show that, since the nineteen-thirties, adherents to the Liberal theory of the state have been regretfully aware that political practice has departed from Liberal principles. Supporters of recent developments have not been lacking, but they have not been able to justify their attitudes in terms of the traditional British theories of representation. Instead, they have attempted to justify them in terms of more recent theories, to which we must now turn.

[1] This last point was elaborated in articles in the *Manchester Guardian*. December 13, 1952, and *Parliamentary Affairs*, vol. 6 (1952–3).

[2] Quoted in Hansard Society, *Parliamentary Reform,1933–1958* (London, 1959), p. 158.

[3] Reprinted in *Parliament: a Survey*, ed. Lord Campion (London, 1952), p. 120.

[4] *The Passing of Parliament* (London, 1952), p. 199.

[5] Ibid., p. 201.

These theories, though they differ widely from one another on some issues, have in common the fact that they reject the individualistic assumptions about society on which the traditional doctrines were based. For this reason, they will be considered under the general heading of 'collectivism and the theory of representation'.

# PART III

# COLLECTIVISM AND THE
# THEORY OF REPRESENTATION

## CHAPTER 6

## Doctrines of Class Conflict

### LIBERAL ASSUMPTIONS

The Liberal view of the state depends on a view of society which is essentially individualistic. It assumes that citizens exercise their political rights as individuals choosing freely among rival candidates, conflicting policies, and differing views of the good life, and not as members of a group or category whose views are determined by that membership. It assumes that, although men's opinions and personal interests vary, there is no fundamental conflict of interests in society of a kind that arrays man against man or group against group. It assumes that, because the conflicts in society are not fundamental, the state can be neutral in its attitude towards them. It assumes that the neutrality of the state will be generally accepted as a fact, and that in consequence minorities will be willing to accept the decision of the majority, knowing that by education and propaganda the minority of today can become the majority of tomorrow.

The enumeration of these assumptions makes clear what has often been pointed out, that the social, economic and political aspects of Liberalism are intimately related. This doctrine developed in a society devoted to free enterprise, in which men were rewarded according to their success as individuals, and in which not much more was expected of the state than that it should maintain order, prevent breaches of the rules like fraud or violence, and generally uphold the conditions in which individuals could pursue their own interests. The idea of a free competition of ideas, based on a fundamental harmony of political interests, went hand in hand with the idea of free competition for profits, based on a fundamental harmony of economic interests.

This is not to say that nineteenth-century Liberals denied the existence of social divisions. Like other commentators, they spoke of the landed gentry, the middle classes, the labouring classes, and so on. But they did not believe that these divisions were barriers, and they did not think that there was anything in the nature of an irreconcilable conflict between one class and another. In the language of modern sociology, they thought of classes as status groups which graded individuals according to their rank in society. The three-class status system with which we are now familiar appears to have emerged in conversation and writings in the 1830's,[1] and it bears the marks of its middle-class origin in that it contrives to put the middle class in the most favourable position. The distinction between middle-class and working-class people in this system is that the former are more successful and therefore presumably more talented and industrious than the latter. The distinction between members of the middle and upper classes is that the latter, by accident of birth, do not need to work for their living. In terms of Victorian middle-class moral values, the middle class therefore emerge as the most virtuous section of the community, as their publicists were not slow to suggest. Politically, the essential point is that people were thought to be free to move up and down the social scale as their fortunes waxed or waned, and it was believed that members of all classes had the same interest in the growth of material prosperity and the maintenance of ordered government. As Palmerston said in a famous speech in 1850:

'We have shown the example of a nation, in which every class in society accepts with cheerfulness the lot which Providence has assigned to it; while at the same time every individual of each class is constantly striving to raise himself in the social scale.'[2]

### DOCTRINES OF CLASS CONFLICT

There is a world of difference between this view and what is now familiar to us as the Communist view of a class system based not on status but on power, in which there is an irreconcilable conflict of interest between different classes. In capitalist societies this conflict is said by Communists to be simply one between the two remaining classes: those who own the means of production and those who do not. If this view were correct, there would be no place for Liberalism, for there would be no possibility of the state being neutral in the class struggle. Inevitably, the dominant class would use the state as a means to further its exploitation of the subordinate class. Members

[1] 1833 saw the publication of John Wade's *History of the Middle and Working Classes*, which was something of a milestone in the development of class-consciousness. For a discussion of changes in linguistic usage, see Asa Briggs, 'The Language of "Class" in Early Nineteenth-century England', in Asa Briggs and John Saville, *Essays in Labour History* (London, 1960).

[2] Quoted in ibid., p. 71.

of the subordinate class would have no interest in supporting such a system; indeed, their emancipation could be achieved only by its collapse. In this situation, the Liberal ideals of toleration and free speech would be meaningless, for men's political views would be determined by their economic position, and John Stuart Mill's argument that truth would emerge from the clash of opinions would be no more than a piece of bourgeois myth-making.

This view has been characterized as Communist because at the present time most of those who hold the view are members of or sympathizers with the Communist Party. In this form the view derives from the writings of Karl Marx, though the account that Marx himself gave of the relations between class and politics was a good deal more subtle than that usually propagated by his followers. However, long before Marxist ideas had achieved any influence in this country some British writers had challenged Liberal views about the relations between the classes.

In the 1820's several writers influenced by Robert Owen developed economic theories based on the labour theory of value, drew attention to the conflict of interest between employers and workers, and demanded that labour should get an increased share of the material product. Between 1830 and 1834 a number of workers' organizations were established. Some of these were unions confined to one trade, such as those of the builders, cotton spinners, and potters. Others attempted to recruit members from all trades, the largest being the Grand National Consolidated Trades Union founded in 1834, with aims that were social and political as well as economic.[1] In the same period the doctrine of class conflict was propagated by men like William Benbow, the London publisher and coffee-house owner, and T. B. O'Brien, editor of the *Poor Man's Guardian*.

However, these early workers' organizations were not successful— the Grand National Consolidated Trades Union collapsed within a few months of its formation—and the theorists who propagated doctrines of class conflict in this period did not have much influence on events. The Chartist Movement of 1838–48 numbered both O'Brien and Feargus O'Connor—another advocate of class conflict —among its leaders, but its stated aims as a movement were entirely compatible with Liberal principles. The six points of the Charter— manhood suffrage, annual Parliaments, voting by ballot, equal electoral districts, the abolition of property qualifications for candidates, and payment of Members—imply an acceptance of Liberal ideals rather than their rejection in favour of a belief in the inevitability of class conflict.

[1] See Asa Briggs, *The Age of Improvement* (London, 1959), pp. 289–94, for details of these organizations.

What is much more important than these workers' movements is that during the middle decades of the century the rapid growth of industry and industrial towns created what could reasonably be called a working-class pattern of life, and that observant people of all classes realized that the interests and values of people whose lives were shaped by that pattern were very different from those of the middle and upper classes. People followed Disraeli's example in talking of 'the two nations', and in the debates on Parliamentary reform in the 1860's both some of the supporters and some of the opponents of reform talked in terms of 'the balance of classes'.[1] That shrewd observer of the political scene, Walter Bagehot, based his hopes that reform would be accomplished without upheaval not on the Liberal ground that the franchise would lead to the education of the masses but on the very different ground that the deferential habits of the working classes would lead them to vote for their social superiors.[2]

## LABOUR REPRESENTATION

Within three months of the passage of the 1867 Reform Act the London Working Men's Association, as if anxious to disprove Bagehot's contention, published a manifesto calling for 'the Direct Representation of Labour in Parliament'.[3] This movement did not outlast the general election of the following year, but it was the first blow in a long controversy among labour spokesmen as to whether, and if so how and for what purpose, the labour movement should try to secure independent representation at Westminster. Many trade unionists were sceptical of the advantages of political action. Those who agreed on the need for this kind of action were bitterly divided among themselves, and they can, at the risk of some oversimplification, be divided into three categories. First, there were those whose aim was to secure the election of working men who would sympathize with labour interests as Radical or Liberal candidates. Another group wanted labour candidates to be independent of established parties, but proposed aims and methods not very different from those of existing Radicals. A third group demanded that labour representatives should be committed to a policy of class warfare which was incompatible with the assumptions of Liberalism and with the principles upon which Parliamentary government was then based.

The story of the rise of the political labour movement is well

[1] See *Essays on Reform* (London, 1867).
[2] See *The English Constitution* (London, 1867), chapter 8.
[3] Quoted in G. D. H. Cole, *British Working Class Politics: 1832–1914* (London, 1941), p. 38.

known and amply documented.[1] Its most interesting feature in this context is the prolonged and eventually successful struggle waged by a handful of Socialists to persuade the trade unions, first, to enter politics, and second, to adopt Socialist objectives. The leaders of the London Working Men's Association were Radicals, not Socialists, and in their 1867 manifesto they argued that working-class M.P.'s would not 'stand isolated as a class' but would 'blend with the other members in the performance of the usual duties expected from members of the legislature'.[2] The founders of the Labour Representation League (1869–81) had similar views, and in a manifesto issued in 1875 the League declared: 'We have even sought to be allied to the Great Liberal Party, to which we, by conviction, belong.'[3] The supporters of the 'Lib–Lab.' movement after 1874 achieved this aim.

After 1880, however, Socialist ideas began to make a serious impression on British political life. In 1881 Engels wrote a series of fairly influential articles in the *Labour Standard*, the Democratic Federation was founded, and H. M. Hyndman published his book *England for All*. Hyndman, a business man who did more than anyone else to introduce Marxist ideas to the British people, later persuaded the Democratic Federation to adopt a programme which included the immediate nationalization of the land, the banks, and the railways.[4] In the following years several Socialist newspapers were launched, including *The Labour Elector*, founded by H. H. Champion in 1888, *The Workman's Times*, edited by Joseph Burgess, and—most successful of all—*The Clarion*, founded by Robert Blatchford and A. M. Thompson in 1891. In the same period a number of Labour electoral associations were formed in industrial constituencies, and in 1893 a meeting of delegates from these associations formed the Independent Labour Party (henceforth I.L.P.).

At this meeting two divergent attitudes regarding representation were revealed. One group of delegates held that I.L.P. branches and members in constituencies where no I.L.P. candidate was nominated

---

[1] The most straightforward account is that by G. D. H. Cole in *British Working Class Politics: 1832–1914* and *The Labour Party From 1914* (London, 1948). Fuller accounts of shorter periods will be found in Henry Pelling, *The Origins of the Labour Party: 1880–1900* (London, 1954), and Frank Bealey and Henry Pelling, *Labour and Politics: 1900–1906* (London, 1958). There is a useful collection of documents in Henry Pelling (ed.), *The Challenge of Socialism* (London, 1954).

[2] Quoted in Cole, *British Working Class Politics: 1832–1914*, p. 44.

[3] Quoted in ibid., p. 72.

[4] See 'Socialism Made Plain', quoted in Pelling, *The Challenge of Socialism*, pp. 130–2.

should be free to support whichever local candidate they preferred. The other group regarded all non-Socialists as class-enemies and held that I.L.P. members should in no circumstances support them: if no Labour candidate were nominated in a constituency the right course would be to abstain rather than vote for a man who, even if he were a Radical, was in the final analysis an ally of the capitalists and an enemy of the working class. The first attitude was compatible with the Liberal view of the constitution; the second attitude, with its insistence that political attitudes were economically determined, was not.

At the inaugural meeting of the I.L.P. the first attitude was supported by a vote of 62 to 37, and at each successive annual conference the more moderate members were in the majority. Nevertheless, the minority was sizeable and its members remained unconvinced. In 1900, at the inaugural meeting of the Labour Representation Committee, one group of delegates urged that only candidates who advocated class warfare should be sponsored. This view was rejected, but so was the view that the Committee should support any candidate, no matter what his social origins and connections, who sympathized with the aims and demands of the Labour movement. Instead, the conference decided that Labour candidates should be chosen only from among members of organizations associated with the I.L.P. or the co-operative movement.

By taking this decision, and by not defining its policy except by saying that it would support legislation in the labour interest, the Labour Representation Committee adopted, as its name implied, the view that its function was to represent a class rather than a viewpoint. In this way it rejected the Liberal theory of representation in favour of a collectivist theory. In 1906 the Committee changed its name to the Labour Party without redefining its purpose. It was not until 1918 that the Labour Party adopted a constitution which committed it to an objective other than the representation of the working class in Parliament. This new objective was defined in clause 4 of the Constitution: 'To secure for the workers by hand or by brain the full fruits of their industry and the most equitable distribution thereof that may be possible, upon the basis of the common ownership of the means of production, distribution, and exchange and the best obtainable system of popular administration and control of each industry or service.'

## SOCIALIST VIEWS SINCE 1918

The policy adopted by the Labour Party in 1918 can be summarized in the phrase: Socialism by Parliamentary means. This policy owed more to the Fabians than to the Marxists, who in 1920 established the Communist Party as a rival organization competing for working-class support. But it is a rather ambiguous policy in some respects, and how far it is compatible with the Liberal view of the constitution is a matter for debate. Opinions within the Labour Party on this question have been so divided that it is necessary to talk of the attitudes of groups of members rather than of the Party as such.

Clearly there is some common ground. All groups within the Party have rejected the Liberal assumptions that the state is and should be neutral as between classes, and that the function of the representative system is to reflect a wide range of individual opinions on matters of policy. They have held instead that since free enterprise systematically favours the interests of the upper and middle classes at the expense of the working class, deliberate action by the government is needed to correct this state of affairs. They have insisted that such action will only be initiated by a body of M.P.'s who regard it as their duty to advance the interests of the workers, and that a vital function of the Labour Party is to secure the election of these representatives. To this extent all Socialists have rejected the Liberal theory of representation.

Beyond this there is an important division. Some Socialists have argued that the Parliamentary institutions which have largely been built on the basis of Liberal assumptions are not suitable for either the transition to or the government of a Socialist society. They have suggested that Liberal institutions, like Liberal theories, were the product of a particular period of social development, and have no general validity beyond this period.

Most Labour leaders, including all those who have held the office of Leader of the Parliamentary Labour Party, have disputed this view. They have argued that although Liberal theories are outdated, Liberal institutions are not, and the maintenance of the Parliamentary system should be regarded as an essential aim of Labour policy. They say that in practice Labour is no more a class party than the Conservative Party is, and they insist that Labour is as determined as the Conservative Party to uphold the established institutions of representative government.

Conservatives have been sceptical of these latter claims. They have insisted that both by its actions and by the speeches of some of its less cautious leaders Labour has stamped itself as a class party rather than a national party, and they have pointed to the fact that in general elections Conservative candidates derive about half their votes from industrial workers and their families in denial of the suggestion that the same could be said of their own party. A second line of argument draws attention to the provisions of the Labour

Party Constitution whereby the formal power to make Party policy is vested in the Party's Annual Conference and, between conferences, in its National Executive Committee. This apparent subjugation of Parliamentary leaders to external authorities has been said to conflict with the principles of the British Parliamentary system. A third argument put forward by some Conservatives is that the Labour Party's professed aim, the nationalization of the means of production, distribution and exchange, would necessarily involve the destruction of Liberal institutions if it were achieved.

A certain amount of support for the view that Socialism is incompatible with the maintenance of Liberal institutions can be found in the writings of Socialist intellectuals between the wars. Thus, in 1920 Sidney and Beatrice Webb recommended that Parliamentary institutions should be substantially re-modelled under a Socialist régime. They also made clear that in their view the achievement of Socialist economic policies should take priority over the maintenance of Liberal freedoms, and they argued that:

'Especially during the stage of transition from a predominantly capitalist society it may be necessary to prohibit the publication of newspapers with the object of private profit or under individual ownership as positively dangerous to the community.'[1]

Later, in 1931, Harold Laski gave a series of lectures in the University of North Carolina that were permeated by a sense of despair for the future of democracy. Capitalism had failed to resolve its contradictions; conflict between rich and poor was increasingly sharp and increasingly open; representative government was under attack from both Left and Right; and Britain, in common with other Western countries, was veering inexorably towards social revolution. Parliamentary democracy in Britain had been built on the twin foundations of continuous economic expansion and general agreement about 'the fundamentals of political action'.[2] But from the 1880's onwards these foundations were gradually worn away by the growth of working-class demands and the Labour Party on the one hand and the reduction in the rate of economic expansion, followed by a series of economic crises, on the other.[3] This process reached its culmination in the crisis of 1931 which resulted in the accession to power of a coalition government which 'moved drastically to the right' while the Labour Party 'moved with equal fervour to the left'.[4] Compromise seemed no longer possible and open conflict, once Labour was returned to power, appeared almost inevitable. At best, said Laski,

[1] *A Constitution for the Socialist Commonwealth* (London, 1920), p. 270.
[2] *Democracy in Crisis* (London, 1933), p. 33.
[3] Ibid., pp. 35–7.   [4] Ibid., p. 38.

'the attainment of power by the Labour Party in the normal electoral fashion must result in a radical transformation of Parliamentary government. Such an administration . . . would have to take vast powers, and legislate under them by ordinance and decree; it would have to suspend the classic formulae of normal opposition. If its policy met with peaceful acceptance the continuance of Parliamentary government would depend upon its possession of guarantees from the Conservative Party that its work of transformation would not be disrupted by repeal in the event of its defeat at the polls'. At worst, conditions would lead to a revolutionary situation and 'men would rapidly group themselves for civil war'.[1]

In a lecture given to the Fabian Society in 1932 on 'The Present Position of Representative Democracy' Laski seemed even more certain that Parliamentary institutions had outlived their usefulness. 'It is obvious', he said, 'that any view which places confidence in the power of universal suffrage and representative institutions, unaided and of themselves, to secure a permanently well-ordered commonwealth is seriously underestimating the complexity of the issue. Such a view not only gravely exaggerates the power of reason over interest in society; it also misconceives the dynamic nature of the purpose which representative democracy is seeking to achieve.'[2]

In a later passage Laski summarized the situation in still more radical terms. 'In any society, in fact, the state belongs to the holders of economic power; and its institutions naturally operate, at least in the main, to their advantage. But by establishing political democracy they offer to the masses the potentiality of capturing the political machinery and using it to redress the inequalities to which the economic régime gives rise. Where that position arises, they are asked to co-operate in the abolition of the advantages they enjoy. Such co-operation has rarely been offered deliberately or with goodwill; and it has been necessary, as a rule, to establish by force a new legal order the institutions of which permit the necessary adjustments to be made. It appears likely that we are approaching such a position at the present time.'[3]

A similar analysis was made at about the same time by John Strachey in his celebrated book *The Coming Struggle for Power*. Other left-wing writers of that period were more concerned than Laski and Strachey were to retain at least the forms of Parliamentary democracy, but were alarmed because they envisaged that a Labour government would find its legislation rejected by the House of Lords and its policies sabotaged by the civil service. Stafford Cripps said

[1] *Democracy in Crisis* (London, 1933), pp. 87–8.
[2] H. J. Laski and others, *Where Stands Socialism Today?* (London, 1933), p. 3.
[3] Ibid., p. 24.

that if it appeared 'that there was any real danger of such a step being taken, it would probably be better and more conducive to the general peace and welfare of the country for the Socialist government to make itself temporarily into a dictatorship until the matter could again be put to the test at the polls'.[1]

These views were expressed in the depths of economic depression and shortly after the political crisis of 1931 had shaken the faith of many Socialists in the ability of a Labour government to carry out its policies in face of opposition from the Treasury and the Bank of England. It is fair to say that the leading members of the Parliamentary Labour Party, such as C. R. Attlee, Herbert Morrison, and Arthur Greenwood, never shared these opinions, and had no intention whatever of leading their Party in an attack on Parliamentary institutions. It is also true that after 1945 both Cripps and Laski repudiated their earlier views: Cripps by his speeches and actions as President of the Board of Trade and Chancellor of the Exchequer, Laski in his book *Reflections on the Constitution*.[2]

These earlier views are nevertheless important, for they point to a problem of political theory. Most Socialists reject the individualistic assumptions of Liberals about the nature of society and of politics. Logically they must also reject the Liberal theory of representation which is based on these assumptions, and the problem is to know with what theory they replace it. The Communist answer is in its way logical but it leaves no room for the continuance of representative democracy. Some Socialist intellectuals have flirted with Communist ideas or have put forward ideas of their own which would have led to the abandonment of Liberal institutions if they had been adopted. The Parliamentary leaders of the Labour Party have rejected these ideas and have insisted that the maintenance of representative democracy is an essential part of Labour's plans. The question which consequently arises is this: what theory or theories have been invoked by Socialists (and other collectivists who would not call themselves Socialists) to justify their belief in a representative democracy which is not based on Liberal assumptions?

The answer to this question is that two or three quite different theories have been invoked. Some political theorists and politicians have adopted a theory based on the organic view of society, which will be discussed in the following chapter. Others have believed that the solution lay in the representation of groups rather than of individuals or classes. This view will be discussed in Chapter 8. Others again have staked their faith on a theory of party democracy, which will be discussed in Chapter 9.

[1] Stafford Cripps and others, *Problems of a Socialist Government* (London, 1933), p. 46.  [2] Manchester, 1951.

# CHAPTER 7

# The Idealist View of Politics

## PHILOSOPHICAL IDEALISM

With the notable exception of Burke, the most influential British political theorists from the time of Hobbes to the 1870's paid little or no attention to the concept of the community. Many agreed with Bentham that 'the community is a fictitious body'; others simply ignored it. During the middle years of the nineteenth century, in particular, the individualistic ideas of the Utilitarians and the classical economists achieved a kind of dominance in political discussion. There was, of course, no shortage of writers who dissented from these ideas. On the one hand, there were Conservative politicians like Disraeli and social reformers like Shaftesbury who insisted on the importance of strengthening the bonds of mutual dependence between members of the national community. On the other hand, there were men of letters who in one way or another protested against the inhumanity of a society based on a belief in competition for individual profit. Robert Southey and S. T. Coleridge, Charles Dickens and Charles Kingsley, Matthew Arnold and Thomas Carlyle, John Ruskin and William Morris can all be included in this category. But none of these was primarily a political philosopher, and none produced a theory of politics which was sufficiently coherent to be set against the theories of the philosophical radicals.

On the level of political theory, some opposition to Utilitarian ideas was offered by the early Socialist thinkers. However, they replaced the belief in individualism either by the doctrine of class solidarity or by the Owenite belief that small communities should be created, a belief which was itself based on the view that communal ties did not exist and could not be created in society as a whole. The early Socialists did not, and could not have been expected to, develop theories emphasizing the dependence of individuals on the national community. John Stuart Mill's ideas were moving somewhat in this direction, but although he exposed the inadequacies of Benthamism he did not provide a coherent alternative to that philosophy. It was not until the last two decades of the century that a small group of Oxford dons, trained to admire the Greek conception of the good life rather than that of the Manchester School, put forward a coherent theory of politics based on the belief that men's lives and values are shaped by the community in which they live.

The most influential members of this group was T. H. Green, who delivered a course of lectures in 1879–80 that were subsequently published as *Lectures on the Principles of Political Obligation*.[1] The theory developed in these and Green's other lectures was not so much a new theory as a new version of a classical theory, ultimately derived from Plato, and appearing in different forms in the work of Rousseau, Kant and Hegel. Its assumptions differ radically from those on which Utilitarianism is based.

In the first place, Green (like Bradley) rejected the Utilitarian assumption that men's actions are determined by their anticipation of pleasures and pains, and that their over-riding aim is to maximize the total of personal pleasures that they experience. Green argued that men's ambitions include the wish to develop their personalities in ways they think good, and that their idea of what is good, both as a form of behaviour and as a line of development, depends on the values of the society in which they live. Man is by nature a social being, and this means that he is also a moral being. A thoughtful man, Green said, will regard his 'well-being' as 'the thought of himself as living in the pursuit of various interests which the order of society—taking the term in the widest sense—has determined for him; interests ranging perhaps from provision for his family to the improvement of the public health or the production of a system of philosophy'.[2] The ideals which shape his behaviour and aspirations will be common to all members of his society, and his realization of these ideals will contribute to the welfare of all. If individuals have ambitions which conflict with these ideals, their pursuit will not, in the long run, benefit their personalities.

Secondly, Green insisted that 'will, not force, is the basis of the state'.[3] Whereas Utilitarians regarded the state as a necessary evil, based on force, Green saw it as an essential agent for the promotion of the common good, based on the common will. It should command obedience not because it possesses coercive powers, but because its citizens recognize that its existence enhances their freedom to pursue worthwhile objectives. The aim of its legislation should be to promote the good life of its citizens, mainly—since compulsory morality is a contradiction in terms—by removing hindrances to the good life.

This was an idealistic view of the nature of the state, and Green

---

[1] By 'influential' is meant influential outside the world of academic philosophers. Within that world F. H. Bradley, whose *Ethical Studies* was published in 1876, was probably more influential than Green.

[2] *Prolegomena to Ethics* (Oxford, 1929), p. 275.

[3] *Principles of Political Obligation* (London, 1941), Section G.

did not pretend that any existing state completely conformed to it. Since the view was proposed as an ideal, its validity was not affected by this disparity. On the basis of these central arguments Green elaborated a number of subsidiary arguments about the rights of citizens, the right of the state to punish, and the rights of the state in particular fields of legislation. He did not discuss the problems of representation and political responsibility at any length but an attitude to these questions is implicit in his writings, and has been developed by some of his followers.

## IDEALISM AND THE THEORY OF RESPONSIBLE GOVERNMENT

The Idealist theory offers an answer which is different from that of the Utilitarians to the fundamental problem of the theory of responsible government: the problem of how a government can respond to public demands and movements of public opinion without being irresponsible in the sense of pursuing inconsistent policies. The Utilitarian view that this is possible because there is a natural harmony of interests in society was plausible, up to a point, so long as there were no effective demands for state intervention in economic and social affairs. But as soon as effective demands of this kind developed, as they did in Britain in the 1870's, the conflicts between the interests of the various groups which would be affected by this intervention became obvious. The Idealist theory attempts to meet this difficulty by distinguishing between the immediate and private interests of citizens, which are apt to be in conflict, and their 'true interests', which are not in conflict.

This distinction flows from Rousseau's distinction between the 'will of all' and the 'general will'; and the clearest discussion of it is to be found in the writings of Bernard Bosanquet, who was one of Green's pupils.[1] Bosanquet argued that the ideal state should seek to further the real interests of its citizens rather than their apparent wants, on the ground that 'what we really want is something more and other than at any given moment we are aware' that we want.[2] Moreover, since we all want to lead a harmonious social life, our real interests cannot lie in the pursuit of objectives which would conflict with this aim. In fact, Bosanquet asserts, 'if everyone pursued his *true* private interest he would pursue the common interest'.[3]

The main weakness of this line of argument is that Bosanquet asserts as a proposition what is in fact simply a tautology. The lack of conflict between citizens' true interests, in this theory, is implicit in Bosanquet's definition of a true interest, which '*necessarily* has just

[1] See *The Philosophical Theory of the State* (London, 1899), particularly Chapter V.  [2] Ibid., p. 119.  [3] Ibid., p. 114.

the characters which the true universal has as against the collection of particulars, or the General Will against the Will of All'.[1] It follows that the theory cannot be tested empirically. If enquiry should show that some citizens have interests which are directly opposed to those of others, all that could be said would be that, in Bosanquet's terminology, some if not all of these interests were apparent rather than true.

In spite of this weakness, the theory does point to a distinction which can be recognized as both genuine and important. It is perhaps best defined as a distinction between citizens' immediate interests as individuals and their long-term interests as members of society. For instance, on the question of tariffs there is a sharp conflict of immediate interest between many manufacturers, who see an advantage in high tariffs to protect their products from foreign competition, and most consumers, who want low tariffs to keep prices down. But the long-term interests of both manufacturers and consumers are bound up with the rate of economic growth and the maintenance of Britain's economic position as a trading nation, and if the question of tariffs is considered in relation to these factors the conflict of interest is likely to be much less sharp. Another example is the controversy over the establishment of 'smokeless zones', in which there is a conflict of immediate interest between manufacturers of smokeless fuels on the one hand and householders who want to burn cheap fuels in their grates on the other. This conflict becomes much less sharp if householders can be persuaded to view the matter in terms of their long-run interest in the creation of a more healthy environment for themselves and their children.

It is clear that this distinction exists. It is probably safe to assert that there is much less conflict between citizens' long-term social interests than between their immediate private interests. It would be unreasonable to assert that there is *no* conflict between long-term interests, unless these are defined in such a way as to make this a necessary truth, as they were by Bosanquet. But one of the achievements of the Idealists was to focus attention on this distinction and on the problem of eliciting the highest measure of common agreement, which they called the common will, from the mass of particular opinions and interests that exist in relation to any sphere of government activity.

### IDEALISM AND THE THEORY OF REPRESENTATION

To the Idealist, the purpose of the representative system is not to mirror the immediate interests that exist, but to make possible a

[1] See *The Philosophical Theory of the State* (London, 1899), p. 114, my italics.

process of discussion in which the common interest will emerge and be recognized. The British Idealists and their followers never accepted Rousseau's view that discussion would inhibit the emergence of the common will; on the contrary they argued that free discussion at all levels is essential to its emergence. In their view, the chief merit of the British political system was that it enabled governmental decisions to be reached as the result of this kind of discussion.

The most eloquent exponents of this view were A. D. (later Lord) Lindsay and Sir Ernest Barker. Lindsay argued that: 'Democracy is based on the assumption that men can agree on common action which yet leaves each to lead his own life—that if we really respect one another's personality we can find a common framework . . . within which the free moral life of the individual is possible. How that can best be attained can be discovered by discussion.'[1] Lindsay compared the government of the modern state with that of the small voluntary society, such as the Society of Friends, and suggested that the problem of political organization in large societies is to find ways of securing something equivalent to the sense of the meeting. Government must always be based on public opinion, but this is not to be estimated by the mere counting of heads. Voting has its place, but it is rather as a check—as a way of ensuring that the discussion is not dominated by any one group—than as a positive method of determining what will best serve the common purpose. 'The purpose of representative government', said Lindsay, 'is to maintain and preserve different points of view, in order to make effective discussion possible . . . it is democratic in so far as it is recognized that every one, just because they have their own life to lead, has something special and distinctive to contribute . . . it gets over the impossibility of large-scale discussion by dividing the unifying of differences through discussion into several stages. But . . . this belief that every one has something to contribute does not mean that what every one has to say is of equal value. It assumes that if the discussion is good enough the proper value of each contribution will be brought out in the discussion'.[2]

The same general argument was related more specifically to British institutions by Sir Ernest Barker.[3] He argued, following Green, that 'democracy which rests merely on the will of number rests merely on force'.[4] The real basis of democracy, he claimed, is the 'discussion of competing ideas, leading to a compromise in which all the ideas are

[1] *Essentials of Democracy* (2nd edn., London, 1935), p. 33.    [2] Ibid., pp. 40–1.
[3] It is not suggested that Barker embraced all the views of the Oxford Idealists; he did not, for instance, share their theory of knowledge; but his views on politics bear a strong family resemblance to theirs which makes it appropriate to include them in this chapter.    [4] *Reflections on Government* (London, 1942), p. 36.

reconciled and which can be accepted by all because it bears the imprint of all'. In Britain this discussion proceeds through four stages. The first stage is the formulation of the issues by a process of discussion within and between the political parties; the second is 'the choice between party programmes, and between the representatives of those programmes, which is made by the electorate';[1] the third is the discussion between these representatives in Parliament; the fourth is the discussion at cabinet level, when the general trends of political opinion are translated into specific decisions.

Barker specifically denied the validity of the view that the authority of each stage derives from that of the preceding stage, so that the cabinet is subordinate to the will of Parliament and Parliament is subordinate to the will of the electorate.[2] He argued that instead of a hierarchy of authorities, there is a division of labour between authorities which interact constantly with one another. As a result, he claimed, the differences of view between groups in society have the chance of being reconciled at various stages of the debate and at various levels of generality.

## THE POLITICAL INFLUENCE OF IDEALISM

If political theories become widely accepted or influential it is usually because they suit the needs and temper of the time. This was true of Utilitarianism in the second quarter of the last century and it was equally true of Idealism in the final quarter. The moralistic spirit of the times demanded a philosophy more uplifting than that based on the hedonistic assumptions of Bentham and James Mill, while the political reformers of the period wanted a theoretical justification for their plans to extend the activities of the government in ways that could not easily be justified in Utilitarian terms. Idealism met both these needs, and it had the additional advantage of being a style of philosophy well suited to the intellectual preferences of the ruling classes, educated as they mostly were in the classical tradition. T. S. Eliot's comment on F. H. Bradley is relevant to the school as a whole: 'He replaced a philosophy which was crude and raw and provincial by one which was, in comparison, catholic, civilized, and universal.'[3]

This philosophy was accepted, in part or in whole, by a wide variety of political theorists, political leaders, and public servants. Among political theorists, what is remarkable is the evident influence of Idealism even among writers who did not regard themselves as adherents to the Idealist view. Thus, L. T. Hobhouse devoted one of

[1] *Reflections on Government* (London, 1942), p. 41.   [2] Ibid., p. 50.
[3] T. S. Eliot, *Selected Essays* (London, 1934), pp. 410–11.

his books to a vigorous attack on the theories of Hegel and Bosanquet, saying in a preface that Hegel's philosophy had laid the foundation of the 'false and wicked doctrine' of the glorification of the state, the 'visible and tangible outcome' of which was to be seen in the bombing of London in 1917.[1] Yet in his book on *Liberalism* Hobhouse accepted all the main tenets of the Idealist theory: he explained that Liberals now believed in the organic theory of society; he described liberty as 'primarily a matter of social interest, as something flowing from the necessities of continuous advance in those regions of truth and of ethics which constitute the matters of highest social concern';[2] and he asserted that 'an individual right . . . cannot conflict with the common good, nor could any right exist apart from the common good'.[3] And in a later book on *The Elements of Social Justice*[4] Hobhouse again demonstrated his very considerable debt to the philosophical Idealists.

H. J. Laski was another writer who, while criticizing the Idealists on numerous occasions, was nevertheless clearly influenced by their views. In 1929 he wrote a lecture in which he said that 'a true theory of liberty . . . is built upon a denial of each of the assumptions of Idealism'.[5] But only a few years earlier he had leaned heavily upon Green's work in his discussion of rights and duties in *A Grammar of Politics*,[6] and in 1928 he wrote a report to the Inter-Parliamentary Union which included the following sentence: 'The underlying thesis of Parliamentary government is that discussion forms the popular mind and that the executive utilizes the legislature to translate into statute the will arrived at by that mind.'[7]

To trace the influence of a theory on practical politics is necessarily more difficult than to trace its influence on subsequent political ideas. Political decisions are influenced by a great variety of factors, and even when a politician justifies a decision in terms of a particular theory of politics it is difficult to be certain that he would not have reached the same decision if his theoretical assumptions had been different. There is a sense in which the writings of the English Idealists both pointed to the need and provided a justification for the collectivist policies that were subsequently adopted. But it is not clear whether this should be adduced as evidence of the influence of Idealism or as a partial explanation of the appeal of Idealism. Most historians would prefer the second alternative.

[1] L. T. Hobhouse, *The Metaphysical Theory of the State* (London, 1918), p. 6.
[2] *Liberalism* (London, 1911), pp. 124–5.
[3] Ibid., p. 127.　　　　　　　　　　　　　　　　　　[4] London, 1922.
[5] *Liberty in the Modern State* (first published 1930, Penguin edn., London, 1937), p. 58.　　　　　　　　　　　　　　　　[6] London, 1925.
[7] H. J. Laski and others, *The Development of the Representative System in our Times* (Geneva, 1928), p. 13.

We are on safer ground if we leave on one side the question of the possible influence of Idealist theories on policy and deal instead with their influence on politicians' understanding of the nature of the political process. This kind of understanding can come only from teaching and experience, and if teaching precedes political experience it is likely to shape the lessons drawn from that experience. Many of Britain's political leaders in the first two decades of the present century were educated at Oxford and exposed to the influence of T. H. Green and the other Idealist philosophers. Those who were members of Green's own college, Balliol, included Milner, Curzon, Haldane, Asquith, and Grey; and in the next generation J. Ramsay MacDonald, though never at Oxford, had educated himself in the writings of the Oxford Idealists. The influence of these theories on Haldane's approach to politics has been discussed in a very interesting essay by C. H. Wilson.[1] In this chapter there will be space only to add a few comments on the two prime ministers, Asquith and MacDonald.

Asquith's biographers have told us of his 'ardent admiration' for T. H. Green.[2] While Asquith was not greatly interested in the more metaphysical aspects of Green's thought, he acquired from his studies at Oxford an understanding of politics as a process of discussion between reasonable men who shared the same fundamental values. His approach to problems of government was marked, on the one hand, by a belief that discussion and negotiation would eventually produce a solution that would be accepted by all parties and, on the other, by an intense dislike of any violent or unconstitutional action which would interrupt or distort this process. He had little or no understanding of the position of a minority which felt so strongly about an issue that it was prepared to break the rules in its campaign for what it considered to be its rights.

These attitudes were illustrated by Asquith's policies as Prime Minister. His repeated refusal to yield to the demand for female suffrage was based not so much on an objection in principle to this reform as on his abhorrence of the methods of the suffragettes. In the 1912–13 session he offered a free vote on the issue and admitted that he could share neither the enthusiasm of the advocates of this reform nor the vehemence of most of its opponents.[3] But as the suffragette campaign grew more violent Asquith became determined not to yield to its demands. For a minority—or for that matter, for a majority—to try to impose its will by force was to destroy the fabric

---

[1] See C. H. Wilson, *Haldane and the Machinery of Government* (London, 1957).
[2] J. A. Spender and C. Asquith, *Life of Lord Oxford and Asquith* (London, 1932), vol. I, p. 36.
[3] See ibid., vol. I, pp. 358–61.

of democratic government, as he conceived it. Such action made it impossible for a common agreement to be achieved by discussion and compromise. It followed that it would be wrong to consider granting the reform until the suffragettes abandoned their unconstitutional methods of campaigning. They did so when war broke out, and in 1917 Asquith supported the proposal to enfranchise women, giving as one reason for his change of attitude the fact that 'since the war began, now nearly three years ago, we have had no recurrence of that detestable campaign which disfigured the annals of political agitation in this country, and no one can now contend that we are yielding to violence when we refused to concede to argument'.[1]

During the same period Asquith had to deal with the agitation against Home Rule in Ireland. It is fair to say that in doing so he again displayed a complete lack of comprehension of the position of a minority which felt so strongly about an issue that it was prepared to flout the conventions of constitutional government. He was convinced that Home Rule was in the general interest of both Britain and Ireland, and that most voters in both countries had shown their understanding of this. While he regretted that a minority composed of about one-fifth of the Irish people disliked the plan, he thought it was their duty to discuss the matter in an amicable fashion so that a measure of common agreement could be reached. He could not understand the obstinacy of leaders who said simply that they would not accept Home Rule, and would resist it by any means open to them. He refused to believe in the possibility of civil war some time after most observers had accepted that this was a very real possibility.[2] His biographers say, and they might have put it more definitely, that he was 'so staunch a believer in the processes of argument, debate and election, that he perhaps failed to reckon with the passions that had been unloosed both in Ireland and in Conservative circles in England'.[3]

These examples expose a limitation in Asquith's understanding of politics which was common to most of those who subscribed to the Idealist theory. They were so impressed with the need for the decisions of the government to reflect the common will of society that they ignored the fact that there are some issues on which no common will exists or can be created. This is a criticism which could not be levelled against Rousseau, the originator of the idea of the general will. He specified very clearly that there could be no general will except in a homogeneous society whose members all adhered to the same civil religion, and that even when these conditions were

---

[1] *House of Commons Debates*, 5th s., v. 92, c. 470.

[2] See, for instance, his speech in Dublin in July 1912, quoted in Spender and Asquith, op. cit., vol. II, pp. 19–20.　　　　[3] Ibid., vol. II, p. 56.

satisfied there would be no general will on issues which, by their nature, ranged one section of society against another. In the early years of the present century A. J. Balfour issued a similar kind of warning, in rather different terms. But English Idealists paid scant attention to these warnings, perhaps because they believed that British society was sufficiently homogeneous for them to be unnecessary. The result is that their understanding of politics tended to break down when sharp sectional differences were exposed. The suffragette campaign was one instance; the Irish question was another; the conflict between Muslims and Hindus in India was a third; and the general strike of 1926 may possibly be cited as a fourth. It is perhaps significant that Asquith's biographers say that 'the iniquity of the general strike seemed to him so patent, so glaring that he thought the facts need only be stated to carry conviction to every mind'.[1]

The other Prime Minister who accepted many of the views of the Idealists was J. Ramsay MacDonald. His biographer has said that his social ideas were influenced by his biological studies,[2] and there is clearly some truth in this, but the view of politics that is presented in his book *Socialism and Government* is nearer to the Idealist view than to any other. In this he defined the state as 'the organization of a community for making its common will effectual by political methods',[3] and he discussed the relation between the individual will and the common will in terms rather similar to Bosanquet's exposition in *The Philosophical Theory of the State*. 'The actions of legislatures', MacDonald wrote, 'can but express the will of the community—not of a class, or of a majority, or a minority, or a party, but of the community.'[4] And later he explicitly rejected the doctrine of class representation to which the Labour Party (of which he was then secretary) was officially committed. Socialists, he maintained, were not interested in the representation of classes, or of interests, or of property. Their concern was 'that good government which is the result of an accurate representation of the State personality', and their object in advocating adult suffrage was 'to make the social experience of all adults . . . available for the State'.[5]

Elsewhere, MacDonald maintained that 'the Radical idea of majority rule is wrong, because it is the general will and not the majority that governs'.[6] The general will is to some extent indicated by the majority vote, but 'the representatives returned by the majority have to observe the wish as of the minority in their actions'.[7] It

---

[1] Spender and Asquith, op. cit., vol. II, p. 372.
[2] Lord Elton, *Life of James Ramsay MacDonald* (London, 1939), p. 112.
[3] *Socialism and Government* (London, 1909), vol. I, p. 4.
[4] Ibid., p. 21.    [5] Ibid., pp. 46–7.    [6] Ibid., p. viii.    [7] Ibid., p. 80.

follows that the representative should not take instructions, for he 'represents society, he is not the delegate of the majority that elected him'.[1]

The knowledge that MacDonald held these views helps us to understand some of his actions. For instance, in 1911 he supported the contributory principle embodied in Lloyd George's National Insurance Bill, although the Fabians and most of the Labour leaders were opposed to this. He supported it because he thought it better to retain an element of personal responsibility in matters of this kind than for the workers to depend on 'state philanthropy'.[2] His basic political attitudes were also reflected in his views on women's suffrage, on which he again differed from many of his colleagues. He supported this reform on the ground that as women's experience differed from that of men, their opinions ought to be represented in the process of political debate. But he would not agree that women had a natural right to vote, nor would he accept what he called the 'colonial argument of no taxation without representation'.[3] Further, he did not agree that women ought to have more influence than men on decisions relating to the employment of women in factories or public houses, for he insisted that these were social problems that should be dealt with by society as a whole rather than by any particular group within society. These views separated him from many Labour leaders, as did his repeated condemnations of the violence of the suffragettes' campaign. MacDonald opposed violence of any kind, including the civil disobedience campaign propagated by Gandhi and the 'direct action' favoured by a number of his colleagues in the Labour movement.[4]

MacDonald's attitude to the General Strike and his behaviour in 1931 were also in accord with his general approach to politics. His decision to form a national government in 1931 had unfortunate consequences for the Labour Party (which subsequently expelled

[1] *Socialism and Government* (London, 1909), vol. 1, p. 83.

[2] See Elton, op. cit., pp. 207–9.

[3] Quoted in Benjamin Sacks, *J. Ramsay MacDonald* (Albuquerque, New Mexico, 1952), p. 7.

[4] See M. S. Venkataramani, 'Ramsay MacDonald and Britain's Domestic Policies and Foreign Relations, 1919–1931', in *Political Studies*, vol. VIII (1960). R. E. Dowse has pointed out that between 1918 and 1922, when MacDonald was not in Parliament and the Parliamentary opposition to the government was ineffective, MacDonald suggested that some kinds of direct action might be justified if the government itself engaged in unconstitutional action or threatened to involve the country in an aggressive and unwanted war. But it is clear that this would have been direct action to protect the *status quo*, not to change it. See R. E. Dowse, 'A Note on Ramsay MacDonald and Direct Action', in ibid., vol. IX (1961).

him) and ruined MacDonald's reputation in left-wing circles.[1] But no impartial student can doubt that, rightly or wrongly, it was based upon a conviction that in a situation of serious economic crisis the most important need was the preservation of national unity. He felt that his actions, unpopular though they were with most members of his own party, reflected the common will and would be endorsed by the majority of voters at the next election, as indeed they were.

It seems clear from these examples that the theories of the philosophical Idealists influenced not only the subsequent course of academic political thought but also the way in which practical politicians looked at the political process. The individualistic approach to politics passed out of favour towards the end of the last century, and political discussion in terms of the Utilitarian calculus was replaced, in part, by discussion in terms of concepts like the common will, the social ethic, and the organic unity of the nation. But it cannot be said that the theory of representation which Lindsay and Barker developed on this basis has become widely accepted as a satisfactory account of the functions and purpose of the British representative system. Unlike the Marxist views discussed in the previous chapter, it cannot easily be dismissed as untrue. But it is too vague and perhaps too complacent to be entirely convincing, for it is precisely at those moments of crisis when interest in the foundations of our political system is greatest that the limitations of the Idealist approach to politics are exposed.

[1] MacDonald's actions in 1931 created such bitterness among writers who felt that he had 'betrayed the left' that the events were subsequently misrepresented and MacDonald himself was vilified in a long series of articles and books. For details, see R. Bassett, *Nineteen Thirty-One: Political Crisis* (London, 1958).

# CHAPTER 8
# Theories of Group Representation

The reaction against political individualism in Britain took three main forms. Some writers maintained that society consisted essentially of competing (or warring) social classes; some thought it more appropriate to look upon society as an organic whole; and others insisted that the basic units of social life were groups and associations. This last view was by no means novel, for it had its roots in medieval ideas about the nature of society. In more recent times it was reflected in eighteenth-century ideas about the representation of interests as well as in Burke's insistence on the virtues of 'the little platoon'. In the nineteenth century it suffered a temporary loss of favour, but in the first two decades of the twentieth century it blossomed out again in a rather different form.

In this period the group view of society derived fresh impetus and a new slant from two loosely associated movements of ideas. One, which consisted of ideas of a rather abstract kind about the nature of society, is generally known as Pluralism; the other, which consisted of ideas about political and industrial organization, is generally known as Guild Socialism. The two sets of ideas moved on different levels, as did their exponents; the Guild Socialists being much more concerned with practical questions than the Pluralists. But it must be said straight away that the two doctrines are almost equally difficult to define in precise terms.

## PLURALIST IDEAS

The doctrine known as Pluralism had three main strands, which cannot easily be related except in the very loose sense that they all contributed to the same movement of ideas. The first strand was an attack launched by several academic lawyers, most notably F. W. Maitland, on the concept of legal sovereignty that had held a central position in English jurisprudence from Austin to Dicey. Maitland, under the influence of the German writer Otto von Gierke, argued that permanent groups within society have personalities and wills which should be recognized as just as real, from the legal point of view, as those of individuals. They have what may be called juristic personalities which exist independently of state recognition, for such groups and associations are logically prior to the state, not created by it. It follows that the rights of such groups should be respected by the state, and their duties acknowledged; they should be able to sue and equally they should be capable of being sued.[1] This doctrine was apparently accepted by the Lords of Appeal responsible for the Taff Vale judgement of 1901, in which it was held that a trade union, though not a corporate body, could nevertheless be sued for damages.[2]

A very similar point of view to Maitland's was advanced by J. N. Figgis, who argued that churches and other voluntary associations had rights which the state should respect. The national society, in Figgis's view, was a federation of groups and communities to which the first loyalty of citizens was owed; and the claim of such groups and communities to legal recognition and rights depended on the fact that, in this sense, they were prior to the state itself. Figgis also insisted that groups and communities had personalities, and should be granted some of the legal privileges normally given to persons. 'It is perfectly plain', he said, 'that a community is something more than the sum of the persons composing it—in other words, it has a real personality, not a fictitious one.'[3] And he went on to draw attention to the case of *Free Church of Scotland v. Lord Overtoun*,[4] in which the House of Lords had refused, despite eloquent arguments by counsel, to accept the principle that the Free Church could be accorded the right that would be granted to a person to change its mind on a point of doctrine and dispose of its property in a way that was consistent with its new, but not with its old, doctrinal position.

A rather different contribution to Pluralist ideas was made by a number of social psychologists, of whom the most eminent was William McDougall, who developed the concept of 'the group mind'.[5] This concept is now as dead as the dodo, and we need not go into the matter except to note that the currency of the concept at the time lent support to those who wished to accord groups a vital place in their political theories. On the one hand could be found eminent lawyers who asserted that groups had juristic personalities; on the

[1] See F. W. Maitland, Introduction to O. von Gierke, *Political Theories of the Middle Ages* (London, 1900) and *Collected Papers*, ed. H. A. L. Fisher (Cambridge, 1911), vol. III, pp. 304–20; also Ernest Barker, *Political Thought in England: 1848–1914* (London, 1915), Chapter 6.

[2] For brief details, see G. D. H. Cole, *British Working Class Politics: 1832–1914* (London, 1941), pp. 167–9.

[3] J. N. Figgis, *Churches in the Modern State* (London, 1913), p. 250.

[4] [1904] A.C. 515.

[5] See McDougall's *Social Psychology* (London, 1908) and, more particularly, *The Group Mind* (Cambridge, 1920).

other could be found eminent psychologists who asserted that groups had minds. In this general climate of thought it did not seem unreasonable for political theorists to assert that groups were living entities within society which deserved special recognition within the political system.[1]

Theorists of this kind contributed the third and, from our point of view, most interesting strand of the movement of ideas known as Pluralism. The main concern of these theorists was to show that the claims widely made for the omnipotence of the state were invalid. In the last chapter L. T. Hobhouse was cited as a writer who was in general accord with the views of the philosophical Idealists but was worried because these views seemed to afford no clear basis for defining the limits of state action. Among scholars of the succeeding generation A. D. Lindsay, Ernest Barker, Harold Laski, and G. D. H. Cole all found themselves (for a time) in rather a similar position. They had rejected the individualistic assumptions of Victorian Liberals on both philosophical and sociological grounds; they could give no credence to Mill's distinction between self-regarding and other-regarding actions; but at the same time they were unwilling to accept that the state was morally entitled to take whatever action the government of the day thought would be in the best interests of the nation.

For a period of about ten or fifteen years following 1914 these writers thought that an answer to this dilemma might be found by insisting on the importance of voluntary groups and associations in society. Though they could see no basis for the claim that individuals had rights against the state, they suggested that groups and associations had rights which the state ought not to curtail. They developed this point of view in a variety of ways.

Lindsay wrote an article in 1914 in which he referred to groups as corporate personalities within society. He suggested that they attracted deeper loyalties than the state, which was of necessity a much more heterogeneous association, and he claimed that if groups were left a wide measure of freedom they would prove effective agencies of social co-ordination.[2] Barker wrote sympathetically about Maitland's ideas in the survey of recent political thought which he published in 1915. He said in this that:

[1] McDougall's work is cited in the bibliography of G. D. H. Cole's *Social Theory* (London, 1920) and is referred to, directly or obliquely, by several of the writers who contributed to the Pluralist movement.

[2] See Lindsay, 'The State in Recent Political Theory', in *The Political Quarterly*, vol. 1 (1914). The phrase 'social co-ordination' was very popular in this period: it was overworked by G. D. H. Cole and crops up frequently in other Pluralist writings.

'If we are individualists now, we are corporate individualists. Our "individuals" are becoming groups. . . . Every state, we feel, is something of a federal society, and contains within its borders different national groups, different churches, different economic organizations, each exercising its measure of control over its members.'[1]

Barker warned his readers that 'we must not push too far our claims on behalf of group-persons',[2] but he was quite clear that claims should be made, and that 'associations which are living and acting like persons under social recognition' should be accorded both legal and political recognition.[3]

Laski approached the matter in a slightly different way. He maintained that it was not only morally wrong to assert that the state was omnipotent, but also, as a matter of fact, mistaken. In a series of works he pointed out that no government could enforce its will against the determined opposition of important groups within society, whether these be churches, trade unions, or employers' organizations. It followed that the theory of sovereignty should be revised to take account of the federal nature of society and the dependence of the state upon the support of other human associations.[4]

None of these three writers espoused this doctrine for more than a few years. Lindsay and Barker moved towards philosophical Idealism, and not much trace of Pluralism is to be found in their later works. Laski ceased to be so concerned about the limits of state action after the onset of the economic depression, when he began his long and inevitably unsuccessful demonstration of how to be a Liberal and a Marxist at the same time.

G. D. H. Cole's attachment to Pluralism is of a different order, both because he constituted the most vital of the several links between Pluralism and Guild Socialism and because he remained loyal to these doctrines until his death in 1959. Cole's main theoretical contribution is to be found in his book *Social Theory*, published in 1920. In this he rejected individualism and identified himself as a follower of Rousseau.[5] At the same time he dissociated himself from the English Idealists on the ground that they had made the doctrine of the real will into a 'colossally fraudulent justification of "things as they are" '.[6] Interestingly, he cited Bosanquet's writings as 'an

---

[1]*Political Thought in England: 1848–1914* (first pub. Oxford, 1915; second edn. 1928), p. 181.   [2]Ibid., p. 180.   [3]Ibid., p. 178.
[4]See H. J. Laski, *The Problems of Sovereignty* (London, 1917), *Authority in the Modern State* (London, 1919), *Foundations of Sovereignty* (London, 1921), and *A Grammar of Politics* (London, 1925).
[5]See *Social Theory* (London, 1920), pp. 6–9.   [6]Ibid., p. 93.

awful example' of this tendency and referred to Hobhouse's work as 'an excellent onslaught' upon it.[1] In Cole's view society was neither a collection of individuals nor an organic whole, but a complex of functional associations whose activities were co-ordinated by another association known as the state.

On the basis of this view Cole set out to provide new answers to a number of political problems, and in Chapter 6 he attempted 'to restate the theory of representation in a truer form'.[2] This restatement has only a little of the clarity that distinguishes many of Cole's later writings, and it will be helpful to reduce it to a set of propositions. First, Cole maintained that true representation 'is always specific and functional': it is impossible to represent men as men, but possible to represent 'certain purposes common to groups of individuals'.[3] It follows, second, that elections based on geographical constituencies can only result in misrepresentation, and the best hope for democracy is 'to find an association and method of representation for each function' in society.[4] This would involve, third, the replacement of Parliament by 'a system of co-ordinated functional representative bodies',[5] each concerned with particular interests and activities. This plan would mean that citizens with a variety of interests would have a number of representatives, and Cole suggested that the familiar slogan 'One man, one vote' should be replaced by a new slogan: 'One man as many votes as interests, but only one vote in relation to each interest.'[6]

Cole was certainly not the only writer to suggest this kind of reform. In 1910 someone writing under the pseudonym of Candidus had published a short book entitled *The Reform of the Electorate Based Upon the Professions and Trades in place of Local Constituencies*, and in 1917 A. H. Mackmurdo wrote a pamphlet called *Electoral Reform; Voting by Occupations*. Candidus took the view that democracy required 'a real grouping of non-conflicting interests that one man may represent, and for this we need some sifting process that shall class the people into *consistent* and *organic* groups'.[7] He suggested that this sifting process should be provided by occupational guilds which individuals would join. There would be a guild for each occupation, or two guilds if those who followed the occupation were divided into employers and workers; the members of each guild would elect a guild council; the guild councils would elect Members of Parliament; and the system would be so arranged that employers' guilds and workers' guilds would enjoy equal representa-

---

[1] See *Social Theory* (London, 1920), p. 93n.  [2] Ibid., p. 104.
[3] Ibid., p. 106.  [4] Ibid., p. 108.
[5] Ibid.  [6] Ibid., p. 115.
[7] Op. cit., p. 16, italics in the original.

tion in Parliament. It is clear that Candidus, like Cole, was one of those who formed a bridge between the Pluralists and the Guild Socialists, to whose ideas we must now turn.[1]

## GUILD SOCIALIST IDEAS

Guild Socialist ideas had three sources which were somewhat different in spirit. One source was the movement of ideas discussed in the previous section, which led a number of writers to look upon the powers and organization of the state in a rather new light. Another source was the Syndicalist movement in France. Nobody of any consequence in Britain advocated Syndicalism in its continental form, for mistrust of the state in this country was not so great as to lead people to wish to dispense with it altogether. But a number of labour leaders, most notably Tom Mann, were influenced by Syndicalist ideas and advocated the creation of industrial unions (as opposed to craft unions) and the eventual establishment of a form of industrial self-government.[2]

A third source was the nostalgia for an earlier form of economic organization that was engendered by writers who looked with horror on industrial capitalism and wanted to restore to the worker the sense of craftsmanship and control over his own activities that, in their view, workers had enjoyed in medieval times. John Ruskin, William Morris, Hilaire Belloc, and G. K. Chesterton all contributed in different ways to this nostalgic mood, which was quite widespread between about 1890 and 1914. The Guild Socialist movement derived its name as well as many of its ideas from the writings of three men who viewed economic and social affairs in this way. A. J. Penty, who published *The Restoration of the Guild System* in 1906, has been described as 'an extreme and consistent medievalist, with an uncompromising hatred of inventions and machinery and of division of labour'.[3] It would not be unfair to apply the same description to S. G. Hobson and A. R. Orage, who spread Guild Socialist ideas in their weekly journal, the *New*

---

[1] In addition to the works cited, there was a good deal of discussion about functional representation and allied questions in the journals of the period. As an example, see the three articles contributed by J. A. R. Marriott to *The Fortnightly Review*: 'Quo Vadis' (February 1920), 'Soviet v. Parliament' (October 1920), and 'President or Premier?' (November 1920).

[2] See Henry Pelling (ed.) *The Challenge of Socialism* (London, 1954), chapter 13. It is worth noting that Cole himself said that Guild Socialism in Britain was the parallel to Syndicalism in France. See G. D. H. Cole, *Self-Government in Industry* (London, 1917), p. 321.

[3] Alexander Gray, *The Socialist Tradition* (London, 1946), p. 441.

*Age.*[1] All three writers wanted to see the establishment of industrial guilds, on medieval lines, through which the producers in each industry would have a large measure of control over the industry in which they worked.

There were clearly basic differences of outlook between progressive political theorists like Cole, militant unionists like Mann, and romantic medievalists like Penty and Hobson. But for a time they all had similar objectives; the movement produced a considerable flurry of ideas and publications;[2] and Margaret Cole has said that in 1914 and for some years after 'the majority of young intellectual socialists' were supporters of Guild Socialism.[3]

The theory that emerged from this movement was essentially a theory of industrial organization under socialism. The Guild Socialists wanted ownership of industry to be in the hands of the nation, but control of industry to be in the hands of industrial guilds composed of representatives of the workers. But this was also a theory of political organization because it asserted that the existing machinery of representative government should be excluded from the control of industrial affairs. The Guild Socialists wanted to see the creation of another system of representative institutions, based on the guilds, which would exist side by side with the Parliamentary system. This new system would be hierarchical in structure and would be headed by a Central Guilds Congress which would have the task of resolving conflicts and securing co-ordination between the various industrial guilds. The relations which would exist between the Central Guilds Congress and Parliament were never defined with any precision. It was generally assumed that Parliament (either under that name or under some other) would continue to exist, but with truncated powers and stripped of its claims to sovereignty. But what would happen in case of a conflict between Parliament and the Guilds Congress was not made clear.

The Guild Socialists published so much, written so hastily, and

---

[1] Other publications by these three include Penty's *Old Worlds for New* (London, 1917), and *A Guildsman's Interpretation of History* (London, 1920); Hobson's *National Guilds and the State* (London, 1914), and *Guild Principles in War and Peace* (London, 1917); Orage's *National Guilds* (London, 1914) and *An Alphabet of Economics* (London, 1917).

[2] The following is a selection of other books published by members of the National Guilds League in this period: Bertrand Russell, *Roads to Freedom* (London, 1919), R. H. Tawney, *The Sickness of an Acquisitive Society* (London, 1920), Frank Hodges, *Nationalisation of the Mines* (London, 1920), M. B. Reckitt and C. E. Bechhofer, *The Meaning of National Guilds* (London, 1918), G. D. H. Cole, *The World of Labour* (London, 1913), *Self-Government in Industry* (London, 1917), *Chaos and Order in Industry* (London, 1920), and *Guild Socialism Re-stated* (London, 1920).

[3] Margaret Cole, *The Story of Fabian Socialism* (London, 1961), p. 153.

containing so many variations on their theme, that it is almost impossible to choose quotations which fairly summarize their views. But perhaps the following brief extract from one of Cole's later books on the subject will give an impression of their rather vague attitude to the problems of political organization.

'The omnicompetent state, with its omnicompetent Parliament, is thus utterly unsuitable to any really democratic community, and must be destroyed or painlessly extinguished. . . . Whatever the structure of the new society will be, the Guildsman is sure that it will have no place for the survival of the *factotum* state of today.'[1]

## PARLIAMENT AND INDUSTRY

The Guild Socialists' main opponents on the political left were Sidney and Beatrice Webb, who thought that workers were insufficiently educated to control industry and who believed that in any case national efficiency demanded national control of economic life by agencies of the state. However, it is an interesting indication of the climate of opinion in this period that the Webbs accepted that existing representative institutions might be inadequate to deal with this extended burden of responsibility. They suggested that there was a case for a Social Parliament, side by side with the existing Parliament, to deal with economic and social affairs.[2] Since they thought the new Parliament should be elected in the same way as the old, this was a proposal not for the representation of particular groups but for the representation of the whole community for a particular purpose. As such it is not directly relevant to our theme, though it is clearly related to the same movement of ideas.

In the event, the Webbs and their followers were more successful than the Guild Socialists in influencing the leaders of the Labour movement. The I.L.P. committed itself to Guild Socialist objectives in 1922, but when the Labour Party drew up plans for the nationalized industries these provided for control to be vested in national boards whose members would be appointed by the government. The cause of workers' control lost ground first as a result of the failure of the general strike, secondly when Herbert Morrison's plans for the nationalization of transport were accepted by the Labour Party between 1932 and 1934, and thirdly when the Trades Union Congress came out against workers' control in the report on nationalization which it produced in 1944. The whole issue is now virtually dead, and the ideas discussed in this chapter have had no practical effect on British institutions.

[1] *Guild Socialism Re-stated*, p. 32.
[2] See *A Constitution for the Socialist Commonwealth of Great Britain* (London, 1920).

The Webbs's plan for a co-Parliament to deal with social and economic affairs has also been ignored, and since the war the only people who have toyed with this kind of idea have been members of the political right. Both L. S. Amery and Christopher Hollis have suggested that there is something to be said for the establishment of a House of Industry, elected on a basis of occupational constituencies, which would relieve Parliament of much discussion of industrial matters, though remaining subservient to Parliament.[1] These suggestions have met with no direct response, though post-war governments have tried various other ways of ensuring that detailed discussion of economic and industrial problems takes place not in Parliament but between representatives of the industries, trade unions, and ministries most directly involved. The establishment of the National Economic Development Council is the latest and in some ways the most ambitious move in this direction.

This points to the main reason why the ideas of group representation that were canvassed so actively forty years ago have now fallen out of fashion. Since the 1920's the rapid extension of the economic activities of the government has been paralleled by an equally rapid extension of the political activities of economic interest groups. Trade unions and trade associations do not need any new institutions to represent their interests, for these are already represented in a variety of ways. Government departments hear representations from the affected interests before any important decisions are taken. The numerous official committees which deal with economic affairs normally contain representatives of the trade unions and trade associations concerned. When Parliamentary debates are held on economic questions a leading part in the debates is played by M.P.'s who act regularly as spokesmen for the groups with which they are associated.

These kinds of representation are enjoyed not only by trade unions and trade associations but by any organized group which represents a genuine interest. Ex-servicemen are represented through the British Legion, motorists through the motoring organizations, and people who enjoy fox-hunting through the British Field Sports Association. This is representation in the first sense of the term, as defined in Chapter 1, and not representation through a formal process of election. But it is highly effective, and nobody who is familiar with the flexible pattern of relationships existing between interest groups and the government would now see any advantage in trying to replace it by a system of functional representation through elections to specially constituted agencies.

[1] See Christopher Hollis, *Can Parliament Survive?* (London, 1949), p. 120, and L. S. Amery, *Thoughts on the Constitution* (Oxford, 1947), pp. 64–8.

# CHAPTER 9

# Party Democracy

## PARTY GOVERNMENT

One of the features common to the traditional theories of representation discussed in Part II of this book is that no account is taken of the possible role of organized parties. It is something of a paradox that disciplined parties developed at the same time that the Liberal view of the constitution, with its assumption that M.P.'s would act independently, was gaining general acceptance. By and large, Liberal writers have either ignored or regretted the growth of mass party organizations and their influence in the representative system. J. S. Mill, for instance, simply ignored the existence of political parties. Acton, also writing in the 1860's, thought their activities were disgraceful.[1] Later Liberal writers, some of whom have been mentioned in Chapter 5, have generally regretted the growth of party discipline and have suggested that this is one reason for the decline which they profess to see in the quality of Parliamentary democracy.

Conservative and Labour supporters are alike in rejecting this attitude and in believing that party management is helpful in the transaction of Parliamentary business. Both the main parties are of course highly organized at Westminster, and in the majority of Parliamentary debates each party presents a united front on the main issues at stake.[2] The Conservatives handle the problems of party management more smoothly than their opponents, and since the last war they have been rather more successful in avoiding open divisions within the party. But there is little practical difference between the two parties, either in the importance that they attach to party management or in the day-to-day means by which they carry it out.

There is a difference, however, in the way in which supporters of the parties discuss party management. Conservative writers, if they mention it at all, invariably assume that party discipline follows naturally from the loyalty of members to their leaders, and therefore needs no justification. More frequently, they simply take it for

[1] See *Essays on Church and State* (reprinted London, 1952), pp. 406–10.
[2] See P. G. Richards, *Honourable Members* (London, 1959), for an account of the behaviour of back-bench M.P.'s.

granted. The topic is not mentioned in Quintin Hogg's *The Case for Conservatism*[1] or in any of the numerous Conservative Party pamphlets published since 1945. In contrast, writers with Labour leanings have always been ready to justify party discipline in terms of a theory of representation.

## THE JUSTIFICATION OF PARTY DISCIPLINE

The justification of party discipline generally offered by left-wing speakers and writers can easily be summarized. In the first place, it is claimed that electors now decide how they will vote according to the policies of the parties rather than according to the personalities or individual opinions of the candidates. It is said to follow that a general election gives the victorious party a mandate to put its policies into effect, and that M.P.'s who were elected on that party's platform have an obligation to support the party in Parliament even though its policies may occasionally conflict with their personal views. Only by acting as a disciplined block, it is said, can these M.P.'s ensure that the popular will expressed at the polls is translated into legislative and executive action.

The objection is sometimes made to this view that electors do not in practice have a free choice of policies at the polls, but simply a choice between two or three policies of which none may correspond to the electors' real wishes. The Labour answer to this objection is that political parties should be (as the Labour Party is) democratically organized, so that all who are interested in policy can play a part in framing it. And they would add that the parties themselves should encourage people to take an interest in policy (as the Labour Party does) by producing a constant flow of pamphlets about current issues, by organizing conferences and debates and programmes of political education, and by convincing the rank-and-file member that a genuine opportunity exists for him to influence the party's decisions. In this way, it is said, the ordinary citizen can be given a continuing role in the democratic process, and the policy of a party winning a general election can rightly be regarded as embodying the will of the majority.

In describing this as a Labour doctrine it is not intended to suggest that all members of the Labour Party subscribe to it. There are differences of opinion among members on this as on other matters, and since 1955, and more particularly since 1959, some of the Party's leaders have drawn attention to the disadvantages of firm electoral commitments. As a result, the party seems now to have moved away from its earlier practice of issuing a list of industries which it pro-

[1] London, 1947.

posed to nationalize if it won the next general election. On the other hand, in 1962, these same leaders made play with the doctrine of the electoral mandate in connection with the proposal that Britain should join the Common Market. All in all, it seems fair to regard the arguments outlined in the previous two paragraphs as being characteristically Labour arguments, and this adjective will be used in the remainder of the chapter with the implicit qualification that not all Labour Party members accept the arguments in full. The arguments themselves will now be considered in relation to recent developments in British politics.

## THE ELECTORAL MANDATE

The idea of the electoral mandate is by no means new. On several occasions before the rise of the Labour Party the electorate voted in the knowledge that their behaviour at the polls would determine not only the composition of the government but also the policy to be followed upon the dominant issue of the day. In 1831 the King's Speech prior to the dissolution stated that one of the purposes of the election was to refer to the people the question of whether the system of Parliamentary representation should be reformed, and in the election many candidates gave pledges regarding their attitude to reform should they be elected. In 1868 the dominant issue of the election was the proposal to disestablish the Irish Church, and Gladstone's victory was regarded as giving him a mandate for disestablishment. In 1906 the election was fought on the issue of free trade *versus* protection, after Balfour, as Prime Minister, had stated that it would be beyond 'the limits of constitutional propriety' for the government to introduce protection without having first referred the question to the electorate.[1] Finally, both the elections of 1910 were dominated by specific issues: that of January by the rejection by the Lords of the Government's 1909 budget, and that of December by the proposal to curtail the powers of the House of Lords.

But although the idea of the mandate is not new, it has never occupied anything like the same place in Liberal and Conservative thought that it has in Labour thought since 1918. Neither Liberals nor Conservatives have ever embraced the view that a party should go to the electorate with a set of concrete proposals which, if successful, it is thereby mandated to put into practice. Their concept of the mandate has been, and is, much more vague. In the first place, they have argued that the party which wins an election has 'a mandate to govern', it being understood that, unless the election happens to have been dominated by a single issue (which is exceptional), the govern-

[1] *House of Commons Debates*, 4th s., v. 131, cc. 678–9.

ment should be free to pursue whatever policies it thinks appropriate. This usage of the term amounts to little more than an acknowledgement of the fact that, since the reform of Parliament, the government's political and moral authority has rested upon its popularity with the voters at the previous election.

Secondly, it has often been asserted that a ministry's 'mandate to govern' does not necessarily entitle it to introduce a major change of policy, of a kind likely to arouse intense public controversy, if the electors have not had the chance to express their views on the subject. This is a very vague principle (if principle it be), and it has been the subject of a good deal of controversy. Peel ignored it in 1846 and Gladstone did the same in 1886, when he introduced his Home Rule Bill. On the other hand, neither Balfour in 1903–5 nor Baldwin in 1923 was willing to introduce tariff reform without first getting a mandate from the people (which in the subsequent elections the people refused to give). But if these examples and that of the elections of 1910 suggest that the principle was acquiring general acceptance, later examples point the other way. The Conservative Government of 1924–29 had no mandate for the decision to return to the Gold Standard in 1925, which was said to be justified by economic necessity, or for the introduction of the Trade Disputes Bill of 1927, which was said to be justified by the general strike. And when a general tariff was introduced in 1932 this was done a few months after an election in which the government had secured nothing more precise than a 'doctor's mandate' to do whatever seemed best for the national economy.

The truth is that Liberal and Conservative leaders have invoked the principle when political conditions made this tactically appropriate, but have felt free to ignore it in other circumstances. And even though they have sometimes fought an election on one dominant issue, they have regarded this as an exceptional circumstance and have never accepted that a political party is under any obligation to present the electorate with concrete proposals. They maintain that the government should judge each issue on its merits and in relation to the opinions expressed in Parliament and the country, and should not feel that its hands are tied by pledges made some time previously in the possibly different circumstances of an election campaign.

The Labour approach to the question of the mandate is very different. In the first place, it has always been one of the principles of the British trade-union movement that leaders and delegates should not only be elected but should be mandated to pursue policies endorsed by the members. Labour politicians with trade-union backgrounds have instinctively tended to assume that the same principle should apply to the government of the nation. In the second place, Labour politicians have never accepted the view of the older parties that politics, involving as it does a constant process of compromise and adjustment, is an activity which requires a substantial degree of independence on the part of those who engage in it.

On the contrary, Labour supporters believe that their representatives are elected in order to transform society. This is, indeed, the central belief that has, until recently, united the various groups that make up the Labour Party. In this view politics is not a matter of compromising between interests and opinions, but a matter of advancing towards a known objective. Drawing comfort from military analogies, Labour politicians have tended to speak of themselves as comrades-in-arms, preserving unbroken ranks in face of the class enemy, and working together to overcome obstacles in the advance towards a more just social system. 'Our claim to office', states a recent party pamphlet, 'is not just that we can manage things better than the Conservatives; we aim to create a different and better society.'[1]

This approach to politics naturally leads members of the Labour Party to look upon the doctrine of the mandate in a rather different light from that of the older parties. Most Labour politicians feel that at each general election it is the duty of the Labour Party to present the electorate with a manifesto setting out the reforms that the party proposes to introduce, if returned to office, during the life of the following Parliament. They feel that, if successful, the party would have a mandate to translate this programme into action and should do so unless circumstances change radically in the intervening period. This attitude was frequently expressed during the life of the Labour Government of 1945–50. The Government's first major bill, the Trade Disputes and Trade Unions Bill of 1946, was defended not only on its merits but also on the ground that, whereas 'the Baldwin Government of 1927 had no mandate whatever from the electorate to pass the 1927 Act . . . this Government has a definite mandate from the electors to repeal the 1927 Act'.[2] Subsequent Government bills were defended in similar terms, both inside and outside Parliament. And in 1947 the Vice-Chairman of the Fabian Society struck a note that was often to be repeated in the long debate on steel nationalization when he said that 'any retreat by the Government on the question of iron and steel would be regarded as a betrayal of their election pledges by the great majority of the Party's supporters both in the House and in the country'.[3]

In 1949 the National Executive Committee issued a policy state-

[1] Labour Party, *Look Forward* (London, 1961), p. 3.
[2] T. O'Brien, M.P., in *House of Commons Debates*, 6th s., v. 419, c. 231.
[3] John Parker, *Labour Marches On* (London, 1947), p. 65.

ment for discussion at the Party's Annual Conference in which they stated: 'We take pride in the conscientious care with which we framed our election programme for 1945 and in the democratic rigour and efficiency with which the Labour Government has kept trust with the people by carrying that programme through.' Now, in 1949, 'we have a solemn task. We have to make a new programme for the coming election which will determine the government of Britain for the next five years.'[1] This programme was worked out in the following months and was published in a manifesto setting out 'the principles and policy upon which the Labour Party will fight the General Election of 1950'.[2] It is therefore clear that the doctrine of the mandate was taken seriously by the Labour Party not only when the party was in opposition but also, what is much more significant, when the party was in power. Whether the doctrine has any general validity is another question.

## THE VALIDITY OF THE DOCTRINE OF THE MANDATE

In so far as the doctrine is prescriptive, it cannot be proved or disproved by empirical evidence. It may be that parties ought to frame specific programmes, that electors ought to vote according to their estimate of these programmes, and that the government of the day ought to feel bound to put its programme into effect. These are propositions that can be discussed, but cannot be established or refuted.

The Labour doctrine is partly of this nature, but it is also to some extent descriptive. Labour publicists maintain that Labour voters not only should but actually do vote according to their estimate of the Party's programme. It is on this basis that the claim is made that a Labour Government has (or would have) a popular mandate for its policies. On this topic a good deal of empirical evidence is now available, but it gives very little support for this proposition.

The first detailed survey of the political opinions of British voters was made in Greenwich at the time of the 1950 general election. In this survey electors were asked to state whether or not they agreed with five propositions embodying the main items of Labour policy and five propositions embodying the main items of Conservative policy. Of the Labour voters[3] questioned, the proportions agreeing with Labour propositions ranged from 79 per cent (who agreed with Labour's policy on full employment) to 49 per cent (who agreed with Labour's attitude to nationalization). The average proportion was

---

[1] *Labour Believes in Britain*, p. 30.
[2] *Let Us Win Through Together* (1950), p. 12.
[3] Actually the figures relate to those who intended to vote Labour.

only 61 per cent. On the other hand, many Labour voters agreed with Conservative propositions which clearly conflicted with Labour policy. The proportions doing this ranged from 21 per cent (who agreed that 'Socialism is a stepping-stone to Communism') to 65 per cent (who agreed that 'Our foreign policy should be based on "Empire First" '). The average proportion of Labour voters agreeing with Conservative propositions was 41 per cent.[1] As there was an apparent tendency for voters to agree with the propositions when in doubt, it is fair to conclude that not more than three-fifths of the Labour voters in this constituency were in general agreement with the Labour Party's policies, while the proportion who agreed with all the Party's policies was considerably smaller.

The authors of this study also constructed an index of political opinion by scoring the answers to all the questions. This index showed that only 32 per cent of Labour voters were moderately or strongly pro-Labour in their opinions while 30 per cent were slightly pro-Labour and 38 per cent were neutral or pro-Conservative.[2]

A rather different approach to the importance of the party programme in an election was followed in a study of the 1951 election in a Bristol constituency. In this survey voters were asked why they had voted the way they had. In their replies, only 31 per cent of the repondents mentioned anything that could possibly be classified as a policy or issue, and among Labour voters the proportion was only 26 per cent.[3] The authors of this study give reasons for their view that the proportion of electors actually influenced by a policy or issue was much smaller than this. First, many of the voters who mentioned particular issues also indicated, elsewhere in the same interview, that they did not consider these issues were important in this election. Second, two-thirds of those who mentioned issues 'were staunch party supporters who would have voted the same way in any case'.[4] It follows, the authors conclude, that 'the maximum proportion of voters whose vote was primarily decided by an issue or issues cannot have been more than 10 per cent, and may have been much smaller'.[5]

In the same constituency in the 1955 general election further evidence was gained of the relative unimportance of party policies in influencing voters, whether they were Labour supporters or not. In this study Labour voters were asked their views on two Labour propositions and two Conservative propositions. In all four cases more agreed with the propositions than disagreed, the largest majority

[1]See Mark Benney, A. P. Gray, and R. H. Pear, *How People Vote* (London, 1956), pp. 140–1.     [2]Ibid., p. 146.
[3]R. S. Milne and H. C. Mackenzie, *Straight Fight* (London, 1954), p. 120.
[4]Ibid., p. 139.     [5]Ibid., p. 139.

being for the Conservative proposition that 'There should be more scope for free enterprise in this country'.[1] An index of political opinion constructed on this occasion showed that 34 per cent of Labour voters were strongly or moderately pro-Labour in their opinons, 27 per cent were neutral, and 39 per cent were moderately or strongly pro-Conservative.[2]

These figures demonstrate what has now become almost a platitude among students of politics: that the majority of electors do not make up their minds how to vote on the basis of the policies outlined in the election manifestoes. Instead, they are influenced on the one hand by factors such as their occupation, social status, religion, and personal attitude towards society, and on the other hand by the changing public images of the political parties and their leaders.[3] This being so, it is clearly fallacious to believe that success in a general election indicates that the voters have endorsed the policies advocated by the winning party. And the doctrine of the mandate, in so far as it purports to be based on fact, must therefore be condemned as invalid.

Since the justification of party discipline put forward by left-wing writers is partly based on the doctrine of the mandate, the undermining of this doctrine by electoral research makes it even less likely than it previously was that this justification will become acceptable to non-Socialists. It follows that while British political practice is now dominated by the assumption that the Parliamentary parties will behave as disciplined blocks, British political thought still lacks any justification of party discipline that is generally accepted. The consequence is that, when controversies about discipline arise, much public discussion is still conducted in terms of ideas and slogans drawn from the individualistic tradition of earlier times. Since this tradition is explicitly or implicitly rejected by many of the participants, a degree of intellectual confusion inevitably arises.

This was particularly noticeable at the time of the Suez crisis, when a number of Conservative M.P.'s who criticized the Government's actions subsequently found themselves in trouble with their constituency associations. On this occasion Conservatives and others were divided in their sympathies, one group criticizing the M.P.'s in terms that sounded more military than political, the other group drawing on Liberal and Whig arguments to defend the rights of

[1] R. S. Milne and H. C. Mackenzie, *Marginal Seat, 1955* (London, 1958), p. 118.
[2] Ibid., p. 119.
[3] These factors are explored in the three books cited, and also in A. H. Birch, *Small-Town Politics* (London, 1959), Mark Abrams and Richard Rose, *Must Labour Lose?* (London, 1960), and J. Trenaman and D. McQuail, *Television and the Political Image* (London, 1961).

individual Members. The whole episode has been discussed in an excellent book by one of the chief participants, who gives (in the Appendix) a statement of Whig principles which he claims to be as valid today as they were in the eighteenth century.[1]

## INTRA-PARTY DEMOCRACY

Labour's theory of party government stands on two legs: one is the doctrine of the mandate; the other is the belief in intra-party democracy. The first may be valid as an account of how the political system ought to work, but has now been shown to have no validity as an interpretation of current political practice. The second, which is clearly related to the organization and practice of the Labour Party, must now be examined.

The Labour Party's belief in and practice of intra-party democracy does not have ideological origins. That is, to use Michael Oakeshott's terminology,[2] it does not result from an independently premeditated idea about how a political party should be organized. Instead, it results from the application to party organization of the experience and traditions of the trade-union movement. British trade unions have always been elaborately democratic in their internal organization. The early unions were, in the Webbs's phrase, 'primitive democracies', and the 'essential feature of primitive democracy was that everybody took part in the making of decisions'.[3] The close connections and overlap of personnel between the early unions and the Free Churches undoubtedly contributed to this democratic tradition. A historian of the Methodist Church has noted that 'the clearest example of Methodist leadership was provided by its organization. As a religious democracy, practically the whole of its technique was taken over by the political societies.'[4] The unions were equally influenced, and they derived 'atmosphere and fervour, spirit, tone, and method'[5] from the Free Churches.

When the unions got bigger new methods of government were introduced, but 'the belief that each member was equally responsible for the affairs of the union and equally capable of conducting them was not abandoned'.[6] In 1893, when the I.L.P. was formed, the new party decided to govern itself 'by means of a supreme annual con-

[1] See Nigel Nicolson, *People and Parliament* (London, 1958).

[2] See *Political Education* (Cambridge, 1951), p. 11.

[3] B. C. Roberts, *Trade Union Government and Administration* (London, 1956), p. 5.

[4] R. F. Wearmouth, *Methodism and the Working-Class Movements of England, 1800–1850* (London, 1937), p. 216.

[5] R. F. Wearmouth, *Methodism and the Struggle of the Working Classes, 1850–1900* (Leicester, 1954), p. 209.     [6] Roberts, op. cit., p. 5.

ference—a democratic device inherited from the trade unions, but not at that time accepted by any existing political party'.[1] And in 1918 the Labour Party followed the same course when it adopted its constitution. The delegates at the special conference convened for this purpose did not even debate the question, so much was it taken for granted that the constitution would vest policy-making powers in the hands of an annual conference representing all the branches and affiliated organizations of the party.

An institution of this kind, which is part of the tradition or *ethos* of the Labour Movement, hardly needs justification to members of that Movement. As we should expect, therefore, Labour statements on the subject are invariably re-assertions of the belief in intra-party democracy rather than attempts to justify it. A typical example is the following extract from a party pamphlet:

'The Labour Party is a collective expression of democratic sentiment based on the working-class movement and on the constituency organizations of the workers by hand and brain. Accordingly, in the Labour Party, the final word rests with the Annual Party Conference.'[2]

C. R. Attlee's comments on the same topic are in a rather similar vein. Attlee asserts that 'throughout the whole of the constitution of the Labour Party the democratic principle is observed', that 'the local activities of the Labour Party are a practical school of democracy', and that 'the Labour Party in Parliament is governed on democratic principles'.[3] Other Labour spokesmen, who differ among themselves on many issues, are unanimous in their agreement with these assertions and their apparent acceptance of the idea of intra-party democracy.

This idea has never been accepted by Conservatives, Liberals, or independent students of politics. Their objections to it have been based on three slightly different arguments: that it is contrary to the principles of the British constitution; that it would have the effect of exaggerating differences of opinion and thus making compromise less easy; and that it is based on a misunderstanding of the nature of politics and is in fact unworkable.

The first argument has been developed by a variety of people ranging from Sir Henry Maine to R. T. McKenzie. Maine argued that government by party caucus would destroy the independence of Parliament which was the basis of the British system and would

---

[1] H. Pelling, *Origins of the Labour Party: 1880–1900* (London, 1954), p. 232.
[2] *The Rise of the Labour Party* (Labour Discussion Series, No. 1, 1948), p. 14.
[3] *The Labour Party in Perspective* (2nd edn., London, 1949), pp. 75, 82, and 87.

inevitably lead to corruption.[1] Ostrogorski expressed similar fears in his monumental study of British political parties.[2] Nearly half a century later, Winston Churchill raised the matter in the 1945 election campaign. In a broadcast he warned his listeners that a Labour Government, if elected, would have to accept direction from a non-Parliamentary body unknown to the British constitution. More recently, R. T. McKenzie has declared that the 'outmoded theory of intra-party democracy' is based on 'a serious misunderstanding of the nature of party in the British Parliamentary system'.[3]

It is, of course, stretching things rather far to suggest that the Labour Party's mode of organization is in conflict with the British constitution. It would be more reasonable to suggest that this mode of organization is potentially in conflict with one strand of the British political tradition. This strand holds that those who make national policy should be free of commitments. This belief is partially rejected by those who assert that an elected government should feel itself bound to implement the party programme that has been endorsed by the electorate. The rejection becomes complete if it is further asserted that the party programme should be interpreted, and the omissions of the programme rectified, by the annual conference of the party concerned. The justification of party discipline outlined earlier in this chapter, which was formulated some time after party discipline and intra-party democracy were established facts, is an attempt to replace this strand of British political tradition by a doctrine which is said to be more in accord with current practice. It may or may not be a sensible doctrine, but it cannot logically be rejected simply by pointing out that it is novel.

The second line of attack on the doctrine of intra-party democracy is based on the belief that party workers are more extreme in their opinions than party leaders or the electors as a whole, so that an arrangement which puts power in the hands of party workers will tend to sharpen political conflict. This view was first expressed by Bagehot in relation to Liberal and Conservative party workers, whom he described as 'immoderate persons'.[4] It was developed by Lord Hugh Cecil, who said he could hardly imagine a less satisfactory form of government than one in which supreme power rested 'in the hands of extreme partisans and of the statesmen that extreme partisans most admire'.[5] It was a source of grave danger, he felt, that political authority in Britain lay 'alternately in the hands of one of

[1] See *Popular Government* (London, 1886).
[2] *Democracy and the Organisation of Political Parties* (London, 1902).
[3] In *Political Studies*, vol. IV (1956), pp. 96–7.
[4] Quoted in N. Nicolson, op. cit., p. 166.
[5] *Conservatism* (London, 1912), p. 236.

two knots of vehement, uncompromising and unbalanced men'.[1] In recent years this kind of argument has been commonly used in relation to Labour Party workers, whom the right-wing and independent press tend to regard as fanatics and zealots.

In point of fact, there is some evidence that the more active party workers in both main parties are more extreme in their political views than either the Parliamentary leaders or the main bulk of electoral supporters. This is only a tendency, and it is not by any means true of all areas or all workers in any area. But by and large, local Labour parties either support or are to the left of the Labour leadership on questions of policy, and very rarely to the right, so that the political centre of gravity of the local parties is somewhat to the left of the position of the Parliamentary leaders. In much the same manner, the political centre of gravity of local Conservative associations is somewhat to the right of the position of the Parliamentary leaders.[2]

A recent analysis of resolutions submitted to the annual conferences of the two parties in the years 1955-60 has provided statistical support for these generalizations. In both parties something like half the resolutions submitted were on points of sectional interest that could not be classified as left, right, or centre. Of the other Labour resolutions 58 per cent were to the left of party policy as against 40 per cent in support of party policy and only 2 per cent to the right of party policy. Of the Conservative resolutions that could be classified in this way, 52 per cent were to the right of party policy as against 41 per cent in support of party policy and only 7 per cent to the left of party policy.[3] To many people, this indication of the distribution of attitudes among party members would constitute an argument against the view that they should be given any formal powers to determine party policy. It is widely regarded as one of the sources of strength of the British political system that the leaders of the two main parties, dealing with the same problems, and appealing to the same marginal voters, have a natural tendency to move towards one another in their policies. In so far as active party members are more extreme in their views than the party leaders, any arrangement which strengthened the influence of the members on party policy would reduce the effectiveness of this tendency towards

[1] *Conservatism* (London, 1912), p. 238.

[2] This has been neatly illustrated in diagrammatic form by David Butler in his article, 'The Paradox of Party Difference', in *The American Behavioral Scientist*, vol. IV, No. 3 (1960).

[3] These figures have been adapted from those given in Richard Rose, 'The Policy Role of English Party Militants', in *American Political Science Review*, vol. 56 (1962). It should be noted that Rose himself draws a slightly different conclusion from his material.

consensus. People who value consensus can therefore reasonably argue that, in the present state of British party politics, intra-party democracy is undesirable.

In assessing this argument, however, it is important to note that the preference for consensus is not itself based on empirical evidence. No doubt a certain degree of consensus is necessary for the maintenance of a democratic system, but it has never been shown that Britain is anywhere near the limit in this respect. Radicals could plausibly argue that the British political system could tolerate a good deal more political conflict than at present exists, and if this be the case this whole argument against intra-party democracy loses much of its force except for those who wish to preserve the present pattern of political attitudes at Westminster.

The third argument against the doctrine of intra-party democracy asserts that it is based on a misunderstanding of the nature of politics. In this view the activity of government simply does not and can not consist in the translation into practice of premeditated policies which have been adopted by a party conference. Such policies, it is said, will nearly always seem irrelevant to the real problems of government as these are seen by those responsible for dealing with them. Realistic policies cannot be framed in isolation from the day-to-day activity of administering the affairs of state; in fact it is better to speak not of policies being framed but of policies emerging from the constant interplay between administrative requirements, sectional pressures, and intimations of public opinion and social need. In this view the doctrine of intra-party democracy must be rejected not so much because it is undesirable as because it is unworkable. In order to assess this view we must consider the attempts made by the Labour Party to put the doctrine into practice.

## INTRA-PARTY DEMOCRACY IN PRACTICE

This is a controversial topic both inside and outside the Labour Party. One student of Labour Party affairs has concluded that the whole concept of intra-party democracy is something of a sham.'The relations of a Labour Government to the Parliamentary Party and to the Party outside Parliament', declared R. T. McKenzie, 'are in no significant respect different from the relations of a Conservative Ministry to its supporters'.[1] McKenzie based this conclusion on a study of the party in the period up to 1954. He observed that the Parliamentary leaders were so sure of the support of the largest trade unions that they were rarely if ever in danger of failing to get

[1] *British Political Parties* (London, 1955), p. 426.

the support of the Annual Conference for the policies which the Parliamentary leaders advocated. He noted that on the infrequent occasions when Conference passed resolutions contrary to the wishes of the leaders, as in 1947 and 1948 when Conference called for the abolition of tied cottages, the leaders were able to ignore the resolutions. He concluded that the Labour Party's own picture of itself is 'highly misleading',[1] and that in practice its organization is oligarchic rather than democratic.

As it happens, events in the years immediately following the publication of this book suggested that McKenzie had generalized too hastily from the facts at his disposal. In the period which he studied most closely the Parliamentary leaders had the support of the leaders of the largest trade unions, and it was plausible to assert that the party was dominated by a handful of men through the operation of the block vote at the annual conference. But this was a temporary phenomenon rather than a permanent characteristic of the Labour Party. Another writer has shown that the trade unions are usually divided in their attitude to policies sponsored by the Parliamentary leaders,[2] and subsequent developments have demonstrated that the unions can be swung into opposition to these policies as effectively (though perhaps not so easily) as they can be swung into support.

Between 1954 and 1960 the Labour Movement was sharply divided on a number of issues, of which German re-armament and nuclear disarmament were the most important. Each autumn the Parliamentary leaders sought the support of the Annual Conference for their policies, and the existence of the union block-votes, far from guaranteeing the success of the Parliamentary leaders, had the effect of bringing the contest forward to the union conferences held earlier in the year. One result was that there were several summers in which the domestic political news was dominated by stories of debates, manoeuvres and the marshalling of votes within the Labour Movement in preparation for some critical vote at the Annual Conference in October.

In situations of this kind the Parliamentary leaders were in a difficult position. To make an effective appeal to the loyalty of wavering groups they had to say that the rejection of their policy would create serious difficulties for the next Labour Government, but this kind of appeal inevitably suggested that the leaders would regard the Conference decision as binding. In this way the leaders won some of their majorities at the price of strengthening the general belief in the

[1] *British Political Parties* (London, 1955), p. 582.
[2] Martin Harrison, *Trade Unions and the Labour Party* (London, 1960), chapters IV and V.

sovereignty of Conference and so making the situation more difficult for their successors.

Thus, in a debate on a resolution opposing German re-armament in 1954, C. R. Attlee said that if the resolution were passed and a Labour Government were elected, 'in any subsequent negotiations with Russia the Secretary of State will enter already tied and bound, because the Russians will know that under no circumstances will there be any re-armament of Western Germany'.[1] Later in the same debate Herbert Morrison declared that 'if the Executive motion were lost today we should be in a chaotic situation in the House of Commons . . . Supposing a Labour Government is returned, which is quite possible, are we going to be faced as a government . . . with a situation in which we are tied and fettered and cannot think in relation to the facts of a changing situation?'[2] And three years later Aneurin Bevan struck the same note when he said in a debate on nuclear disarmament: 'if you carry this resolution and follow out all its implications . . . you will send a British Foreign Secretary . . . naked into the conference chamber. . . . If any Socialist Foreign Secretary is to have a chance he must be permitted to substitute good policies for bad policies. Do not disarm him diplomatically, intellectually, and in every other way before he has a chance to turn around'.[3] The clear implication of these statements was that the Parliamentary leaders felt they would be bound to comply with Conference decisions on these subjects.

In 1960, as everyone knows, the Annual Conference rejected the defence policies advocated by the Parliamentary leaders and the National Executive Committee. Besides rejecting the official motion on defence, the Conference passed motions committing the Party to unilateral nuclear disarmament, the rejection of NATO defence policy, and opposition to American missile bases in Britain.

The question of whether the leaders of the Parliamentary Party were bound by Conference decisions, frequently debated but never settled, now assumed crucial importance. In the summer of 1960 several new attempts to answer this question had been made. In July a pamphlet by the General Secretary of the Party was published which stated:

'Every constituency sends delegates to Annual Conference . . . When a resolution comes up, delegates speak to it and vote on it. And when the vote has been taken, the decision reached is the final word on the

[1] *Report of the 53rd Annual Conference of the Labour Party, 1954*, p. 94.

[2] Ibid., p. 108. See also the discussion in Saul Rose, 'Policy Decision in Opposition', in *Political Studies*, vol. 4 (1956).

[3] *Report of the 56th Annual Conference of the Labour Party*, 1957, p. 181.

subject. The delegates' voice is supreme in determining the policy of the Party.'[1]

But in the same month another pamphlet by the same author was published containing a different interpretation of the scriptures. This one stated:

'Because we are a democratic party there are several centres of decision within our] movement . . . The Parliamentary Party is one centre of decision-making, the National Executive Committee another, and the Annual Conference a third. Policy therefore cannot be laid down, it must be agreed.'[2]

Also in July, the National Executive Committee adopted a statement on the constitutional position which was subsequently issued to all affiliated organizations. This declared that a resolution passed by the Annual Conference of 1907 'remains the definitive statement of the relationship between the Parliamentary Labour Party and the Party as a whole'. The 1907 resolution was as follows:

'Resolutions instructing the Parliamentary Party as to their actions in the House of Commons be taken as the opinion of the Conference, on the understanding that the time and method of giving effect to these instructions be left to the Party in the House in conjunction with the National Executive.'

The statement went on to note that 'the Election Manifesto . . . on which its members are elected is the one thing to which, under the Constitution, the Parliamentary Party is bound'.[3]

The most interesting aspect of these statements is that they demonstrated the extreme difficulty of upholding the theory of intra-party democracy to which the Labour Party had always been committed. The theory survived over the decades because, until 1960, Party and trade-union leaders always succeeded in preventing the Conference from rejecting an official policy on a major issue to which both the Parliamentary leaders and the majority of Labour M.P.'s were firmly committed. When the 1960 Conference rejected the official policy on defence the majority of Labour M.P.'s were faced with a serious dilemma: either they had to ignore the Conference decision, and thus reject the theory of party democracy to which they had always paid lip-service, or they had to disregard their own convictions as to what would be best for the nation and advocate a

[1] *This is the Labour Party*, July 1960.
[2] *Labour in the Sixties*, July 1960.
[3] *Constitution of the Labour Party*, August 1960.

policy which would be in direct conflict with the one which they had advocated at the time of their election only twelve months earlier.

In the event most Labour M.P.'s ignored the Conference decision and supported the policies advocated by the Leader of the Parliamentary Labour Party. In the following months most of the Parliamentary leaders not only ignored the Conference resolutions but actively campaigned against them, with the result that the 1961 Annual Conference reversed all the more important decisions on defence policy that had been reached twelve months earlier. The consequence of these developments is that the doctrine of intra-party democracy is not likely to be taken so seriously in the future as it has been in the past.

It would perhaps be rash to draw the conclusion that intra-party democracy is completely unworkable. The proper conclusions would seem to be that it has not been put fully into practice in Britain; that the recent experiences of the Labour Party make it more unlikely that it will be put into practice; and that if in the future another attempt is made to put it into practice the chances are that the consequences will be unfortunate for the party concerned.

It follows from this that the theory of intra-party democracy is of no more help than the doctrine of the mandate in providing a justification for the present system of disciplined party government in Britain. Possibly it is a mistake to seek a justification. The system works, and those who understand it are mostly content to accept it. But the urge to justify political institutions is natural to politicians and political theorists alike, and another kind of argument is frequently used by those who are sceptical of the theories discussed in this chapter. This argument is in terms of a view about responsible government rather than in terms of a theory of representation. It is held that the extension of government activities in recent decades has created a situation in which effective party management is essential if the government is to be truly responsible. To assess this view it is necessary to consider the nature of responsible government in Britain, which is the subject of the following chapters.

# PART IV

# RESPONSIBILITY IN BRITISH POLITICS

## CHAPTER 10

## Collective Responsibility

### THE PRINCIPLE

In Chapter 1 we distinguished three usages of the term 'responsible' when applied to groups taking political decisions. It is used to signify that the decision-makers are responsive to public opinion; it is used to signify that their decisions are prudent and mutually consistent; and it is used to signify that they are accountable for their actions to another body, such as Parliament. And while critics commonly assert (or imply) that governments should be responsible in all these senses, it is clear that there is no necessary link between them. Responsiveness and consistency are desirable ends that are wholly compatible only in rare combinations of circumstance. Accountability is not an end in itself so much as a means whereby one or (to some extent) both of the other ends may be secured. The great virtue of ministerial accountability to Parliament, say admirers of the British constitution, is that it gives ministers enough independence to pursue consistent policies without giving them so much independence that they can safely ignore public opinion.

Ministerial accountability to Parliament has two aspects: the collective responsibility of ministers for the policies of the government and their individual responsibility for the work of their departments. Both forms of responsibility are embodied in conventions which cannot be legally enforced. Both conventions were developed during the nineteenth century, and in both cases the practice was established before the doctrine was announced. Thus, the convention of collective responsibility was developed between 1780 and 1832, but the concept of 'responsible government' appears not to have been introduced into British political debates until as late as 1829, and then in relation to Canada rather than Britain.

On May 14th of that year E. G. Stanley (later Lord Derby) presented a petition to the House of Commons which had been

131

signed by over 3,000 citizens of Upper Canada and which asked, among other things, for 'a local and responsible ministry—not stating very clearly of what kind'.[1] In the following years the term was used a good deal by the advocates of constitutional reform in British North America, who demanded that the British Government should accept 'the principle of responsible government'. In a despatch to the new Governor-General of Canada in 1839, Lord John Russell noted that 'it does not appear, indeed, that any very definite meaning is generally agreed upon by those who call themselves the advocates of this principle', and observed that 'its very vagueness is a source of delusion'.[2] However, in the Durham Report, which had been published earlier in the same year, the principle was said to be one of the central features of the British constitution, which the Canadian reformers wished simply to see applied in their own country. Lord Durham's description of the principle of responsible government was as follows.

'In England, this principle has so long been considered an indisputable and essential part of our constitution, that it has really hardly ever been found necessary to inquire into the means by which its observance is enforced. When a ministry ceases to command a majority in Parliament on great questions of policy, its doom is immediately sealed; and it would appear to us as strange to attempt, for any time, to carry on a government by means of ministers perpetually in a minority, as it would be to pass laws with a majority of votes against them. The ancient constitutional remedies, by impeachment and a stoppage of supplies, have never, since the reign of William III, been brought into operation for the purpose of removing a ministry. They have never been called for, because in fact, it has been the habit of ministers rather to anticipate the occurrence of an absolutely hostile vote, and to retire, when supported only by a bare and uncertain majority.'[3]

This statement is worth quoting in full because it was the first clear assertion of what later became known as the convention of collective responsibility. In giving the impression that this was a long-established principle of the British constitution, Durham (who was a Radical) was rather misleading. In fact it had been established only during the previous three or four decades, and securely and irrevocably established only since the Reform Act of 1832. It has been authoritatively stated that in 1815 'the responsibility of the cabinet as a whole was difficult to establish',[4] and the same writer notes that

[1] *House of Commons Debates*, 3rd ser., vol. 21, col. 1332.

[2] The despatch is reprinted in F. P. Lucas (ed.) *Lord Durham's Report* (Oxford, 1912), vol. 3, pp. 332–5.     [3] Ibid., vol. 2, pp. 278–9.

[4] E. L. Woodward, *The Age of Reform* (Oxford, 1938), p. 23.

'no ministry between 1783 and 1830 resigned as a result of defeat in the House of Commons; no ministry before 1830 ever resigned on a question of legislation or taxation'.[1]

It is true that, very much earlier, Walpole had asserted that the ministry should be accountable to Parliament. On February 1, 1739, he told the Commons: 'When I speak here as a minister, I speak as possessing my powers from his Majesty, but as being answerable to this House for the exercise of these powers.'[2] And in 1742, when he was defeated in a Parliamentary division, he resigned. Nevertheless, the convention of governmental responsibility cannot be dated from this occasion. For the convention to be established, three developments were necessary. These were: first, the effective unity of the cabinet; second, effective control of the cabinet by the Prime Minister; and third, the understanding that if the cabinet were defeated in Parliament on a major issue or a vote of confidence, the Prime Minister would have no choice but to resign or ask for a dissolution. It will be helpful to sketch the history of these developments in a few sentences.

The effective unity of the cabinet was established in the period between 1780 and 1815. In 1782 there occurred the first example of the collective resignation of a ministry. When Lord North resigned in anticipation of a certain Parliamentary defeat, all his ministers, with the one exception of the Lord Chancellor, resigned with him. Following this, Pitt, during his long term of office from 1783 to 1800, did a great deal to develop the convention that cabinet ministers, whatever their private disagreements, should present a united front on major issues of policy. In 1792 Pitt secured the dismissal of the Lord Chancellor, who had criticized the Prime Minister's policies in Parliament. Another date of some significance is 1812, when an attempt to form a government drawn from opposed groups was rejected as 'inconsistent with the prosecution of any uniform and beneficial course of policy'.[3] It is rarely, if ever, possible to give a precise date for the establishment of a convention, but it seems safe to say that cabinet unity had become the rule by about 1815.

Since this date public disagreements between ministers have been rare,[4] although it is clear from memoirs and other evidence that private disagreements have been frequent. Since the ill-fated 'agreement to differ' of 1932 (which resulted in the resignation only eight

[1] E. L. Woodward, *The Age of Reform* (Oxford, 1938), p. 23.

[2] Quoted in W. C. Costin and J. S. Watson, *The Law and Working of the Constitution: Documents 1660–1914* (London, 1952), vol. 1, p. 217.

[3] A. Todd, *On Parliamentary Government in England* (2nd edn., London, 1887), vol. II, p. 142.

[4] Jennings cites nine cases between 1835 and 1937. See W. I. Jennings, *Cabinet Government* (Cambridge, 1937), pp. 218–20.

months later of the ministers who were in the minority), there has been no occasion on which cabinet ministers have disagreed in public. In 1940 Winston Churchill publicly supported Neville Chamberlain, even though Chamberlain's critics were asking for Churchill to take his place. In 1950, when a junior minister not in the cabinet criticized the Government's agricultural policy and resigned immediately afterwards, The *Economist* commented that he 'would have been in a stronger position if he had resigned first and made his criticisms afterwards, rather than transgress an accepted rule of the constitution'.[1] In 1958, when the Chancellor of the Exchequer resigned because of a disagreement with other ministers on a question of economic policy, no hint of the disagreement reached the public before the resignation was announced.

The second necessary development was effective control of the cabinet by the Prime Minister. This could not be established during the early part of George III's reign, when the position of the Prime Minister was overshadowed by the power of the monarch. In this period cabinet ministers were 'the King's ministers' in fact as well as in form; they had separate access to the King; and it was still possible for the King to dismiss the Prime Minister and appoint one of his former colleagues in his place. This situation changed as the result of a series of fortuitous circumstances. When Pitt was Prime Minister (from 1783 to 1801 and from 1804 to 1806) he achieved a personal ascendancy over his ministers that enabled him to dominate the cabinet. George III's declining health in his later years weakened his authority, and the Prince Regent was never to be taken seriously as a politician. Nor did his brother, William IV, make any attempt to exercise personal initiative in the manner of his father. In 1837, when the young and inexperienced Victoria acceded to the throne, she leant heavily upon the advice of Lord Melbourne. From then onwards the Prime Minister was in effective control of his cabinet. During Victoria's reign there were several occasions on which the Queen succeeded in persuading her Prime Minister not to give a place in the cabinet to a politician whom she thought unfit for office,[2] but this is best classified as an exercise of influence rather than power. Her objections were generally on personal rather than political grounds (an example is her objection to Sir Charles Dilke because he had been involved in a divorce suit), and she did not go so far as to tell her Prime Ministers whom they should appoint instead.

The third necessary development was the understanding that the Prime Minister should resign or ask for a dissolution if his ministry were defeated in Parliament. This did not exist when Pitt formed his

[1] The *Economist*, April 22, 1950.
[2] The occasions are discussed in Jennings, op. cit., pp. 49–53.

government in 1783. In the first two years of this ministry he refused to resign despite numerous defeats in Parliament and he did not ask for a dissolution until he judged (correctly) that the moment was favourable to the chances of his supporters. However, during the following decades there was a change of attitude on this question. In 1830 Wellington resigned without hesitation when his ministry was defeated on a motion regarding the civil list and faced defeat on a much more important motion in favour of reform; and after the Reform Act it quickly became regarded as axiomatic that the government must respond to a Parliamentary defeat on a major issue. Peel put this into words when he resigned in 1835, saying that he considered 'that the Government ought not to persist in carrying on public affairs . . . in opposition to the decided opinion of a majority of the House of Commons'.[1]

It follows that between Pitt's appointment in 1783 and the enactment of the Reform Bill in 1832 the three conditions necessary for the establishment of the convention of collective responsibility were all fulfilled. The recognition of this convention as one of the central features of the British system of government owed much to the nature of party politics during the following forty years. During this period party discipline in Parliament was extremely weak; indeed, even to say this is to describe the situation in terms of a concept that did not arise until later. Between the first and second Reform Acts the question was not one of discipline, for the means to enforce this did not yet exist: the question was one of the influence that leaders could bring to bear on their Parliamentary supporters. And, as Bagehot noted in 1867, 'the power of leaders over their followers is strictly and wisely limited: they can take their followers but a little way, and that only in certain directions'.[2] To add to the flexibility of the situation, several of the party leaders themselves changed sides between one ministry and the next.

In these middle decades of the century, the collective responsibility of the cabinet to Parliament became a cardinal feature of British politics. Lord John Russell, who had questioned the meaning of the principle in 1839, accepted its implications without hesitation in 1852 and 1866, in each case resigning immediately his government was defeated in Parliament. Between 1832 and 1867 no fewer than ten governments were brought to an end by adverse votes in the Commons;[3] in eight cases the Prime Minister resigned and in the other two he secured a dissolution. In these years not a single

[1] *House of Commons Debates*, 3rd ser., vol. 27, c. 980–2.
[2] *The English Constitution*, p. 124.
[3] The dates were as follows: 1841, 1846, 1851, February 1852, December 1852, 1855, 1857, 1858, 1859, 1866.

government lasted the entire life of a Parliament, from one general election to the next.

It is largely on the experience of these years that the doctrine of collective responsibility is based. It began to appear in text-books in the 1860's and 1870's. Todd devoted a chapter to it in 1867,[1] and in the same year Bagehot made several references to its consequences. The House of Commons, he said, 'is a real choosing body; it elects the people it likes. And it dismisses whom it likes too'.[2] 'The distinguishing quality of Parliamentary government,' he declared, is that the public 'can, through Parliament, turn out an administration which is not doing as it likes, and can put in an administration which will do as it likes.'[3] Five years later the doctrine was stated more formally by E. A. Freeman. 'What we understand by the responsibility of ministers,' he wrote, 'is that they are liable to have all their public acts discussed in Parliament.' While impeachment had passed, 'the unwritten constitution makes a vote of censure as effectual as an impeachment, and in many cases it makes a mere refusal to pass a ministerial measure as effectual as a vote of censure'.[4] In this unwritten constitution, the cabinet is 'a collective body bound together by a common responsibility'.[5] In the following decade the doctrine was stated more briefly by A. V. Dicey: 'the cabinet are responsible to Parliament as a body, for the general conduct of affairs'.[6]

## COLLECTIVE RESPONSIBILITY IN THE TWENTIETH CENTURY

It is now three-quarters of a century since Dicey wrote. In this period the doctrine of collective responsibility has been proclaimed by innumerable politicians and restated by innumerable commentators. It is part of the Liberal theory of the constitution, but it has been defended as much by Socialists and Conservatives as by Liberals. It has acquired the status of a sacred principle of British government.

In fact this doctrine, like other parts of the Liberal theory of the constitution, is largely a codification of the developments and theories of the years between the first and second Reform Acts. In that short period of thirty-five years Parliament dominated the executive as it never did before and has never done since. The diminution of Parliamentary power as a result of the growth of party discipline since 1868 has been discussed in general terms in

[1] Op. cit., vol. II.  [2] Op. cit., p. 116.  [3] Ibid., p. 302.
[4] *The Growth of the English Constitution* (first published London, 1872, 3rd edn., 1876), p. 120.  [5] Ibid., p. 121.
[6] *Law of the Constitution* (8th edn., London, 1931), p. 416.

Chapter 6. One effect of this development has been that, while the doctrine of collective responsibility remains unchanged, its practical importance has been greatly reduced.

Whereas in the thirty-five years leading up to 1867 adverse votes in Parliament forced ten Prime Ministers to resign or ask for a dissolution, in the ninety-four years since 1868 only five Prime Ministers have been put into this position.[1] In the earlier period no government survived for what may now be called a government's normal life, from a general election until the Prime Minister asks for a dissolution, at a time of his own choice, near the end of that Parliament's allotted span. Today a government that was not able to survive in this way would be regarded as distinctly unlucky. Since 1868 most changes of government (apart from those caused by the retirement or ill-health of the Prime Minister) have been brought about not by a Parliamentary reversal but by an adverse vote in a general election.

In so far as this signifies an increase in the direct influence of the people on the government of the country it can be regarded as an advance in democracy. But it is not so much a form of Parliamentary control of the executive as a form of voters' control, exercised through Parliamentary elections. And since elections take place infrequently, it is not clear that the word 'control' is appropriate. The idea underlying the doctrine of collective responsibility is that the government should be held continuously accountable for its actions, so that it always faces the possibility that a major mistake may result in a withdrawal of Parliamentary support. In the modern British political system this simply does not happen. An obvious blunder may lead to an immediate swing of public opinion against the party in power, but the Parliamentary majority normally holds firm and the government may have ample opportunity to recapture public support before the next general election is held. The Labour Government of 1945–50 survived through the fuel crisis of 1947, the collapse of its Palestine policy in 1948, and the fiasco of the ground-nuts scheme in 1949. In 1950 it was returned to power, though with a reduced majority. The Conservative Government of 1955–59 succeeded not only in surviving after the *debacle* of Suez, but in winning an increased majority at the next election.

It is clear that the doctrine of collective responsibility does not occupy the place in the present political system that is commonly claimed for it. It purports to provide an effective sanction for governmental blunders, but it does not normally do so. In times of peace a modern government is not more likely to resign or dissolve

---

[1] In 1885, 1886, 1895, January 1924, and December 1924, Chamberlain's resignation in 1940 should perhaps be added to this list, though he was not defeated in a Parliamentary division.

Parliament when its policies meet with a major reversal than when things are going well, but less likely to do so. In the months following the Suez expedition the opposition leaders frequently quoted the Government's alleged unpopularity in the country as a reason why it should resign, but they knew as well as everyone else that they were simply playing a traditional and somewhat outdated Parliamentary game. A crisis that would have brought down a government a hundred years ago now acts as an opportunity for its Parliamentary supporters to give an impressive display of party loyalty, and stimulates its leaders to hold on to the reins of power until public attention is diverted to a sphere of policy which puts the government in a more favourable light.

To say this is not to say that the doctrine has no useful function. The convention that the government must always present a united front has important and possibly beneficial effects. It compels ministers to be discreet and prevents the sort of confusion that sometimes arises in other countries, for instance the United States, when government spokesmen make pronouncements which reveal differences of view within the administration. It tends to force inter-departmental disputes to the surface at cabinet meetings, when they are generally resolved one way or another. It identifies government policy in a way that provides a clear focus for public discussion, at least when the facts are generally known.

This maintenance of a united front is held in such high esteem by the general public that, significantly, and quite recently, a new linguistic usage has developed. A government is now commonly said to be 'taking responsibility' when it takes a collective decision and uses the whips to ensure Parliamentary support for it, and to be 'shedding' or 'evading responsibility' if it permits a free vote on the matter. The decision to allow a free vote on capital punishment in 1956 was criticized in these terms, and when the Government proposed to allow a free vote on the most controversial clauses of the Street Offences Bill in 1959 the objections from its own back-benchers were so numerous that it changed its mind and put on a two-line whip.

This usage of the term 'responsibility' involves something like a reversal of the traditional meaning, for in the new usage a government is acting 'responsibly' not when it submits to Parliamentary control but when it takes effective measures to dominate Parliament. Perhaps this reversal of meaning indicates as well as any description the gap between the doctrine of collective responsibility and the practice of contemporary politics.

# CHAPTER 11

# Individual Responsibility

## THE DOCTRINE

In one sense the development of the concept of ministerial responsibility for the actions of the executive was a corollary of the withdrawal of the monarch from personal responsibility. 'The great principle of ministerial responsibility for every act of sovereignty . . . is a natural consequence of the system of Parliamentary government which was introduced by the revolution of 1688. It is based upon the fundamental doctrine that the King himself can do no wrong.'[1] In the early part of the eighteenth century this meant that ministers were liable to be impeached by Parliament for mismanagement of public affairs. However, the unsuccessful attempt to impeach Walpole after he resigned in 1742 was the last attempt ever made to impeach a minister for purely political offences. The only two cases of impeachment since that date were those involving Warren Hastings, who was not a minister, and Melville (First Lord of the Admiralty, 1804–5), who was accused (but not found guilty) of personal corruption.

Impeachment fell into disuse because politicians had come to regard 'the loss of office and public disapprobation as punishments sufficient for errors in the administration not imputable to public corruption'.[2] This clear assumption that a minister would have to resign if an administrative error in his department were exposed and criticized in Parliament was shared by most constitutional lawyers and commentators in the second half of the nineteenth century. It forms the basis of the doctrine of the individual responsibility of ministers for the work of their departments.

This doctrine has two strands. The first strand (in terms of logic, if not of history) states that the political head of a department, and only the political head, is answerable to Parliament for all the actions of that department. The positive aspect of this is that Members of Parliament wishing to query any of the actions of a department know that there is one man to whom they may address their

---

[1] A. Todd, *On Parliamentary Government in England* (2nd edn., London, 1887), vol. 1, p. 273.

[2] These oft-quoted words are from T. B. Macaulay, *Hallam*, in *Works* (Edinburgh edition), vol. V, p. 228.

questions, who cannot evade the duty of answering them. The negative aspect of it is that civil servants are not answerable to Parliament for their actions, and are protected from political controversy by the minister. As Gladstone said: 'In every free state, for every public act, some one must be responsible; and the question is, who shall it be? The British Constitution answers: "the minister, and the minister exclusively"'.[1]

The second strand of the doctrine states that the minister must receive 'the whole praise of what is well done, the whole blame of what is ill'[2] in the work of his department; and that in consequence he must resign if serious blunders are exposed. Evidence for the importance attached to this second strand of the doctrine is to be found not only in text-books about British government but in 'a veritable canon of Parliamentary *obiter dicta*'.[3]

This is the doctrine. It is a vital part of the Liberal theory of the constitution. And it is, indeed, the basis of the claim that in Britain, there being no separation of powers, the actions of the administration are controlled by the people's representatives in Parliament.

The suspicion that political practice does not entirely correspond with this doctrine has been voiced frequently since 1930, and is to be found in a few publications before that date. The arguments put forward are of two kinds. First, it has been pointed out that in practice very few ministers have resigned in response to Parliamentary criticism of the work of their departments: innumerable errors have been exposed but in most cases the minister concerned has simply refused to offer his resignation. Since the power to bring about a minister's resignation is the only sanction Parliament can apply in cases of administrative error, the fact that this power is apparently nominal rather than real is said to indicate that Parliament's control of the administration is also nominal rather than real. Second, it has been asserted that the doctrine of ministerial responsibility is used to prevent the development of other means of Parliamentary control of the administration which might be more effective, such as the use of specialized committees. In this view the doctrine, far from ensuring that the departments are subservient to Parliament, actually serves to protect the departments from Parliamentary control.

These arguments will be considered separately, the first in this chapter and the second in Chapter 12.

[1] *Gleanings from Past Years* (London, 1879), vol. 1, p. 233.
[2] J. S. Mill, *Considerations on Representative Government*, p. 264.
[3] S. E. Finer, 'The Individual Responsibility of Ministers', in *Public Administration*, vol. XXXIV (1956), p. 379.

## MINISTERIAL RESIGNATIONS

That relatively few ministers have resigned in direct response to Parliamentary criticism of the work of their departments is not so much an argument as a fact. There were no cases of this happening between Melville's impeachment in 1805 and Lord John Russell's resignation in 1855. Until the middle decades of the century it was, indeed, often difficult to pin responsibility for the activities of a department on any one man. As Todd notes, it was the administrative reforms of this period that led to 'the general substitution of concentrated responsibility in the hands of a minister of the crown, for the indefinable and irresponsible authority of boards'.[1]

After 1855 resignations in response to criticism occurred from time to time, but according to Finer there were only 16 cases in the following hundred years.[2]

This figure may in one sense be a little misleading, for in many cases the indirect result of Parliamentary criticism has been the subsequent removal of the minister to another department. However, this depends not so much on the relations of the minister to Parliament as on his relations with the Prime Minister and his standing in the party. The doctrine suggests that Parliament has the power to compel a minister to resign. The fact that Parliamentary criticism sometimes damages a minister's reputation within his own party is not the same thing, and the distinction is emphasized by the practice of allowing a decent interval to elapse between the Parliamentary criticism and the ministerial changes. Nor is this a distinction without a difference: accordance to the doctrine a minister's resignation or survival should depend on the extent of the error and the severity of Parliamentary criticism, but in practice 'which Ministers escape and which do not is decided neither by the circumstances of the offence nor its gravity, but is the 'haphazard consequence of a fortuitous concomitance of personal, party and political temper'.[3]

It may be helpful to illustrate these generalizations by describing some of the cases that have occurred since the last war. Between 1945 and 1960 there were six outstanding examples of an unsuccessful policy or an administrative blunder for which the minister concerned was severely criticized in Parliament. These were as follows: first, the fuel crisis of 1947; second, the failure of British policy in Palestine, 1945-8; third, the failure of the ground-nuts scheme in 1949; fourth, the Crichel Down affair of 1954; fifth, the Suez expedition of 1956; and sixth, the deaths at the Hola Camp in Kenya in 1959. The list could doubtless be extended, but for the purpose of illustration these six examples will suffice.

[1] Op. cit., vol. II, p. 221.    [2] Op. cit., p. 394.    [3] Ibid., p. 393.

1. *The fuel crisis* of 1947 was sudden and catastrophic. Throughout the autumn of 1946 it had been predicted that there would be a coal shortage in the winter. However, the government operated such elaborate controls over the distribution and use of coal that it clearly had the powers necessary to prevent the shortage dislocating industry. On October 24 Emmanuel Shinwell, the Minister of Fuel and Power, said: 'Everybody knows that there is going to be a serious crisis in the coal industry—except the Minister of Fuel and Power. There is not going to be a crisis in coal, if by a crisis you mean that industrial organization is going to be seriously dislocated'.[1] But on a Friday afternoon in the following February the Minister announced 'to a dumbfounded House of Commons that, as from the following Monday, electricity supplies to industry were to be cut off completely in London and the South-East, the Midlands and the North-West'.[2] The stoppage lasted for about three weeks, unemployment rose to over two millions, and 'the crisis probably lost Great Britain £200 millions of exports'.[3]

This was as clear a case of administrative failure as could be imagined. The Minister did not offer to resign and he was supported in the ensuing debate by the Prime Minister. However, he lost popularity in his party to the extent of being 'ostracized' by many of his Parliamentary colleagues,[4] and eight months later he was moved to the War Office. In so far as Shinwell thereby lost his seat in the cabinet this move can be regarded as a demotion; but his successor did not inherit his cabinet seat, it was stated that the Ministry of Fuel and Power had been represented in the cabinet only during the transition to public ownership in the coal industry, and the personal aspect of the changes was largely obscured from public view.

2. *The failure of British policy in Palestine* was, of course, a catastrophe on a different scale. It involved immense suffering, much loss of life, and great damage to Britain's international reputation. Not one of Britain's changing objectives was achieved, and when the last British High Commissioner sailed away 'he left behind him a country without legal government, administration, police or public services, cut off from the outside world and ravaged by war'.[5] The Foreign Secretary bore the major responsibility for the policies that had led to this disastrous result: indeed at an early stage he had declared that he would stake his political future on his ability to deal with the situation in Palestine.[6] Throughout the whole period

[1] Quoted in John Jewkes, *Ordeal by Planning* (London, 1948), p. 184.
[2] Ibid., p. 182.      [3] Ibid., p. 183.
[4] Shinwell used this term in an article in the *Sunday Times*, Septenber 18, 1960.
[5] Arthur Koestler, *Promise and Fulfilment* (London, 1949), p. 167.
[6] Ibid., p. 180.

of his responsibility he was subjected to strong Parliamentary criticism, both from members of his own party (whom he frequently accused of 'stabbing him in the back') and from members of the opposition. In the debate on the end of mandate the spokesman for the opposition front bench, Oliver Stanley, said: 'I am afraid it will be a humiliating end to the honourable role which hitherto we have played in that country . . . very different from the object for which many thousands of our fellow citizens worked, indeed, died in Palestine'.[1] However, there was no serious suggestion that Ernest Bevin should resign, and there is no indication that he gave so much as a minute's thought to this possibility.

3. *The failure of the scheme to grow groundnuts* on an unprecedented scale in Tanganyika by mechanized methods was much less serious. It involved little more than a loss of money, and its cost, though considerable, was much less than the overall cost of the fuel crisis. Paradoxically, it led to stronger demands for the resignation of the minister concerned than had been expressed in either of the other cases.

The failure of the scheme was revealed when the first report of the Overseas Food Corporation was published in November 1949. This report disclosed 'that anxiety about the scheme had been grounded on fact, that the commercial prospects for its future were, to say the least of it, dubious, and that in addition the internal accounting arrangements had been neglected'. The *Economist* observed that the Minister 'would have done a service both to the groundnut scheme and to his own reputation if he had resigned on the day the Corporation's report was published. . . . Instead, the effect of rising public anxiety has merely been to stiffen Mr. Strachey's determination to cling to office at all costs. . . . On Monday he offered Parliament . . . neither explanation nor apology for the past, ending in a blank wall of defiance'.[2] The paper noted that for over a century it had been accepted that a minister should resign 'if any public undertaking for which he held personal responsibility had manifestly failed',[3] and regretted that this principle was not observed by the Government of the day.

Three months later Strachey was moved from the Ministry of Food to the War Office, when Attlee reconstructed his Government after the general election, but there was no suggestion that this was in any sense a demotion.

4. *The Crichel Down affair* differed from the other five cases in that it involved no direct loss to the country and no obvious failure of public policy. What was involved was simply unfair treatment of an

[1] *H. of C. Deb.*, 5th ser., v. 445. c. 1221.
[2] The *Economist*, November 26, 1949.        [3] Ibid.

individual landowner by the Ministry of Agriculture and the Commissioners of Crown Lands. The landowner was interested in a large tract of farming land which had previously formed part of the estate which his wife had inherited, but which had been acquired by the Government by compulsory purchase for use as a bombing range. When the land was no longer needed for this purpose the authorities refused either to resell it to the heirs of the original owner or to let it in sections to neighbouring farmers who had previously rented these sections and now wished to reincorporate them in their farms. Instead, the authorities decided to equip the land at great expense as a model farm and to let it to a tenant from some distance away whom they had chosen in a rather arbitrary fashion.

The landowner concerned, having attempted without success to secure redress of his grievance through Parliamentary channels, wrote to *The Times* and organized a meeting of local farmers to protest against the decision and demand a public enquiry. The Minister at first refused to accede to this demand. The matter was then taken up by the National Farmers' Union, the Country Landowners' Association, and Conservative Associations in the county concerned. On October 20, 1953 serious disquiet was expressed at a meeting of the Food and Agriculture Committee of back-bench Conservative M.P.'s; on October 22nd the Minister met the landowner and agreed to institute a public enquiry.[1]

On June 15, 1954 the Report of the Public Enquiry was published.[2] It was strongly critical of some of the decisions that had been taken, of the way the negotiations with members of the public had been conducted, and of the behaviour of five of the civil servants concerned. It disclosed that many of the decisions of the Ministry had been based on an inaccurate report made by a junior official who had been denied access to the documents he needed to assess the situation properly. It stated that the public authorities concerned had become 'so infatuated with the idea of creating a new model farm'[3] that they had refused to give proper consideration to the financial disadvantages of the scheme. It noted that highly-placed officials had deliberately attempted to mislead applicants for tenancies into thinking that their applications had received due consideration, when in fact these officials had previously decided, quite without justification, to let the land to someone else. It pointed out that 'a most regrettable attitude of hostility' to the original landowner had been evinced by several officials, this attitude being 'engendered solely by a feeling of irritation that any member of the

[1] See R. D. Brown, *The Battle of Crichel Down* (London, 1955), pp. 84–5.
[2] *Report of the Public Enquiry into the Disposal of Land at Crichel Down*, Cmd. 9176 of 1954. [3] Ibid., p. 27.

public should have the temerity to oppose or even to question the acts or decisions of officials of a government or state department'.[1] It concluded that the landowner had been fully justified in demanding a public enquiry.

On the day this Report was published the Minister of Agriculture (Sir Thomas Dugdale) made a short statement to the House of Commons. 'So far as those criticized are persons . . . and most of them are . . . for whose conduct I am answerable as a Minister of the Crown, the responsibility rests with me. This responsibility I wholly accept'.[2] However, he did not offer to resign, and of the civil servants concerned he said: 'In view of the nature of the errors and of the public way in which they have been exposed, I am satisfied that no further action by me in relation to them is necessary.'[3] If the matter had been left there the doctrine of ministerial responsibility would have served the purely negative function of protecting the civil servants from the usual consequence of serious error.

As it happened, the matter was not left there. Press criticism was severe, and on June 17th the 150-odd members of the Conservative Party's Food and Agriculture Committee again expressed their disquiet at the situation. There followed three meetings of the 1922 Committee, at each of which the Conservative back-benchers made clear their unwillingness to let the matter lie and their demand for some more meaningful gesture than had then been made. The last and most stormy of these meetings was held on July 15th; on July 19th Dugdale had an interview with the Prime Minister; and on July 20th Dugdale announced his resignation. Meanwhile, the Prime Minister had appointed a special committee to make recommendations regarding the future of the censured officials, and these were mentioned by Dugdale in his final speech. The committee recommended that four of the officials could be left where they were (one of them having already been promoted to a different office and another having been moved, at the same level, to take charge of a different Division of the Ministry). However, it was recommended that the most senior official concerned, the Permanent Commissioner of Crown Lands, should be transferred to other duties. These recommendations were accepted by the Government and the last-mentioned official was subsequently moved to a senior post in the Colonial Office.

The Crichel Down affair gave rise to a wave of discussion about the relations between Parliament, ministers, and civil servants. It was claimed by some that Sir Thomas Dugdale's resignation was a re-assertion of the principle of ministerial responsibility, and by

[1] *Report of the Public Enquiry into the Disposal of Land at Crichel Down*, Cmd. 9176 of 1954, p. 31.
[2] Quoted in Brown, op. cit., p. 113.                          [3] Ibid.

others that it was a demonstration of the effectiveness of the traditional British way of providing a remedy for administrative mismanagement.

This second claim was certainly false. The mismanagement in this affair was not exposed as a result of questions put by the landowner's M.P. to the Minister, which is the traditional method of approach. This method was tried, but it met with no success. The mismanagement was in fact exposed as a result of a combination of four factors, all of which were somewhat exceptional. First, the aggrieved citizen had the persistence, the energy, the education, the social standing, and the resources necessary to conduct a prolonged campaign in his own cause.[1] Second, he secured the support of the National Farmers' Union, which probably enjoys more influence in Whitehall than any other single pressure group. Third, the enquiry was conducted by a barrister of exceptional brilliance and independence of mind. Fourth, the Minister was willing to publish the report of the enquiry, which was not legally necessary. The fact that the redress of an undoubted grievance required such a combination of factors should properly be disturbing, rather than reassuring, to those who believe that the British system offers an adequate protection to citizens against the misuse of governmental power.

5. *The story of the Suez expedition* of 1956 is complicated and controversial, but its outlines are well known. Opinions differ as to whether or not the whole project should be condemned on moral grounds. Leaving this question on one side, it is clear that those who planned the action misjudged the relative strengths of the Israeli and Egyptian armies, the speed with which Anglo-French forces could be brought into action, and, most important of all, the reactions of the United States and the United Nations. The result of these disastrous miscalculations was an expedition which achieved none of the aims which were said at the time to justify it, which jeopardized Britain's relations with her most powerful ally, and which ended in a humiliating withdrawal.

No minister resigned as a result of the vehement Parliamentary criticism of this expedition. Sir Anthony Eden resigned because of ill-health, and it is clear that this was the reason and not simply a face-saving device.[2] The Foreign Secretary and the other ministers directly involved stayed in their posts.

[1] He was a man of some means who had enjoyed a distinguished career as a naval officer and had served as naval equerry to King George VI. His wife was a member of an aristocratic family and a goddaughter of Queen Elizabeth the Queen Mother. It is interesting to notice that the Secretary of State for War at the time was her uncle by marriage and the Secretary of State for Scotland had been an executor of her father's will.

[2] It is of course possible that he would have stayed in office in spite of his

6. *The deaths at the Hola Camp* in Kenya in 1959 raised the rather difficult question of how far the Colonial Secretary could be expected to take the blame for actions carried out by officials of a colonial government. What happened was that the Kenya Government decided that all prisoners at Mau-Mau detention camps should be made to work, by force if necessary. Since it was known that some of the prisoners would resist a careful plan was prepared for over-coming their resistance. When this plan was put into operation at the Hola Camp eleven prisoners were clubbed to death by warders and a further 22 received injuries which necessitated their admission to hospital. The coroner stated in his report that this was 'entirely unjustified and illegal'.[1]

On the day after this report was published members of the opposition raised the matter in the House, demanded to know what action was to be taken, and suggested that the Colonial Secretary might resign.[2] The Colonial Secretary replied that it would be wrong for him to comment on the case until the Attorney-General of Kenya had decided whether to institute legal proceedings against any of the individuals concerned. It was subsequently announced that no charges were to be brought, but that disciplinary action was to be taken against the camp commandant and his deputy. Although these officials had followed the government plan in outline they had deviated from it in detail, and the Kenya Government maintained that it was this failure to keep exactly to the plan that had led to the deaths.

In the following weeks there were two Parliamentary debates on this affair. In each of them Labour Members argued that the Colonial Secretary was responsible to Parliament for the administration of colonial territories, and should therefore resign in face of this clear evidence of maladministration. Their case was strengthened by the fact that a week before the deaths had occurred some of them had asked the Minister to institute an enquiry into the administration of the Kenya prison camps, which he had refused to do. In reply, the Colonial Secretary (Alan Lennox-Boyd) accepted responsibility for the actions of the Kenya Government, but gave two reasons for staying at his post. The first was that this was an isolated incident in a programme for the rehabilitation of Mau-Mau detainees which, judged as a whole, had been outstandingly successful. (Labour members did not deny this.) The second reason was that in his view

health if he had been strongly urged to do so by his senior colleagues, but this is a very delicate question, of which the facts are known only to a small circle of people.

[1] Quoted in *House of Commons Debates*, 5th s., v. 605, c. 254.
[2] Ibid., c. 566.

(from which Labour Members differed) the deaths would not have occurred if the instructions of the Kenya Government had been followed to the letter.

It is perhaps also relevant to mention that at this time Lennox-Boyd was nearing the end of a very distinguished political career. A few months later, as was widely anticipated, he resigned his office, accepted a peerage, and went into business.

The purpose of outlining these cases is not to suggest that the ministers concerned should have resigned. Rather, it is to demonstrate that the practice of British government does not conform to the doctrine of ministerial responsibility, as this is commonly understood. The doctrine appears to provide a sanction for political and administrative error, but it is evident that in these cases there was no relation at all between the gravity of the error and the consequences for the minister concerned. The policy in Palestine, which caused more human suffering than any other policy of the British government since 1945, had only a marginal effect on the minister's reputation. The Crichel Down affair, which was the least serious of the cases cited, brought the minister's political career to an end. The cases provide impressive support for Finer's suggestion that the consequences for a minister of the exposure of failure depend largely on his relations with his party and Prime Minister, and only a little on the extent of the failure. It is quite clear that in this respect the doctrine of the individual responsibility of ministers for the work of their departments is a misleading guide to practice.

## THE SIGNIFICANCE OF THE DOCTRINE

Does this mean that the doctrine is no more than a myth or sham? To say this would be to go beyond the facts. In the first place, the doctrine gives Members of Parliament the right to demand information about any administrative decision from the minister in charge of the department. This is done more often by private correspondence than by a question on the floor of the House, and it enables Members to investigate the grievances and press the claims of their constituents at the highest level. If Members did not have this right, they might be in a much weaker position than they are now to protect the interests of their constituents. Possibly some alternative procedure might be found, but the existing arrangements appear to work well and must be counted as one of the benefits of the convention of ministerial responsibility.

In the second place, there is no doubt that the behaviour of civil servants is affected by the knowledge that, if they make a mistake or offend a member of the public, the matter may be raised in

Parliament a few days later. The name of the civil servant will not be publicly disclosed, but no official likes the prospect of having to justify his actions to his superiors in response to an urgent demand by the minister, knowing that the reputation of the department rests, for the moment, on his shoulders. It is true that as the size of the civil service has increased far more rapidly in the past fifty years than the number of questions asked, the chances of any individual decision leading to a Parliamentary question must have diminished. But there is no evidence that this has led civil servants to stop worrying about the possibility of a question, and no serious reason to doubt the truth of the following comment by a senior official of the Ministry of Labour:

'One may say of the British official that, if he is engaged on a job with no immediate outlet to minister and Parliament, he will still be working tacitly with the sort of notions of relevance that would mean something to them; he must try so to order things, that, of all that can happen, only those things happen which are susceptible of explanation in the Parliamentary context'.[1]

In the third place, the ability to hold ministers to account for their actions in Parliament facilitates the work of the opposition. They can use Parliamentary questions to expose weaknesses in the government's policies and lack of efficiency in the administration. If the matter which is brought to light is both serious and urgent, the opposition may be able to secure the adjournment of the House and hold a full debate on the same day. Failing this, the opposition can move a vote of censure or debate the issue on one of the 26 supply days. If the matter is potentially damaging to the government's reputation, members of the opposition can return to it time and time again by asking questions on its different aspects, as Labour Members did in regard to the Suez expedition. In this way the opposition can bring the government's weaknesses to the attention of press and public, and so hope to win votes in the next election.

If these three points are considered together, it is clear that the convention of ministerial responsibility plays a significant role in the British system of government. It does not normally enable Parliament to secure the resignation of ministers, but this does not mean that its importance is negligible. Whether procedural reforms would enable Parliament to control the administration more effectively through other channels is a question that will be considered in the next chapter.

[1] C. H. Sisson, *The Spirit of British Administration* (London, 1959), p. 123.

# CHAPTER 12

# The Parliamentary Watchdog

## THE LIMITATIONS OF PARLIAMENTARY CONTROL

It is part of the Liberal view of the constitution that Parliament should control the administration through the dependence of ministers on Parliamentary support and the convention of ministerial responsibility for the work of their departments. There are other countries, it is commonly said or implied, where the bureacracy is a law unto itself, but in Britain the administration is kept in check by the vigilance of 'the Parliamentary watchdog'. In practice this control is now limited by two factors. The first is the development of party government, under which ministers are protected from the possibility of an adverse vote in Parliament by the support of the majority party. The second is the immense amount and complexity of government business, which makes it difficult for back-bench M.P.'s to offer informed criticism except in so far as they are briefed by affected interests.

There is no evident way of reversing either of these trends. Some writers have advocated the adoption of proportional representation, giving as one reason that this would reduce the strength of the government party and increase the independence of M.P.'s. But neither of the major parties supports this proposal and it is very unlikely that any party possessing a Parliamentary majority would ever introduce an electoral reform which would have the certain effect of reducing the majority of the party winning the next election. Quite apart from this, there is no evidence that the present system of party government is at all unpopular in the country as a whole.[1] Some Liberal critics are worried about the strength of party discipline but it is doubtful if more than a small proportion of the electorate could be persuaded to share their views, even if the matter received more publicity than it at present does.

Equally, there is no general concern about the failure of ministers to resign when administrative blunders are exposed, for this is in line with the general tolerance shown in Britain towards people

[1]At the time of writing the two main parties appear to have lost some of their popularity, but this is by no means the same thing. The swing to the Liberal Party in 1961 and 1962 would clearly have been much more pronounced were it not for a general fear of 'weak government'.

who make honest mistakes, whatever job they may happen to be doing.

The growth in the extent and complexity of government business is even less likely to be reversed than the growth of party management. A rough guide to the extent of administrative activities is given by the size of the civil service. In 1881 there were 51,000 non-industrial civil servants; twenty years later there were 116,000; and by 1960 the number had grown to 637,000.[1] Many of these are employed in departments whose activities do not give rise to many Parliamentary questions and debates, such as the Post Office and the revenue departments. If these are excluded the overall numbers are smaller but the rate of increase is greater, from about 40,000 in 1914 to about 311,000 in 1960.[2] Since the amount of Parliamentary time available has hardly increased at all it follows that the amount of time that can be devoted each session to enquiries into any one topic or the activities of any one government office has suffered a considerable decrease.

The complexity and technicality of administrative activities have increased as well as their extent, and it is often said that as a result M.P.'s inevitably know less about the work of the government than they did a century ago. Probably this puts the emphasis in the wrong place. On the one hand, government business has always seemed complex to those concerned with it, and it would be a mistake to suggest that there was once a golden age of Parliament when back-benchers were well informed about the whole range of government activities. On the other hand there is no shortage of specialized and technical information available to those who have the time and inclination to seek it: for instance, the six or seven people who write the commentaries on current affairs in the *Economist* each week show much more specialized knowledge than is usually displayed by back-benchers.

The truth is that it is not one factor but a whole range of factors, reinforcing each other, which produce a situation in which Parliamentary criticism of the administration is generally poorly informed and largely ineffective. In the first place, back-benchers do not have much time to devote to the acquisition of specialized information about administrative matters. They are busy with the internal politics of their own parties; they constantly travel to and from their constituencies, making speeches, attending social functions, and

[1] See W. J. M. Mackenzie and J. W. Grove, *Central Administration in Britain* (London, 1957), p. 7, and *Digest of Civil Service Staff Statistics* (London, annually).
[2] See F. M. G. Willson, *The Organisation of British Central Government, 1914–1956* (London, 1957), chap. 1; and *Digest of Civil Service Staff Statistics.*

meeting electors; they attend to a large correspondence with (in general) inadequate secretarial help, and take up innumerable grievances on behalf of constituents; in many cases they also carry on part-time careers as lawyers, journalists, or business men.

Secondly, as a class back-benchers do not have much incentive to become experts on a wide range of topics. Those who are ambitious may take the advice Lord Woolton gave when he was Chairman of the Conservative Party and specialize on one subject, so that the Whips may get to know that they are reliable people to put up when this subject is debated. But many M.P.'s do not feel it is necessary to do this, and of those who do a high proportion on the government side of the House will be sterilized as critics by being offered posts in the administration. The government now has about 120 posts to distribute among its Parliamentary supporters; some will go to Peers but there remain between 90 and 100 posts to be offered to the more able and industrious members of the majority party in the House of Commons.

A third factor is the greatly increased tendency of interest groups to negotiate directly with the administration, of which more will be said in later chapters. One effect of this is to reduce still further the incentive for back-benchers to acquire specialized knowledge of the affairs with which these groups are concerned. For instance, any M.P. with a general interest in agriculture knows that agricultural policy is determined, within limits set by the cabinet, by direct negotiations between the National Farmers' Union and the Ministry. If the negotiations break down at any stage, the subsequent Parliamentary debate is dominated by government spokesmen on the one hand and spokesmen briefed by the Union on the other. In these circumstances it is not surprising that few M.P.'s are inclined to spend much time making an independent study of agricultural affairs.

A fourth factor is that defence and foreign affairs, which loom larger in government policy and government expenditure than ever before in peacetime, are wrapped in a veil of secrecy and discretion. This is only partly a matter of the Official Secrets Act, for Winston Churchill showed in the 1930's that this need not prevent effective criticism of defence policy. Much more important than this is the existence of a tradition of secrecy and discretion which the leading members of both main parties generally respect. The government's problems at any time are apt to be broadly similar to those which the leaders of the opposition experienced when they were last in power and which they expect to experience again when they are next in power; as a result observance of this tradition is not only good form but is also usually good tactics.

All these factors impose a more severe limitation on Parliamentary control than does the growth of party discipline. John Stuart Mill said that Parliament's functions were 'to watch and control the government: to throw the light of publicity on its acts: to compel a full exposition and justification of all of them which anyone considers questionable: to censure them if found condemnable'.[1] If M.P.'s were well informed about all the government's activities Parliament could perform the first three of these functions, even if party solidarity prevented it performing the fourth. But if M.P.'s do not know exactly what the government is doing they cannot perform any of these functions effectively. It was awareness of this that led one Member to observe that 'the House of Commons is in great danger of becoming the administration's Pekinese, able maybe to snarl and snap a bit after the event but never possessed of that current knowledge which is so essential if we are to have any chance of performing the function of watchdog'.[2]

## CONTROL BY COMMITTEE

Only one way has been found of overcoming these limitations. This is the institution of specialized committees to supplement control by Parliament as a whole. There now exist four select committees of the House of Commons, one each on Public Accounts, Estimates, Statutory Instruments, and Nationalized Industries. These committees have (with one exception) been established since the development of party government,[3] and their rules of procedure take account of this development. It has been said that they do not either 'formulate or criticize policy', which is the task of the House as a whole: 'what they scrutinize is the application of policy'.[4] Since policy itself is not normally under discussion, and since a vote critical of some aspect of administration is not interpreted as a defeat for the government, the normal compulsion to vote according to party lines does not operate in these committees. In consequence, 'party plays little part in the working of the committees to scrutinize and control'.[5]

The composition and activities of these committees have been

[1] *Considerations on Representative Government*, p. 172.
[2] John Peyton, M.P., quoted in the *Economist*, April 2, 1960.
[3] The Public Accounts Committee was established in 1861, a few years before effective party government was developed; The Estimates Committee dates from 1912, though it lapsed (as such) during each war; the Statutory Instruments Committee was formed in 1944; and the Select Committee on Nationalized Industries dates from 1955.
[4] K. C. Wheare, *Government by Committee* (Oxford, 1955), p. 207.
[5] Ibid., p. 248.

described elsewhere[1] and it is unnecessary to give a further account of them here. Two of the committees, those on Statutory Instruments and Nationalized Industries, have won almost unanimous approval from politicians and commentators. The former does a dull but essential piece of work with quiet efficiency; the latter has made an auspicious start on its more exciting task of scrutinizing the activities of public corporations which are free from the traditional forms of Parlimentary control. The financial committees have been the subject of greater controversy, and some of the arguments used in regard to them are interesting because they illustrate the divergence of opinion that exists on the nature of the proper relations between Parliament and the administration.

## THE FINANCIAL COMMITTEES

The main criticism of the organization of the two financial committees has been that neither of them is able to examine current expenditure with the object of preventing extravagance. The Estimates Committee has a staff which is neither large enough nor expert enough (in the absence of any trained accountants) to scrutinize the estimates in detail. All that it can hope to do is to pick out a few problems and departments each year for examination. The Public Accounts Committee is assisted by the Comptroller and Auditor-General, whose staff of about 500 are continuously engaged in the audit of departmental accounts. The main purpose of this audit is to ensure that expenditures have been duly authorized, but if an apparent example of gross extravagance were disclosed the auditors would discuss it with the officials concerned and with the Treasury. A note on this might then be included in the annual report of the Comptroller and Auditor-General to Parliament, made in the following year. There is statutory provision for a special report to be made in cases of urgency, but this has never been done. As the discussions of the Public Accounts Committee are based entirely on the Comptroller's annual reports, it follows that any enquiry into extravagance is bound to be delayed until a considerable time after the money has been spent.

In 1946 a plan to overcome this limitation was presented to the Select Committee on Procedure by Sir Gilbert Campion, then Clerk to the House of Commons. He suggested that a new Public

[1] See A. H. Hanson, 'The Select Committee on Statutory Instruments', in *Public Administration*, vol. 27 (1949); B. Chubb, *The Control of Public Expenditure* (Oxford, 1952); Sir Frank Tribe, 'Parliamentary Control of Public Expenditure', in *Public Administration*, vol. 32 (1954); Wheare, op. cit., chap. 8; Mackenzie and Grove, op. cit., chaps. 18 and 20.

Expenditure Committee should be established which would combine the functions of the two existing financial committees. This new committee could consider the accounts and estimates for a three-year period (the preceding, current, and forthcoming years), and could have the services of the Comptroller and Auditor-General and his staff. This plan was supported by some members of the Select Committee but was opposed by all the witnesses who had positions of authority, including the Speaker, the Comptroller and Auditor-General, the Leader of the House of Commons, and the official spokesman for the Treasury. Some of their arguments are illuminating.

If the arguments are put in logical order, first place must go to the view put forward by a Government spokesman that current expenditure does not exist, all expenditure either having already been made or being about to be made. The proposal to check current expenditure, it was suggested, therefore fell to the ground as being impossible of achievement. Second place must go to the Treasury view that it was impossible to conceive that the existing arrangements could be improved upon. 'You have now your two committees', said the Financial Secretary to the Treasury (W. Glenvill Hall), 'and you have in addition the Departments in Whitehall and over them the Treasury. . . . We think there you have as much machinery as it is possible for human society to set up to cover this particular field.'[1] Third place goes to the view put forward by the same witness, at the same interview, that if the machinery of scrutiny were improved this would be very unpopular in Whitehall. When asked to explain this more fully, he referred to the antipathy in Whitehall to the 'trained clerks' who had assisted the wartime Committee on National Expenditure:

'I think the apprehensions at the time were that the trained clerks were, so to speak, taking such an interest in the current administration, looking for trouble and ferreting out things, that they were almost becoming quasi-executive or administrative themselves. That was the fear, and therefore, these fellows in Whitehall felt that there were some sleuths over at the Palace of Westminster running side by side with them, trying to trip them up.'[2]

This was an unusually frank summary of the Whitehall attitude towards Parliamentary control of the administration. It is therefore interesting to note that an almost identical attitude was adopted by

[1] *Third Report of the Select Committee on Procedure in the Public Business*, H.C. 189–1 of 1945–46, p. 114.
[2] Ibid., pp. 112–3.

Herbert Morrison, then Leader of the House of Commons. Morrison, like Glenvill Hall, asserted, first, that existing arrangements did not need to be improved, and second, that an improvement might embarrass the administration.

Mr. Morrison: 'I have just this sneaking suspicion that some day some M.P. of capacity will get hold of the expenditure of a Government Department and make a great speech on the floor, and tear that Department to pieces and prove its extravagance. If he did it he would be rendering a great public service and put fear into the hearts of the rest of them. It has not been done for a long time'.
Viscount Hichingbrooke: 'How is he to do that without having an organization which goes into the work of the Departments, subjects civil servants to cross-examination, and which provides him with the information on which to base that speech?'
Mr. Morrison: 'I do not know'.[1]

On the second point, Morrison observed that the proposed committee would 'make major enquiries and special short-term enquiries into current complaints. That would be a big change and I think would be a nuisance to Departments. I do not say the House should not be a nuisance to Departments. One of the functions of Parliament is to be so; but nevertheless Parliament has a duty to take account of the running of Departments'.[2]

These statements throw a certain amount of light on the nature of the British constitution. It is commonly said that whereas the United States Constitution is based on the doctrine of the separation of legislative and executive powers, the British constitution provides for continuous control of the administration by Parliament. In practice the U.S. Congress, through its Appropriations Committees, exercises a much closer control over the expenditures of the administration than Parliament is able to exercise over the expenditures of the departments in Whitehall. And proposals designed to increase the effectiveness of Parliamentary control have usually been opposed by all those in positions of authority, who argue, in substance, that effective control would be undesirable.

On this occasion the Financial Secretary to the Treasury and the Leader of the House of Commons were supported, in slightly different terms, by the Speaker and the Comptroller and Auditor-General. The Speaker invoked the constitutional doctrine that only the minister is responsible for matters of policy. If the proposed committee were to probe at all deeply into departmental affairs, he said, 'the minister would pull them up and say: "This is not your

[1]*Third Report of the Select Committee on Preceedure in the Public Business,* H.C. 189–1 of 1945–46, p. 111.　　　　　　　　　　　　　[2]Ibid., p. 114.

business; it is mine. It is policy". He would put his foot down—
and I think rightly too. He cannot share responsibility with anybody else'.[1]

The constitutional propriety of the Speaker's contribution cannot
be questioned. But since any question is a question of policy if the
minister decides that it is a question of policy, the real meaning of
this doctrine is that Parliamentary enquiries into departmental
activities can always be halted if the department concerned thinks
they are likely to create difficulties.

The Comptroller and Auditor-General relied upon a different
argument. In a statement outlining the position of the holder of his
office, he said:

'His officers are not generally as well qualified as the responsible
department or the Treasury to form opinions as to the amount of
money required to carry out a given policy. At present departments
willingly furnish the auditors with all information and facilities
necessary to carry out the audit duties laid down by Parliament,
but these happy relations might be disturbed if information obtained
from departments were used to criticize departmental policy or
decisions taken by a minister after the expression of conflicting
views within the department or in correspondence between the
department and the Treasury'.[2]

In considering this argument it must be remembered that while the
Comptroller is formally a servant of Parliament he is appointed to
his office by the Crown, which means that in practice he is chosen
by the Permanent Secretary to the Treasury from among the fifty
or sixty most successful civil servants of the time. Partly because of
this, he occupies a rather ambivalent position in relation to the
spending departments. On the one hand, he is the servant of Parliament charged with auditing and if necessary investigating their
accounts; on the other hand, he clearly sees it as his duty to stand
between Whitehall and Parliament and to protect civil servants from
questioning by politicians except when he thinks this is desirable.
When pressed by members of the Select Committee as to why the
Public Accounts Committee should not discuss current as well as
past expenditure, he replied that it was helpful for departments to
have 'an opportunity of giving their explanations to me before I
report to Parliament', and added:

'It would be very difficult for me to be putting questions to depart-

[1] *Third Report of the Select Committee on Proceedure in the Public Business*,
H.C. 189–1 of 1945–46, p. 84.                                    [2] Ibid., p. 188.

ments and examining a particular matter, and ultimately selecting certain matters for report to Parliament itself, if at the same time I and my officers were advising a committee of Parliament'.[1]

It is also relevant to note that, as the Comptroller and Auditor-General admitted, the officers of his Department are not well qualified to decide whether other departments have been extravagant in their expenditures. The Exchequer and Audit Department does not enjoy anything like the status of the French *Cour des Comptes* or the German *Bundesrechnungshof*; its staff are recruited from school-leavers and have a position equivalent to that of Executive, not Administrative, Class officers; and in practice their functions are to see that the books are properly kept and that expenditures conform to the rules, not to assess the wisdom of departmental spending.

There was thus a considerable weight of official opposition to Campion's scheme. In spite of this the Select Committee on Procedure recommended that Parliament should consider a reform on the lines he had suggested. Inevitably, this recommendation was rejected by the Government and by a large majority in the House of Commons. Since that date, however, there have been one or two changes designed to improve the effectiveness of the Select Committee on Estimates. It has acquired the services of a number of Parliamentary clerks who, while not trained accountants, are nevertheless able to guide the Committee through the mass of departmental accounts and statistics. It has increased in size and has divided itself into six sub-committees, each of which works on a different aspect of administration or a different department. As a result, the Committee 'succeeds each year in turning a beam of light on perhaps a dozen major items of expenditure, which it investigates in some detail'.[2]

Up to the time of writing, the Committee's reports have very rarely been debated in Parliament, because the government does not allot any time for this and the opposition is normally reluctant to devote any of its limited time to a subject which is unlikely to excite public opinion. However, in July 1960 the Home Secretary, following pressure from Conservative back-benchers, announced a concession to critics of this situation. In future, he said, three days in each session would be allotted to debates on the reports of the financial committees: one day found by the Government, one day promised by the opposition, and one day taken from private members. At

[1] *Third Report of the Select Committee on Proceedure in the Public Business*, H.C. 189–1 of 1945–46, p. 197.
[2] Mackenzie and Grove, op. cit., p. 324.

the same time he announced that the Estimates Committee would be increased in size so as to permit the creation of a seventh sub-committee; that this extra sub-committee would be given facilities to examine the Supplementary Estimates which are presented each spring; and that the Committee would be asked to report each autumn on the principal variations between the estimates for the current and forthcoming years so as to make it possible for the latter to be amended in the light of the Committee's report and the Parliamentary debate on it. These changes promise a slight increase in Parliamentary discussion of the estimates. If all goes well they may also lead to a slight extension of the influence of the Estimates Committee, within the limits set by the established relationship between Parliament and the administration in regard to public expenditure.

## PARLIAMENTARY CONTROL OF EXPENDITURE

The official view of the nature of this relationship has been indicated by the late Sir Frank Tribe, Comptroller and Auditor-General from 1946 to 1953. Acknowledging that the American system of Congressional control is more logical than the British system, he went on to say that 'it frequently results in providing the government with less money to spend on a given service than the departments concerned have persuaded the President is really necessary for the proper conduct of their work, and to our way of thinking such constant Parliamentary interference with the job of governing a country must prejudice executive efficiency'.[1] The use of the word 'interference' is illuminating, suggesting as it does that Parliament is not directly involved in government.

On this view Parliament's powers in relation to public expenditure are purely formal, save for the activities of the Public Accounts Committee in relation to the audit of government records. The responsibility for checking departmental estimates and securing economy in administration is said to rest squarely on the shoulders of the Treasury, though the Treasury may indeed be helped by the financial committees of Parliament. The responsibility for checking extravagance which arises not from administrative inefficiency but from political decisions is thought to rest with the opposition and the electorate. On this view the main factor that checks ministerial extravagance is simply the knowledge that money spent on, say, research into space travel is more difficult to defend in public debate and less likely to bring out votes at the next election than the same sum devoted to an increase in social service payments or a reduction

[1] H.C. 189–1 of 1945–46, p. 381.

in taxation. There is little doubt that this view of the situation corresponds substantially, though not entirely, with current practice.

There is, indeed, another way of describing things, according to which Parliamentary control of expenditure is one of the central features of the constitution. The basis of this view is the history of Parliament itself, for the 'power of the purse' was Parliament's main weapon in its long struggle to break the power of the monarchy and to establish its own independent authority. 'The finance of the country is ultimately associated with the liberties of the country', said Gladstone; 'it is a powerful leverage by which English liberty has been gradually acquired'.[1] And while some early constitutional concepts were replaced by the Liberal view of the constitution that developed in the nineteenth century, the belief that Parliament should control public expenditure was given a central place in Liberal doctrine.

This belief has never been realized except in a formal way. The Liberal view that Parliament controlled the policy of the government through the convention of collective responsibility was a reasonable guide to practice for several decades of the Victorian period, but has become increasingly outdated in the twentieth century. In contrast, the Liberal view that Parliament should exercise financial control of the administration has never been much more than an aspiration.

## THE DEBATE ABOUT SPECIALIZED COMMITTEES

Quite apart from the question of controlling expenditure, there is growing dissatisfaction with Parliament's ability to control the work of the administration. Many people have sought a way of improving the situation, and the proposal that has most frequently been made is that specialized committees of the House of Commons should be created, each concentrating on the affairs of a department or group of departments. The many reforms along these lines that have been suggested have varied in detail. In some schemes the committees would be mainly responsible for dealing with the committee stage of legislation relating to their field of specialization. In others the committees would be mainly concerned with scrutinizing the work of the departments and discussing administrative problems. In others again the committees would have power to examine the estimates of the departments. In many schemes it has been suggested that the committees might combine two or more of these functions. A very convenient guide to recent proposals of this kind has been published[2] and they need not be summarized here. It is perhaps

[1] Quoted in Paul Einzig, *The Control of the Purse* (London, 1959), p. 3.
[2] Hansard Society, *Parliamentary Reform: 1933–1958* (London, 1959), pp. 62–84.

worth noting, however, that the advocates of specialized committees include Lloyd George, L. S. Amery, Sir Stafford Cripps, and Jo Grimond among politicians; Sir Ivor Jennings, Harold Laski, and D. W. Brogan among academics; and two recent Clerks to the House of Commons, Lord Campion and Sir Edward Fellowes.

The advantages of establishing a system of specialized committees are fairly clear. First and foremost, they would enable Members to acquire the detailed information about the work and problems of the departments which is essential if they are to conduct intelligent debates on administrative matters and on legislation framed to meet administrative needs.[1] Second, they would enable Members to acquire information about and to criticize those aspects of defence policy which are now shrouded in secrecy. As there is great reluctance to hold secret sessions of Parliament in peacetime, Members are now generally ignorant of a sphere of policy which is of vital importance and which involves the expenditure of 30 per cent of government income. Members of Parliament now 'know less about the disposition of British forces than do the members of defence committees of foreign legislatures',[2] and defence policy is effectively free of Parliamentary control. To some extent this could be remedied by the creation of a Committee on Defence which meet in private. Third, it could be expected that specialized committees would discuss administrative problems in a non-partisan way, as already happens in the four existing committees but is rare in the charged atmosphere of the House itself. Fourth, membership of a specialized committee would help Members of the opposition not only to criticize the Government in an informed way but also to prepare themselves to take over responsibility for the departments if they should win an election.

These arguments and others have been canvassed on numerous occasions—in speeches, articles and books, in debates in the House, and before the Select Committees on Procedure of 1930–31, 1945–46, and 1958–59. They have met unyielding opposition from the spokesmen of whatever government happened to be in power. The arguments of the government spokesmen have usually been brief and can easily be summarized.

First, it has been asserted that Britain should not try to copy the institutions of foreign countries. In his evidence to the Select Committee on Procedure of 1945–46 Herbert Morrison said: 'Parliament is not a body which is organized for current administration—not in this country. They have had a go at it in France and the United

---

[1] This argument was developed as long ago as 1918 in the *Report of the Committee on the Machinery of Government*, Cd. 9230.
[2] *Parliamentary Reform: 1933–1958*, p. 77.

States, and I do not think too much of it.'[1] A subsequent Leader of the House has used a similar argument in a slightly more sophisticated way. In a debate on procedure in 1958 R. A. Butler referred to specialized committees as 'committees a l'Americain or, perhaps, a la Francaise,' and warned the House that 'if we were to adopt the Standing Committee a l'Americain, we would be doing something absolutely opposite to British constitutional development'.[2] In the debate on the Report of the Select Committee on Procedure of 1958–59 Butler returned to the same theme, observing that the proposal to establish a colonial committee 'smacks to me far more of Capitol Hill and the Palais Bourbon than of the Parliament in Westminster'.[3] In the same debate another Member insisted 'how dangerous it is to argue that, because abroad they have this method of dealing with foreign and colonial affairs and defence, we should deal with them in the same way'.[4]

Statements of this kind are valuable for their emotive force rather than for their logic. In so far as a reference to French government conjures up an unfavourable image in British minds, it is an image (now out of date) of a weak and unstable executive. But the weakness and instability of the French executive before 1958 resulted from the large number of parties represented in the National Assembly, not from the committee system. The reference to American experience is equally irrelevant, for the relations between Congress and the Executive have been shaped by the U.S. Constitution and the absence of effective party discipline at the national level. Most observers agree that, given this situation, the Congressional committees have been fairly successful in bridging the gap between the two arms of the government. It must be concluded that the argument from French and American experience is rather obscure.

The second argument that is usually put against the proposal to create new specialized committees is that this would, in the words of the Select Committee's Report, 'constitute a radical constitutional innovation'.[5] This general assertion has been given specific content in more than one way. First, it has been said that the scrutinizing activity proposed for the committees would mean the abandonment of the principle that the minister is individually accountable to the House as a whole for the work of his Department. Thus, Morrison said of the I.L.P. proposals that were put to the Committee on Procedure of 1929–31 that they 'challenge the vital doctrine of the responsibility of ministers to Parliament as a whole'.[6] In 1958 the Leader of the House said that 'a sitting specialist committee' would

---

[1] Loc. cit., p. 111.     [2] *House of Commons Debates*, 5th s., v. 581, cc. 762–3.
[3] Ibid., v. 609, c. 42.     [4] Ibid., c. 149.     [5] Ibid., p. xxv.
[6] Herbert Morrison, *Government and Parliament* (London, 1954), p. 159.

'blur ministerial responsibility'.[1] And in debates in the House several speakers have made the point that it would be contrary to tradition, and possibly unfair to ministers, if specialist committees were to share the power now enjoyed only by the House of calling ministers to account for the work of their Departments.

An allied but slightly different argument is that such an innovation would be unfair to private Members. The Select Committee of 1945–46 took this line when it rejected Campion's proposal that the report stage of bills should be taken in committee:

'The main objection in Your Committee's view is to the principle of the scheme. The removal of the report stage of bills from the floor of the House would be, in the words of Mr Speaker, "a drastic interference with the rights of private Members" . . . and the suggestion which Sir Gilbert Campion makes to meet this objection— that a Member who was not a member of a standing committee could move amendments without the right to vote—is entirely contrary to the traditional practice of the House'.[2]

A similar point was made by the Select Committee of 1958–59 in relation to the proposal to set up a committee on colonial affairs:

'It would seem more appropriate that colonial affairs, in view of their undoubted importance, should be discussed upon the floor of the House . . . Discussion in a committee, which could not comprise more than a small proportion of the House, would mean that many Members would be prevented from expressing their opinions.'[3]

The weakness of this argument and of the argument about ministerial responsibility is that neither of them answers the case put by the advocates of specialized committees. In essence this case rests on three propositions: (*a*) that Parliament ought to control the administration; (*b*) that the present arrangements for achieving this end are inadequate because M.P.'s lack knowledge about administrative affairs and the House lacks time for detailed discussion; (*c*) that the creation of specialized committees would go some way towards remedying this inadequacy.

It is no answer to this case to say that the reform would constitute a breach of traditional practice, because this is what the reform is intended to be. It is no answer to say that control through specialized committees might become more effective than control through ministerial accountability at Question Time, since this is what is hoped. It is no answer to say that discussion in committee would

[1] H.C. 92–1 of 1959, Q. 1161.  [2] H.C. 189–1 of 1945–46, p. VII.
[3] H.C. 92–1 of 1958–59, p. XXV.

deprive other Members of their theoretical right to discuss the matter in the House, because one of the main points made by the advocates of reform is that in many fields Members are unable to exercise this right effectively. In short, these arguments are no more relevant to the discussion than the appeal to French and American experience.

If most of the arguments used by the opponents of the proposed reform are irrelevant, on what is their opposition based? It can hardly be based on a rejection of either the second or third of the propositions listed above, since nobody has seriously attempted to deny their truth. In fact, it is based on a denial of the first proposition, though it is only occasionally that this emerges with any clarity.

One of these occasions was in the Report of the Select Committee of 1958–59, in which this was the only substantial argument (though not the only argument used) against the proposal to create a committee on colonial affairs. Of this, the Report said:

'There is little doubt that the activities of such a committee would ultimately be aimed at controlling rather than criticizing the policy and actions of the department concerned. In so doing, it would be usurping a function which the House itself has never attempted to exercise. Although the House has always maintained the right to criticize the executive and in the last resort to withdraw its confidence, it has always been careful not to arrogate to itself any of the executive power.'[1]

In the subsequent debate on this Report the same note was struck by the Leader of the House, R. A. Butler, who said: 'If the committee were to devote its attention to day-to-day colonial administration, surely there would be a real danger of usurping the functions, not only of colonial governments themselves . . . but also of United Kingdom ministers.'[2] And later an experienced Labour Member, Mr. Philips Price, declared that a colonial committee 'would be particularly wrong, as it would tend to undermine the authority of the executive'.[3] This is not very different from saying that there is a separation of powers which should be respected.

It is important to notice that although most speakers on procedural matters do not use this argument, all the most influential speakers do use it. And so far this view has always triumphed. If this is considered in conjunction with the official attitude towards Parliamentary control of public expenditure, it becomes apparent that the view of the constitution implied by the phrase 'Parliamentary watchdog' is held only by those who have never penetrated the citadel of government. In the light of this it may be appropriate to reconsider the nature of responsible government in Britain.

[1] H.C. 92–1 of 1958–59, p. XXV.
[2] *House of Commons Debates*, 5th s., v. 609, c. 42.          [3] Ibid., c. 148.

# CHAPTER 13

# Responsible Government Reconsidered

## THE LANGUAGES OF THE CONSTITUTION

The discussions reported in the preceding chapter indicate the existence of a certain amount of confusion about the proper role of Parliament in relation to the executive. This confusion is seen most clearly in the debate, now thirty years old, over the proposal to create specialized committees. One important aspect of the confusion appears to be the fact that there are two languages in which the relations between Parliament and the executive are described. One language is that of the Liberal view of the constitution: it talks of Parliamentary sovereignty, of the responsibility of ministers to Parliament for the work of their departments, of the defence of the people's rights through the vigilance of 'the Parliamentary watchdog', of the democratic advantages of a system in which there is no separation of powers between legislature and executive. This is the language used by nearly all back-benchers, nearly all journalists, and most academic commentators. In this language there are no convincing arguments against specialized committees.

The other language is used by civil servants, the Speaker, ministers of the Crown, and opposition leaders who hope soon to become ministers. It talks of the responsibility of Her Majesty's Government for the administration of the country, of the importance of protecting civil servants from political interference, of Parliament's function as a debating chamber in which public opinion is aired. At least one politician of the twentieth century has used this language in the manner of eighteenth-century Tories, referring to ministers' 'primary responsibility to the Crown as the embodiment of the unity and continuity of our national life'.[1] It is more usual to employ newer concepts, such as that the Government has a mandate to put its policies into effect, and is ultimately answerable to the electorate (not Parliament) for their success. In this language Parliament is portrayed partly as a place where grievances are ventilated and partly as a forum for party controversy, conducting a somewhat formalized battle of words for the benefit of press and public. If the constitution is described in these terms it emerges as one in which

[1] L. S. Amery, *Thoughts on the Constitution* (London, 1947), p. 33.

there is an effective, even though not a formal, separation of powers between Parliament and the executive.

This is, in fact, the view of the constitution held by those in power. As a description of what happens it is undoubtedly more accurate than that given in terms of the Liberal view of the constitution. But such is the spell of the Liberal view that most discussion, by those against as well as those in favour of Liberal ideals, is conducted in what may be called 'the Liberal language'. Since the Liberal language implies the Liberal ideals, this results in the curious nature of the intermittent debate about the reform of Parliamentary procedure. In this debate the arguments given in favour of reform are logically superior to nearly all the arguments given against reform, but in the end the proposed reforms are nearly always rejected.


## THE STATUS OF PARLIAMENT

In these two languages Parliament itself appears in two guises. In the Liberal language Parliament is a corporate entity wielding power. It possesses sovereignty, it holds ministers to account, it controls the executive. In the other language, which may for convenience be called 'the Whitehall language', Parliament is not a corporate entity so much as an arena or forum. In this arena individual Members air grievances and groups of Members carry on the party struggle. Ministers appear so that, in Morrison's term, Members can 'have a go' at them; debates on large issues are staged so that the opposition may present an alternative policy for the benefit of the electors. It is significant that Captain Harry Crookshank, a former Leader of the House, was shocked by the proposal that the Report Stage of legislation should be taken in committee. 'After all', he said, 'we are sent here to represent particular views, not to coalesce into a corporate body upstairs . . . Oppositions are not sent to make perfect bills out of the government measures'.[1] It is also significant that in the debate on the Report of the Select Committee on Procedure of 1958–59 both the Leader of the House and the leading spokesman for the opposition made a point of reminding members that Parliament is the scene of a constant struggle for power between the parties.

As a language of description the Whitehall language is, up to a point, superior to the Liberal language. In general, Parliament occupies the role cast for it by Whitehall spokesmen. But this is by no means the whole story, and the British political system cannot be understood unless it is realized that in this sphere the Liberal language is the language of criticism, defining an ideal with which

[1] H.C. 189–1 of 1945–46, p. 53.

actual behaviour can be compared. Very occasionally the House of Commons lives up to this ideal and forces the government to acknowledge that (for the moment, at any rate) Parliamentary supremacy is more than a fiction. This happened in 1935, when the House forced the Cabinet to disown the Hoare–Laval pact. It happened, as everyone knows, in 1940, when Neville Chamberlain was forced to resign. It happened twice in 1959, first when the Obscene Publications Bill was drastically amended in committee, and later when the Government was forced to order a full-scale enquiry into an allegation that a policeman in a remote part of Scotland had struck an adolescent boy who had sworn at him. It happened again in July 1962, when the House forced the Home Secretary to revoke a deportation order made under the Commonwealth Immigration Act. Rare as such occasions may be, they are of crucial and continuing importance. The knowledge that, in the last resort, back-benchers can revolt leads ministers to pay more attention to back-bencher's opinions than they otherwise would. And the occasional spectacle of Parliament asserting its latent power almost certainly raises the status of M.P.'s in the eyes of the general public.

Generally Parliament occupies a much more subservient role, even though its debates may make newspaper headlines. Then the Liberal language is used by those who wish to criticize the conduct of Parliamentary affairs. Thus, in 1960 the *Economist* lamented that Parliament was deprived 'of any function save that of running a Punch and Judy show on the front lawn to divert the people from looking through the windows of their government'.[1] In 1957, a *Times* editorial painted an even gloomier picture of the Parliamentary performance:

'The cheap gibes, the incessant accusations and counter-accusations, the mocking "Ministerial cheers" and the inane cries of "Resign", the desperate fighting over things that do not matter, which probably hides from the participants themselves their poverty of ideas about those things that do matter, are all part of the same picture'.[2]

And, lest it be thought that such criticisms are a recent development, it is worth adding a comment by Hazlitt:

'It may appear at first sight that here are a number of persons got together, picked out from the whole nation, who can speak at all times upon all subjects . . . but the fact is that they only repeat the same things over and over on the same subjects'.

As a description, either of the unreformed Parliament or of

[1] The *Economist*, April 2, 1960.      [2] *The Times*, December 23, 1957.

Parliament today, Hazlitt's comment is a little unfair but not substantially untrue. Whether or not this constitutes a criticism of Parliament depends, of course, on the assumptions that are made about its role. In terms of the Liberal view, the comment implies criticism. In terms of the Whitehall view, the comment is no more than an acknowledgement of the fact that staging a party battle for the edification of the electorate involves an endless repetition of party slogans.

## THE PAY AND FACILITIES OF MEMBERS

This divergence of view on the proper function of Parliament provides the key to the understanding of the intermittent debate on the pay and facilities granted to Members. The traditional principle is that Members should be amateurs rather than professionals. This tradition was established when all Members had private incomes and the volume of Parliamentary work was a fraction of what it has become in the twentieth century. Salaries were introduced in 1911, but almost from the start the amount paid was insufficient to form a Member's sole income. It still is insufficient, though at the present time only a minority of Members have private incomes of any size. The remainder have either to practice a profession, to be paid by a pressure group, or to live in relative poverty, unable to afford adequate secretarial assistance and distracted by financial worries.

These facts are well known and have been repeatedly put forward in support of the proposal that salaries should be raised to a level at which they would be adequate as a sole source of income. The opponents of this proposal reply, not by disputing the facts, but simply by repeating that it is desirable for Members to be forced to retain or seek other sources of income. In the words of the most recent Select Committee: 'Few would support the idea of a House of Commons composed principally of full-time politicians in the sense of men and women cut off from any practical share in the work of the nation'.[1] The suggestion has sometimes been made that this argument is a rationalization devised by Conservatives, who do not experience financial difficulties so frequently as Labour Members. But the Labour Government of 1945–51 adopted the same attitude, and more recently Morrison has told the House that 'the health of our Parliamentary institutions should and can only derive from the fact that a noticeable proportion of its Members are doing other

[1] *Report of the Select Committee on Members' Expenses*, 1954, H.C. 72 of 1953–54, p. XXXVII.

things . . . so that this House does not become a closed house, a sort of monastery'.[1]

In terms of the view that Parliament's tasks are to legislate and to control the executive, this argument is inexplicable. It makes sense only in terms of the view that Parliament is essentially, in an eighteenth-century phrase, the grand inquest of the nation.

The question of Members' facilities has to be regarded in the same light. As is well known, Members are given no offices, no secretaries, and only very limited facilities for research. The physical conditions in which they work have been vividly described by Anthony Wedgwood Benn (now Lord Stansgate):

'Each of us has only one place private to ourselves, a locker which is so small that it will not take the ordinary briefcase to be locked away. We have no access to a telephone unless we make the endless, senseless tramp around the corridors waiting outside the kiosks, with our papers, waiting to telephone. No incoming telephone calls can reach us. . . . We cannot even communicate freely with each other. There is no general pigeon-hole where one can put messages for a Member. To circulate hon. Members for the debate today, my hon. Friend had to pay 3d. postage to every Member to whom he wrote'.[2]

If it were seriously intended that Members should shape legislation and be well informed about the work of the administration, the poverty of the facilities granted to them could hardly be defended. It can plausibly be argued that to play a constructive role in the government of the country Members need offices, secretaries, and the assistance of a reference service on the lines of that available to Congressmen and Senators in the United States. From time to time reforms on these lines have been suggested, both by Members themselves and by external critics.[3]

But the suggestions are not accepted, because those in power do not view the functions of Members in this way. R. A. Butler has said: 'I admire the powers of the Senators of the United States, their comfort, their secretaries, their publicity and everything else, but I do not believe that hon. Members can vie with these mighty men'.[4] Their function, he implied, is much more modest: it is to support the government or criticize it, not to take part in it. For this elaborate

[1] In 1959. See *H. of C. Debates*, 5th s., v. 609, c. 98.
[2] *H. of C. Debates*, 5th s., v. 581., c. 683 (1958).
[3] A recent example is Bernard Crick's pamphlet, *Reform of the Commons* (Fabian Tract 319, 1959).
[4] *H. of C. Debates*, 5th s., v. 609, c. 43 (1959).

facilities are not necessary, any more than it is necessary that Members should all be intellectuals.

'They frequently ask me', said Butler, 'how men of genius can contemplate coming into the House of Commons, with its antiquated procedure. The answer may well lie in the mouth of the younger Pitt, who said he could not have run the House of Commons at all had not most of his supporters, the country squires, been extremely stupid. Some degree of stupidity and docility is vital to our affairs.'[1]

## RESPONSIBILITY AND RESPONSIVENESS

At this point it may be appropriate to reconsider the general arguments about responsibility in British government. It will be recalled that we distinguished three usages of the term 'responsible': to signify responsiveness to public demands, to signify accountability, and to signify prudence and consistency on the part of those taking decisions. It was subsequently argued that responsiveness and consistency are both generally regarded as desirable characteristics, even though they are not always compatible, and that the device of ministerial accountability has been justified on the ground that it gives ministers sufficient independence to pursue consistent policies without permitting them to forget their obligation to keep in step with public opinion. In the Liberal view of the constitution ministerial accountability to Parliament appears as the key to the whole system: responsiveness of the government to movements of opinion is said to be ensured by the fact that ministers are answerable to the people's elected representatives.

The discussion in the previous three chapters and the earlier sections of this chapter throws a good deal of doubt on the validity of this view. It is clear that the conventions of cabinet and ministerial responsibility to Parliament are not in themselves very efficient ways of securing that the government is responsive to public opinion between elections. This does not mean that the conventions are of no significance, for they have a number of important functions and effects that have been indicated. Nor does it mean that British governments are not responsive to public opinion. It simply means that Parliamentary control of the executive is only one channel, and not necessarily the most important, through which public opinions and pressures are brought to the attention of the government. Accordingly, Part V of this book will be devoted to a more direct examination of public opinion, the channels through which it is communicated, and the ways in which those in power are influenced by it.

[1] *H. of C. Debates*, 5th s, v. 609, c. 37.

# THE PUBLIC AND THE GOVERNMENT

## CHAPTER 14

## The Nature of Public Opinion

### THE PROBLEM OF DEFINING PUBLIC OPINION

It is commonly asserted that the main function of representative institutions is to ensure that governmental decisions are based on public opinion. Some would claim that this is so much more important than any other function that representative institutions may serve that it should be the sole criterion by which these institutions are assessed. Some would argue that other functions, such as providing a peaceful means of changing the personnel of the government, are equally or more important. But no supporter of representative institutions would deny that the reflection of public opinion is one of their most important functions.

Agreement on this proposition is secured much more easily than agreement on how public opinion should be defined. One reason for this is that the term 'public opinion', in the singular, is no more than a metaphor.[1] Opinions are held by individuals, and the public opinion on any topic can never be more than an aggregate of individual opinions. Very occasionally these opinions will all be identical, but as a general rule they will vary. In this case the nature of the aggregate that is called public opinion will depend on how it is assessed. If equal weight is given to everyone's opinions, one kind of aggregate will emerge. But if more weight is given to the opinions of the informed than to those of the uninformed, or if expressed opinions count for more than unexpressed opinions, or if landowners' opinions are regarded as more valuable than labourers' opinions, the results will be different. Broadly speaking, public opinion polls give equal weight to each person's view, while the political process does not. In this situation it is not surprising to

[1] This point was first made by G. C. Thompson in his *Public Opinion and Lord Beaconsfield* (London, 1886), at p. 29.

171

find that politicians' definitions generally have overtones which reflect their own political attitudes.

An early example is to be found in Bentham's *Constitutional Code*. Bentham regarded public opinion as mass opinion, and he thought its influence was beneficial. 'Public opinion', he wrote, 'may be considered as a system of law emanating from the body of the people . . . To the pernicious exercise of the power of government it is the only check; to the beneficial an indispensable supplement.'[1] This may be contrasted with Peel's reference to 'that great compound of folly, weakness, prejudice, wrong feeling, right feeling, obstinacy, and newspaper paragraphs which is called public opinion',[2] which reflects Conservative scepticism in rather an extreme way. Mid-Victorian Liberals mostly followed Bentham in regarding public opinion as a beneficial influence, but tended to define it as the opinion of the educated middle classes. A philosophical idealist has defined it as a 'deeply pervasive organic force' which 'articulates and formulates . . . the evanescent common will'.[3] Socialists have insisted that it is fairer to speak of working-class opinion and middle-class opinion than to assume that there is a national public opinion. The general rule is that each political group has its own definition.

If we turn to academic discussions of the topic, we find that while the approach is usually less dogmatic than that of politicians, the extent of agreement is not appreciably greater. There is, of course, a good reason for this. The essential difficulty of defining and discussing public opinion is that it cannot be perceived until it is expressed: like an iceberg, nine-tenths of it is out of sight. There is no difficulty about discussing the ways in which opinions on political topics are publicly expressed, but this is not the same as defining and discussing public opinion. Neither politicians nor students of politics can ignore the fact that around most political issues there develops a great body of opinions which are not expressed outside a small circle of close friends and relations unless people are either provoked or invited to say what they think. Anyone concerned with politics is bound to be interested in the factors which influence these opinions, the ways in which they can be manipulated, and the circumstances which determine whether, when, and through what channels they will be publicly expressed. But since these opinions cannot be identified until they are publicly expressed, it is difficult for discussion of these topics to be other than speculative. Anyone who studied physics

[1] Quoted in B. Berelson and M. Janowitz (eds.), *Reader in Public Opinion and Communication* (Glencoe, Ill., 1950), p. 9.

[2] Quoted in James Bryce, *The American Commonwealth* (3rd edn., London, 1895), vol. II, p. 255.

[3] Wilhelm Bauer, article on 'Public Opinion' in *Encyclopaedia of the Social Sciences* (New York, 1930–33), vol. 12, p. 669.

at school is familiar with the point that the mere action of inserting a thermometer into a liquid nearly always makes a marginal difference to the temperature of the liquid. In the case of political opinions the problem is that the stimulus which provokes their public expression may not only have altered the opinions but may have created opinions where none previously existed.

In these circumstances it is not surprising that the literature on the subject falls into several fairly distinct categories, each of which is primarily concerned with one form of expression of political opinions. There is a literature on the influence of movements of opinion among the informed minority who are concerned about politics and take steps to express their personal views. There is a literature about the influence of the views of groups whose material interests are likely to be affected by government action. There is a literature about public opinion polling. And finally, there is a literature about the way in which the politicial views of the ordinary voter are influenced by propaganda and election campaigns. These topics will be discussed in this order in the remaining sections of the chapter.

## THE INFLUENCE OF INFORMED OPINION

The most ambitious attempt ever made to assess the political influence of movements of opinion among the informed minority in Britain is A. V. Dicey's book on *Law and Opinion in England During the Nineteenth Century*.[1] Dicey was concerned not so much with the influence of specific opinions on particular points as with the influence of very broad opinions about the proper functions of government. He maintained that in the nineteenth century English legislation was shaped by three main currents of public opinion. The first, which he called 'old Toryism', was influential from 1801 to 1830; the second, which he called 'Benthamism or Individualism', was influential from 1825 to 1870; and the third, which he called 'Collectivism', was influential from 1865 onwards. He illustrated this thesis by summarizing the ideas and sentiments which lay behind each of the major pieces of legislation passed in the nineteenth century.

The book is brilliantly written but it has been subjected to considerable criticism by historians.[2] It has been faulted on more than a few points of detail, which is not surprising in view of the number

[1] First published London, 1905.

[2] See, for instance, J. B. Brebner, '*Laissez Faire* and State Intervention in 19th Century Britain', in *Journal of Economic History*, Supplement VIII (1948); O. MacDonagh, 'The 19th Century Revolution in Government: a Reappraisal', in *Historical Journal*, vol. I (1958); H. W. Parris, 'The 19th Century Revolution in Government: a Reappraisal Reappraised', in *Historical Journal*, vol. III (1960).

of documents that have become available and the amount of research that has been done since Dicey wrote. Apart from these points, there appear to be two weaknesses in Dicey's historical analysis. The first is that the title he gave to the second current of opinion is rather misleading. On the one hand, Bentham's doctrines do not necessarily lead to legislative individualism but may form the basis of some forms of collectivism. While Dicey acknowledged this in a later chapter and also in a footnote to the Introduction to the Second Edition,[1] he did not give as much weight to it as it deserves.[2] On the other hand, Dicey greatly underestimated the influence of the classical economists on Victorian opinion. It may be true that the economists 'were, in popular imagination, and not without reason, identified with the philosophic Radicals',[3] but it was rather sweeping to dismiss the economists with a sentence or two each and discuss their ideas under the general heading of 'Benthamism'.

The second weakness is that Dicey gives the impression that the middle decades of the last century were the hey-day of *laissez-faire*. He notes that most of the acts of this period were based on individualistic ideas, and on this ground he regards it as a period of legislative individualism. But he fails to point out that the average manufacturer was a good deal freer of state regulation in the eighteenth century than in the nineteenth. From one point of view the mid-nineteenth century was undoubtedly an age of belief in the doctrine of *laissez-faire*: from another it was an age of increasing state regulation of industry, public health, and local government. By emphasizing one aspect and ignoring the other, Dicey gave an unbalanced picture of the period.

Apart from these historical weaknesses, the book may also be criticized on other grounds. It is admittedly speculative. It is also a little vague about definitions. Public opinion is defined on p. 3 as 'speculative views held by the mass of the people as to the alteration or improvement of their institutions' and on p. 10 as 'the wishes and ideas as to legislation held by . . . the majority of those citizens who have at a given moment taken an effective part in public life'. These definitions are by no means identical. The first of them is out of accord with the kinds of opinion that are subsequently analysed in the book, and the use of the word 'effective' in the second of them raises important questions which are not answered directly. And

[1] See p. xxx of 2nd edn. (London, 1924, reprinted 1926).
[2] He might have given more weight to this point if he had had access to all of Bentham's economic writings, some of which were made available for the first time in the volumes edited by W. Stark. See *Bentham's Economic Writings*, 3 vols. (London, 1952–54).          [3] Dicey, op. cit., p. 412.

finally, the book is imbued with a degree of optimism about the rationality of political discussion which most students of politics would now consider excessive.

Partly for these reasons, Dicey's book has had no real successors.[1] Most subsequent writers have brought a more sceptical attitude to their study of the ways in which public opinion is formed and the degree to which it influences legislation. One school of writers has insisted on the importance of group conflict in politics and suggested that the study of public opinion is essentially the study of pressure groups. Another school has insisted on the elements of irrationality in opinion-formation. A fair idea of these respective approaches can be gained by considering the work of A. F. Bentley and Walter Lippmann.

## GROUP CONFLICT

Bentley, writing in 1908, declared that Dicey owed his readers 'a quantitative analysis of public opinion in terms of the different elements of the population which expressed themselves through it. He owed us an investigation of the exact things really wanted under the cover of the "opinion" by each group of the people, with time and place and circumstance all taken up into the centre of the statement. In other words, he owed us a social dissection . . . and not a rhapsody'.[2] This belief that opinions are a 'cover' for group interests was essential to Bentley's view of the political process, which he conceived as being at bottom nothing more than the interplay of group pressures. If this view is accepted Dicey's belief that legislation results from the development of informed opinion in society as a whole must clearly be rejected as naive. 'Public opinion', wrote Bentley, 'is . . . a phenomenon of the group process. There is no public opinion that is not activity reflecting or representing the activity of a group or of a set of groups.'[3]

Bentley's challenging essay was a study in method rather than a study of the political process in operation. His ambition was to 'fashion a tool' which he hoped would be used by others. This hope has been only partially fulfilled. Many writers have analysed the place of organized groups in politics, but they have not attempted that 'social dissection' or 'quantitative analysis of public opinion' for which Bentley pleaded. Instead, they have generally confined

[1] The contributors to the symposium on *Law and Opinion in the Twentieth Century* (ed. M. Ginsberg, London, 1959) did not try to emulate either Dicey's classification of the main currents of opinion or his assessment of the general relationship between public opinion and legislation.

[2] *The Process of Government* (first pub. 1908, 2nd edn. Bloomington, Indiana, 1935), p. 153.           [3] Ibid., p. 223.

themselves to a study of the organization and activities of the groups in relation to the administration and the legislature. In studies of this kind public opinion, if it is discussed at all, is usually discussed in terms of the public relations of the groups concerned.[1]

The failure of subsequent writers to carry out the programme Bentley laid down for them is hardly surprising, since this programme was based on a one-sided view of the nature of politics. To approach an understanding of the process of government it is necessary to account both for the general support given to the political system within which interest groups operate and for the climate of opinion which leads these groups to feel that some (but rarely all) of their objectives may be regarded as legitimate. Bentley and his followers largely ignore the second point, and their attempt to meet the first point by postulating the existence of 'potential interest groups' is something like an admission of the inadequacy of Bentley's main argument. It is difficult to conceive of a quantitative analysis of the opinions of an interest group which does not yet exist.

It must be concluded that Bentley's analysis, stimulating though it is, and valuable in so far as it draws attention to some of the weaknesses in Dicey's argument, does not provide anything like an adequate model for the study of the role of public opinion in politics.

## MASS OPINION AND PUBLIC OPINION POLLING

Both Dicey and Bentley, in their different ways, were concerned with the political influence of informed minorities. Both assumed that these groups behaved in a rational fashion: Dicey believed that legislation was influenced by arguments and opinions about the proper role of government in society, while Bentley believed that conflicting groups based their demands on a rational assessment of their interests. The development of universal suffrage has been followed in recent decades by a shift in interest towards the opinions of the average citizen and a retreat from the assumption that political opinions are normally based on a process of rational consideration. This retreat is associated in Britain with the name of Graham Wallas and in the United States with the name of Walter Lippmann.

In this context Lippmann's work is the more relevant of the two. His study of *Public Opinion*[2] was an onslaught on the rationalistic assumptions about the formation and dissemination of political opinions made by Liberals in the United States and Britain. Lippmann insisted that the average citizen's opinions are based not on a

[1] See A. M. Potter, *Organised Groups in British National Politics* (London, 1961), for a discussion of the activities of British pressure groups in the field of public relations.  [2] New York, 1922.

176

dispassionate analysis of the facts but on the acceptance of stereo-typed views. These stereotyped views invariably distort the picture so as to incline anyone who accepts the views towards one conclusion rather than another. It follows, in Lippmann's opinion, that mass opinion is an unreliable and misleading guide to policy-making, and that democratic institutions which compel politicians to act as the servants of mass opinion can only be regarded as dangerous.

Lippmann's study has not had such a direct influence on other writers as Bentley's. Few people have accepted his sceptical views about the principles of western democracy, though he has restated and amplified them in a more recent book.[1] However, many studies of political opinion have been made which are in the spirit of Lippmann's work. Since 1945 the favoured word has been not 'stereo-type' but 'image'.[2] It has been shown in both Britain and the United States that voters generally choose between parties not because of particular issues but because the image of one party has more appeal to them than the image of the other. And if similar research were conducted into the views of electors between elections, it would undoubtedly show that these views are also based on rather general impressions about the nature of the national interest and the attitudes of the political parties. However, academic students of politics have not conducted much research of this latter kind, and the investigation of public attitudes to day-to-day questions of policy has been left to the public opinion pollsters.

Public opinion polling first achieved political significance in 1936, when the Gallup Poll correctly predicted the result of the presidential election in the United States. The development of the polls since that date has produced a flood of statistics about mass opinion on almost every kind of political issue. It has also produced a small army of analysts and a new academic journal in the shape of the *Public Opinion Quarterly*. The analysts tend to make their own assumptions, explicitly or implicitly, about the nature of public opinion. Writers in the tradition of Dicey assume that public opinion is made up of the opinions of informed minorities who are concerned about political issues and reveal their opinions by political actions. The pollsters assume that public opinion is the aggregate of opinions held by the adult population, as this is revealed in the answers given to questions put by interviewers in the street or on the door-step.

The difference between these definitions is, of course, more than a

[1] *The Public Philosophy* (New York, 1955).
[2] The word was first used in this connection by Graham Wallas in *Human Nature in Politics* (London, 1908). But it fell out of use for a long time before it was revived in the years following the Second World War.

matter of taste. The adoption of the first definition points to the view that governments should be influenced by informed opinion, while the adoption of the pollsters' definition suggests that governments should be influenced by mass opinion. In the early days of the polls this conclusion was frequently drawn. One American writer claimed that opinion polling was 'a forward step in the technique of self-government, which in practical social importance will rank with the original conception of government by the people'.[1] Elmo Roper suggested that government agencies should use polls to allow the public 'to express its wants and its fears, its likes and its dislikes'.[2] George Gallup and his colleagues said that those who were sceptical about government by mass opinion revealed a distrust of the people which differed 'only in degree, and not in essence' from the views of Mussolini and Hitler.[3] An academic commentator suggested that if the Founding Fathers had 'known of public opinion research, they might have made provision in the Constitution for its regular use'.[4]

Not surprisingly, claims of this kind were greeted sceptically in many circles, and in 1949 an energetic counter-attack was published which consisted of a full-scale criticism of the pretensions of the pollsters.[5] In this book Lindsay Rogers pointed out that the questions used by the polls were often ambiguous, that the responses might be affected by the manner of the interviewer, that it could not be guaranteed that answers given in the street or on the doorstep reflected the real views of the respondents, that in any case the respondents had no time to form a considered opinion, and that a simple yes/no answer gave no indication of the intensity or degree of conviction with which the respondent held the opinion. He concluded that the pollsters should be more modest in their claims, and he insisted that it would be very dangerous if those responsible for political decisions were influenced by statistics published by the polls which purported to indicate the state of public opinion.

Whether or not because of Rogers's work, the pollsters have indeed been more modest in recent years. In Britain, in particular, directors of the polling organizations have been careful to point out that statistics about mass opinion are not intended to be a guide to government action. In the words of Henry Durant and his colleagues: 'Polls are not and never can be a substitute for an elected legislature.

[1] Robert Updegraff, quoted in G. Gallup & S. F. Rae, *The Pulse of Democracy* (New York, 1940), pp. 125–6.
[2] Quoted in ibid., p. 275.                                    [3] Ibid., p. 259.
[4] Dorwin Cartwright, 'Public Opinion Polls and Democratic Leadership', in *Journal of Social Issues*, vol. II (1946), p. 3.
[5] Lindsay Rogers, *The Pollsters* (New York, 1949).

The polls simply express the opinions of the people, not their commands.'[1]

Provided that exaggerated claims are not made on their behalf, the polls can undoubtedly be of use to anyone who wants to know the general attitude of the public towards particular topics and policies. The polls do not 'measure public opinion', but they provide one guide among others to the distribution of political attitudes. Their findings may be particularly valuable when public discussion of a topic is dominated by the activities of pressure groups, for the polls can then indicate the degree of support that such groups have secured for their policies.

| Response. | All respondents. | Labour supporters. |
|---|---|---|
| Give up nuclear weapons entirely. | 21% | 31% |
| Pool all nuclear weapons with other NATO countries and rely mainly on American production. | 32% | 26% |
| Continue to make our own nuclear weapons. | 37% | 34% |
| Don't know. | 10% | 9% |

*These figures are reproduced by kind permission of Social Surveys (Gallup Poll) Ltd.

A good example of this occurred during 1960, when discussion of defence policy in the popular press tended to be dominated by reports of the activities and views of the groups in favour of nuclear disarmament. In April 1960 Hugh Gaitskell incurred disfavour in some quarters when he said that he would rather consult a Gallup Poll than an Aldermaston march for an opinion about nuclear weapons. A prominent trade unionist regarded this comment as 'a gratuitous insult to people sincerely demonstrating their feelings', and went on to imply that the opinions of people who were willing to go out and demonstrate their beliefs should be given more weight than the opinions of people who simply answered questions put by an interviewer.[2] This is a perfectly legitimate view as to how public opinion ought to be assessed. On the other hand, the results of polls published later in the year showed that (as Gaitskell had implied) support for unilateral nuclear disarmament was still confined to a minority. The figures are given in the above table: the point about them is not that they showed what policy the Labour Party (or anyone else) ought to adopt, but that they showed that the

[1] British Institute of Public Opinion, *Behind the Gallup Poll* (London, n.d.), p. 31.
[2] The Vice-Chairman of the Scottish T.U.C., quoted in *The Times*, 25 April, 1960.

press reports of the time were misleading in the impression they gave that Labour supporters could be divided simply into unilateralists on the one hand and supporters of a NATO nuclear policy on the other.[1]

It is not known how often the views (or the presumed views) of the inarticulate majority of voters are an important influence in the making of public policy, and it is impossible to say how often they should be. But it is perhaps fair to conclude this section by saying that in the mid-twentieth century the views of the majority cannot be ignored, and that the polls occasionally serve a useful purpose by indicating how these views are distributed.

## THE FORMATION OF PUBLIC OPINION

The considerable amount of research which has been done on the formation of public opinion has produced conclusions which are, on the whole, rather negative. Nevertheless, some of them are worth citing. Before doing so, it is necessary to deal with a question about the conditions in which public opinion can exist.

Some writers have suggested that public opinion, being by its nature the result of a rational consideration of the merits and demerits of a proposed action, can only exist in a free society.[2] There is indeed a Liberal ideal of opinion-formation as a process in which everyone is well informed, communications are completely free, and good ideas triumph over bad. In some ways this is like that other nineteenth-century ideal, the perfect market. Conditions do not correspond to it, but it serves as a standard from which deviations can be noted. To say that public opinion depends on freedom to exchange information and ideas is in fact not very helpful. No society enjoys complete freedom of discussion of every topic, while on the other hand there are no societies in which public discussion is completely prohibited. In the real world freedom is always a question of degree, and some kind of public opinion exists under even the most dictatorial régime.

The pertinent question is not whether public opinion exists, but what kind of public opinion exists. The Liberal argument is that Liberal institutions encourage people to exchange ideas about public affairs, stimulate criticism and argument, and in this way lead people to become more discriminating in their acceptance of opinions and propaganda. Where political debate is restricted people lack the opportunity to assess the arguments for and against proposed

[1] This point was made in the *Gallup Political Index* of October, 1960, at p. 5.
[2] See, for instance, A. L. Lowell, *Public Opinion and Popular Government* (New York, 1913).

courses of action, and public opinion is likely to oscillate between passive acceptance and cynical rejection of the ideas put forward by those in authority. Some light is thrown on this last point by the story of a schoolgirl in Warsaw who, when asked by her father what she had been taught in school that day, replied that the science teacher had told the class that glass was made out of sand. 'Of course', added the little girl, 'the Party made teacher say that.'

If the formation of public opinion depends firstly on the nature of the political and social institutions, it is reasonable to assume that it depends secondly on the media of communication. The development of mass media has made the press, radio and television the most obvious source of information about political affairs, and a good deal of academic research on opinion-formation has been devoted to the influence of these media on mass opinion. However, the results of this research, taken as a whole, suggest that the direct influence of these media is less than most casual commentators assume to be the case.

Research into the influence of the mass media has, almost of necessity, focussed on changes of opinion during elections or at times when particular issues became the subject of intense public controversy. The numerous studies of this kind conducted in the United States have found no evidence that the mass media of communication play a decisive part in the process by which opinions change at these times. In an early study of the influence of radio, Lazarsfeld concluded that 'it was the change of opinion which determined whether people listened rather than their listening determining their change of opinion'.[1] Later and more elaborate studies showed that people exposed themselves mainly to communications with which they were predisposed to agree and that they tended to remember the content only of those items with which they had agreed.[2] These studies suggested that, while the mass media may have the effect of reinforcing some people's opinions, they rarely have the effect of changing opinions. There was some evidence that people who exposed themselves to many communications on political matters were better informed than others, but since better-informed people were more interested in politics and more likely to read or listen or watch political items, it was impossible to determine the nature of cause and effect.

[1] P. F. Lazarsfeld, 'The Change of Opinion During a Political Discussion' in *Journal of Applied Psychology*, vol. 23 (1939), p. 147.

[2] See, for instance, P. F. Lazarsfeld, B. Berelson, and H. Gaudet, *The People's Choice* (New York, 1948); J. T. Klapper, *The Effects of Mass Media* (New York, 1949); W. Schramm (ed.), *The Process and Effects of Mass Communication* (Urbana, Ill., 1954); J. T. Klapper, *The Effects of Mass Communication* (Glencoe, Ill., 1960).

Studies of this kind distinguished between readers and non-readers, listeners and non-listeners, and viewers and non-viewers, in communities in which reading and listening and viewing were widespread. Since people discuss news items with friends and neighbours, the absence of any evidence that exposure to communications affected individual opinions did not prove that the communications had no effect on the community as a whole. They might conceivably have influenced readers and listeners and viewers in ways that were spread throughout the community before the researchers had time to conduct their surveys. Particular interest therefore attaches to a survey which was able to assess the influence of television on a number of whole communities.

It happened that in 1952 only about a third of the counties in Iowa were able to receive television clearly: the rest of the state, otherwise similar, was not adequately served. In a survey of voting behaviour in this state in the Presidential election two hypotheses were tested. The first was that the addition of television to the other campaign media would intensify interest in the campaign and lead to a higher poll. The second was that television would increase public awareness of the issues of the campaign and thus increase support for the Democratic Party, which was known to have greater appeal in terms of issues than it had in terms of candidates. In the event neither of these hypotheses was supported. The conclusion of the study was that there was no significant difference either in turn-out or in party support between those counties in which most electors were able to view television programmes about the election and those counties in which very few electors were able to do so.[1]

Studies made in Britain have reached similar conclusions. The election studies sponsored by Nuffield College have all included chapters on the role of the press in the election campaign, each of which has concluded that, so far as could be told, the press had no direct influence on the result. Surveys of voting in particular constituencies have shown that very few people feel that they have been influenced by the mass media: in North-East Bristol in 1955 only 4 per cent of the electors interviewed cited any kind of propaganda source when explaining why they had voted the way they had, and this includes people who cited local election literature.[2] At the time of the 1959 election a survey was made of the effects of television on political attitudes, and the results were again largely negative.[3] The

[1] See H. A. Simon and F. Stern, 'The Effect of Television upon Voting Behaviour in Iowa in the 1952 Presidential Election', in *American Political Science Review*, vol. 49 (1955).

[2] See R. S. Milne and H. C. Mackenzie, *Marginal Seat, 1955*, p. 161.

[3] See J. Trenaman and D. McQuail, *Television and the Political Image* (London, 1961).

analysis made in this study was so penetrating that some of the conclusions deserve to be cited.

In the first place, the study showed that television viewers were nearly all willing to hear both sides of the argument. Conservative voters made up 50·6 per cent of the audience for Labour broadcasts and Labour voters made up 42·5 per cent of the audience for Conservative broadcasts.[1] A similar conclusion was reached by the authors of the Bristol study, using figures for both radio and television programmes.[2] It seems that British electors are rather more tolerant of their opponents' views than American electors are.[3] Secondly, the study showed that exposure to television programmes enlarged people's knowledge of party policies and election issues: 'the more programmes people viewed the more they learned'.[4] However, this was the only effect of television viewing, which apparently had no effect at all on people's attitudes to the parties or to party policies, and no effect on the reputations of politicians apart from a slight tendency ('of borderline significance') for it to improve Gaitskell's personal standing.[5]

The other sources of information, including radio, the press, and the local campaign, had even less influence than television. They had no direct effect either on people's political attitudes or on their knowledge of party policies. Radio broadcasts and the local campaign had no measurable effect at all, and the only effect of the press was that as people read more they tended to become more sceptical of the message that was being presented to them. Conservative newspapers were read mainly by Conservative supporters, and the more they read about the campaign 'the weaker their loyalty to the Conservative Party became'.[6] The inference that people tended to be slightly repelled by the partisan presentation of political views can be drawn with the more confidence because 'there was a suggestion of a similar (anti-Labour) reaction among readers of a pro-Labour newspaper'.[7]

The authors of this study examined their statistics very thoroughly. They tested the hypothesis that campaign propaganda, while having no direct effect on attitudes, might have 'activated latent attitude changes already determined by some earlier experiences'.[8] The result

[1] See J. Trenaman and D. McQuail, *Television and the Political Image* (London, 1961), p. 88.
[2] Milne and Mackenzie, op. cit., p. 96.
[3] Trenaman and McQuail compared their findings with those of the American survey reported in *The People's Choice*. They concluded that 'the ordinary voter here appears to be more sceptical and also more tolerant than the . . . person described in *The People's Choice*. Op. cit., p. 150.
[4] Ibid., p. 188.  [5] Ibid., p. 192.  [6] Ibid., p. 189.
[7] Ibid., p. 190.  [8] Ibid., p. 200.

was negative. They explored the possible effects of propaganda on various sub-groups of the electorate, with similar results. Their conclusions pointed inescapably to the fact that in this election there was a definite barrier between political propaganda on the one hand and political attitudes on the other. As they said:

'What is established here is not merely an absence of cause and effect but *a definite and consistent barrier between sources of communication and movements of attitude in the political field at the general election.*'[1]

If British electors are so completely resistant to political propaganda in the mass media, what does influence their political attitudes? It has already been shown that the parties, although they engage in a great deal of political education, are not at all successful in persuading the people who vote for them to support the particular policies that the parties are advocating.[2] Pressure groups frequently engage in propaganda aimed at the man-in-the-street, but this is often a sign that the groups concerned have failed to establish satisfactory contacts in Whitehall and Westminster and are resorting to a public campaign because it is the only thing they can do. The record does not suggest that such campaigns are generally effective. Public opinion polls 'indicated that neither the propagandist campaign of 1946–47 against the nationalization of road haulage nor that of 1949–50 against the nationalization of sugar refining moved opinion'.[3] The polls also suggested that the Campaign for Nuclear Disarmament, while it has certainly increased public awareness of the issue, has made more enemies than friends for its cause.

These are campaigns which made a direct attempt to change people's attitudes. Public relations experts suggest that background campaigns, designed to build up a favourable image of an industry or an activity without making any ostensible attempt to change attitudes, are likely to be more successful. The examples usually cited are the campaigns waged since the war to create a favourable image of free enterprise in general and Imperial Chemical Industries Ltd., in particular.[4] While this may well be true, there is no direct evidence for it, and many other factors have been working for the establishment of a more favourable image of private industry than existed in 1945.

Another hypothesis about the formation of public opinion is

---

[1] *Television and the Political Image*, p. 192 (their italics).

[2] See above, chapter 10, particularly pp. 119–121.

[3] Potter, *Organised Groups in British National Politics*, p. 333.

[4] See S. E. Finer, *Anonymous Empire* (London, 1958), pp. 76–82, and Potter, op. cit., p. 333.

that an important part is played by a minority of people who are interested in politics and spread ideas among their acquaintances. There appears to be some evidence for this hypothesis in the United States, where it has been accepted by a number of writers.[1] In Britain some people are certainly more interested in politics than others. In the Greenwich survey it was found that 11 per cent of the electors claimed to be very interested in politics;[2] in Glossop the figure was also 11 per cent, and the same proportion claimed to discuss political matters fairly often;[3] in North-East Bristol 12 per cent of the electors said that they were more likely than other people to be asked about political matters, and also claimed to have discussed politics outside their home during the previous six weeks.[4]

The similarity of these proportions is striking. But to show that a minority of people talk about politics is not to show that they spread ideas among the relatively apathetic. Common experience suggests that people who are interested in politics talk about political questions with each other, but rarely bother (unless they are politicians) to discuss them with people who are not interested. For one thing, such talk would be apt to bore both sides; for another, politics, like religion, is a topic which tends to divide people who wish to work or relax amicably together, and for this reason is generally avoided by common consent. Local surveys have provided statistical support for this impression. In both Greenwich and Bristol it was found that the proportion of people who named personal conversation as a source of information was higher among the interested minority than among the rest of the electors,[5] which is the reverse of what would be expected if the minority were in fact spreading ideas among the rest. In Glossop it was found that 64 per cent of the electors rarely, if ever, discussed politics, while most of the others confined their discussions to a close circle of immediate relations and friends.[6] The theory that mass opinion in this country is shaped by a minority of 'opinion leaders' is therefore not at all plausible. It may be that, as Bryce said, 'ten men who care are a match for a hundred who do not', but if and when this is true it is likely to be because the ten achieve more political influence than the hundred, not because the ten persuade or convince the hundred.

---

[1] See, for instance, Lazarsfeld et al., *The People's Choice*; L. Bryson (ed.) *The Communication of Ideas* (New York, 1948); E. Katz and P. F. Lazarsfeld, *Personal Influence* (Glencoe, Ill., 1954).

[2] Mark Benney, A. P. Gray, and R. H. Pear, *How People Vote* (London, 1956), p. 47.

[3] A. H. Birch, *Small-Town Politics* (London, 1959), p. 95.

[4] Milne and Mackenzie, op. cit., p. 144.

[5] Benney, et al., op. cit., pp. 136–7, and Milne and Mackenzie, op. cit., p. 145.

[6] Birch, op. cit., pp. 95–6.

A few pages back we posed the question: what influences the attitudes of British electors to political questions? The evidence suggests that the mass media of communication have no direct effect on these attitudes, that the immediate influence of political parties and pressure groups is slight, and that we can discount the theory that considerable power rests in the hands of a minority of opinion leaders. It is true that in the long run the behaviour of parties and pressure groups, and the way in which the mass media present political news, must influence people's conception of the political process. But in the long run people are influenced by a multitude of factors which make up their experience of life, on the basis of which they acquire preferences and form judgements. What we know of human behaviour suggests that in this process personal experience invariably counts for more than outside pressures.

The most plausible answer to our question is the simplest answer of all. By and large, people make up their own minds. They are, of course, subject to every kind of influence, from their family, their schools, their occupation, their reading, and the variety of their personal experiences. But it does not seem that knowledge of these factors would enable the social scientist to predict people's political attitudes with any degree of certainty. As Trenaman and McQuail said, towards the end of their study:

'The evidence we have quoted points to the operation of some quite important factor which is not included in any of the variables we have tried to assess. Its effect suggests that it may be what, for want of a more precise term, we call individual judgment.'[1]

If this is accepted it follows that the views of the average voter are perhaps worth a little more than the more sceptical commentators have allowed for. The implication of the suggestion that people's political opinions are determined by stereotypes and images is that these opinions are determined by the mass media of communication and in themselves are not worth a great deal. But if most people distrust their newspapers and are impervious to television propaganda; if they develop and change their views in ways that cannot be predicted and cannot be explained in terms of external influences; and if they nevertheless have fairly definite views on which they are willing to act; in all these circumstances it is at least arguable that the evidence is against the sceptics.

It would not do, of course, to go to the other extreme and suggest that everyone is always well informed and rational. It is clear that the range of political issues on which most people have definite

[1] Op. cit., p. 204.

186

views is fairly small, and that the average voter is apt to be quite ignorant about matters which do not affect him directly. In 1960, for instance, the British Gallup Poll reported that a few days after Macmillan's speech to the South African Parliament about 'the wind of change' 42 per cent of the population had neither read nor heard of the speech.[1] Later in the same year, after a good deal of public controversy about the European trade groupings, and newspaper headlines about 'the Six' and 'the Outer Seven', nearly half the population had not heard of these groups.[2] Eighteen months later, after negotiations had begun for Britain's entry to the Common Market, the position was very different. Most people were aware of the negotiations, and a good deal of discussion had taken place about the probable consequences of Britain's entry. This discussion was concerned not so much with abstract questions like the loss of sovereignty and the future of the Commonwealth as with concrete problems like the effect entry would have on local industries and farmers. A special correspondent of *The Times* reported that 'the lens was . . . focussed upon local employment conditions and the individual's job; beyond that he is likely to be politically myopic rather than politically inert'.[3]

Statistics and reports of this kind undermine the more optimistic claims that are occasionally made about the political wisdom of the man-in-the-street, but they do not show him to be a fool. They suggest that on matters which affect him directly he tends to make up his own mind, possibly in terms of a rather narrow view of the problem. On questions of foreign and colonial policy which do not affect him directly he rarely has the information necessary for an independent judgement to be made, and is normally willing to accept the judgement of his political leaders. This tendency doubtless owes much to the fact that the differences between the parties on such questions rarely go very deep. In these circumstances the existence of apathy is hardly surprising, and in any case apathy is a less serious charge than gullibility. If the evidence showed that the great mass of the electors were gullible this would seriously weaken the Liberal case for representative government. The revelation that people are apt to be apathetic about issues which do not affect them directly does not have this consequence, for it has always been part of the Liberal case that representative institutions would gradually widen the area of political discussion and concern. By and large, the trend of British political behaviour over the past sixty years would seem to support this argument. Certainly it seems clear that when the citizen is invited to take a direct part in the political process by voting

---

[1] *Gallup Political Index*, March 1960, p. 9.    [2] Ibid., July 1960, p. 26.
[3] *The Times*, February 5, 1962.

he makes his decision largely on the basis of his own experience and judgement.

All this relates to the formation of political opinion among the general population. The influence of this kind of opinion is a subject for separate enquiry. The general population decide which party will form a government but politicians decide what policies the government will follow. It is far beyond the scope of this book to examine the whole process out of which government policy emerges. All that can be done is to outline the channels through which opinions about policy are communicated to politicians. This will be the subject of the following chapter.

# CHAPTER 15

# Channels of Communication

'In the eighteenth century . . . anything that deserved to be called public opinion was limited to the opinions of the gentry and the more intelligent part of the middle class, so that in this sense the political machinery provided a sufficient channel for the really efficient forces of political thought.'[1]

The reference to political machinery in this passage must be taken to include not only the formal machinery of elections, Parliament, and government committees, but also the informal arrangements by which members of this limited public who wished to exert political influence were able to enjoy personal contacts with politicians and government servants. The majority of the population did not belong to this public and were excluded from both the formal machinery and the informal arrangements. This did not mean that the excluded majority were completely lacking in political influence. Their activities during the Wilkes affair and on more than one other occasion showed that they were able to make their views felt. But since the normal channels of communication with those in power were denied to them, they had to resort to other channels, largely of their own creation, such as public demonstrations and riots.

There are many countries where the majority of the population are still in this position. In these countries public demonstrations, riots, boycotts and strikes are the means by which the excluded majority express their political views and seek such influence on events as their numbers and organization make possible. In Britain, the establishment of universal suffrage has brought everyone within the pale of the constitution, so that the public (in this usage of the word) now includes the whole adult population. Access to the ballot was quickly followed by access to other established channels. People entitled to vote are also entitled to join or form political parties and to demand assistance from their Members of Parliament. People whose demands are not met are apt to write to the press and to join with like-minded citizens in the formation of pressure groups.

[1] P. A. Gibbons, *Ideas of Political Representation in Parliament, 1651–1832* (Oxford, 1914), p. 10.

Nearly all the channels of communication between public and government are now in principle open to everyone, though in practice some persons and groups have better access to them than others.

The process by which opinions are communicated is of course very complex. Opinions are held in the first place by individuals, and the communications network deals with a multitude of individual views and demands. But individuals join together to advance interests and causes which they have in common, and the resulting groups act both as channels of communication for individual views and as units advancing views and making demands of their own. In the remainder of the chapter this will be taken for granted, and an attempt will be made to outline the main ways in which the channels of communication are used both by individuals and by groups.

## ELECTIONS

Elections constitute the most conspicuous and in one sense the most important channel of communication between the public and their government. At a general election the voters decide which group of political leaders will govern the country during the life of the following Parliament. The election campaign itself is very short, and does not provide much opportunity (as it does in the United States) for politicians to sound public opinion, to fly trial balloons, and to modify or develop their policies in accordance with public response. Occasionally there is direct bidding for votes, as in Churchill's promise to try to secure a 'summit meeting' with Stalin in 1951, or in Gaitskell's various promises about taxation and social benefits in 1959. But there is no evidence that moves of this kind have much effect either on the behaviour of voters or on the policies of the subsequent government. Generally speaking, a campaign of three or four weeks does not give the leaders of each party time to do much more than try to present themselves as a united team of sensible men, with clear ideas as to what they want to do, who deserve to enjoy the confidence of the nation. All the evidence suggests that it is in these terms that they are judged by the electors.

Elections are important partly because they give the public the opportunity to choose between rival teams of political leaders and partly because they are the culmination of a long process, starting soon after the previous election, by which politicians try to build up popular support for themselves and their parties. Relatively few voters make up their minds how to vote on the basis of particular policies, but the general image of each party which is of such crucial importance is itself built up by a continuous debate, inside and outside Parliament, over questions of policy, as well as by the success or otherwise of the government's actions. The election is the occasion on which those voters who have been wavering between the parties finally come down on one side or the other.

The evidence suggests that in post-war elections the 'floating voters' have constituted about 15 per cent of the whole number who voted.[1] As a proportion this is not large, but since the waverers hold the balance between the two main parties their behaviour is crucial. This being so, one of the most significant conclusions of electoral research is that the waverers constitute something like a cross-section of the electorate in terms of such factors as sex, age, occupation and social status.[2] Neither party has been able to win an election on the basis of a purely sectional appeal and, unless there is a fairly drastic change in the distribution of political allegiances, neither party is likely to be able to do so. The figures show that at each election the change in the voting behaviour of the electorate as a whole has been reflected fairly faithfully in the behaviour of various sub-groups within the electorate. It is this that makes it possible to talk of a swing in the opinion of the nation, at least in relation to the merits of the main political parties. And it is this also that compels the parties to continue to try to appeal to all sections of the community.

So long as this situation continues, and no party becomes so strong that it can afford to ignore the floating votes, politicians will remain anxious to avoid unpopularity with any sizeable group. It follows that, while election campaigns themselves are too short to be very effective as channels of communication, the prospect of elections keeps politicians continually receptive to the opinions of their constituents. It is not difficult to find examples of the practical consequences of this. Electoral considerations must have played some part in the Conservative Party's announcement that it would abolish petrol rationing if it were returned to power in 1951, in the decision to abolish conscription in 1957, in the Conservative pledge in 1959 that there would be no further relaxation of rent control in the life of the next Parliament, and in the practice that all post-war governments have adopted of raising old-age pensions in the months immediately preceding a general election. It is a common characteristic of these examples (and others which could be mentioned) that they are all issues which affected the personal lives of large numbers of individuals. In a sense this indicates both the limitations and the

[1] See A. H. Birch and Peter Campbell, 'Voting Behaviour in a Lancashire Constituency', in *British Journal of Sociology*, vol. 1 (1951); Benney, Gray and Pear, *How People Vote*; Milne and Mackenzie, *Marginal Seat: 1955*; and Birch, *Small-Town Politics*.

[2] See the first three of the surveys listed in footnote 1.

special significance of the part played by elections in the policy-making process: the opinions of individuals count for everything and those of organized groups for very little. The same cannot be said of any of the other channels of communication between the public and their government.

## PARTIES

Almost everyone takes part in a general election, but the scale of participation in other forms of political activity is inevitably smaller. It is not always realized, however, that the proportion of the electorate who contribute to the funds of a political party in Britain is probably higher than in any other country. The only major party which publishes regular figures of membership is the Labour Party, which had 6·4 million members in 1959.[1] The Co-operative Party had 11 million subscribers in the same year, but there is a good deal of overlap between the two and the annual subscription to the latter is nominal. The Conservative Party has not published a membership figure since 1953, when the total was 2·8 million, but there is no reason to think that the present total is very different from this. The Liberal Party is even more secretive and its membership can only be guessed at: the writer's guess is that it is between 75,000 and 150,000. The Communist Party has about 35,000 members and the Welsh Nationalists and the other minor parties have a few thousand between them.

In addition, each party has a young people's section which caters for supporters aged 16 to 25. The Young Conservative organization is by far the most successful of these, having 1,500 branches and about 150,000 members. The Young Socialists, the Young Liberals and the Young Communist League can probably muster about 50,000 members in all.

If all these figures are added together, and it is assumed that about half the subscribers to the Co-operative Party belong also to the Labour Party, and about half the members of the youth sections are under 21, we arrive at the conclusion that about 15 million adults in England and Wales are subscribing members of a political party, which is almost half the total electorate of 30·9 million.

This is a very high proportion, and of course it gives a somewhat exaggerated impression of the degree of political interest in the country. In the first place, the Co-operative Party subscribers do not make individual decisions to subscribe but do so automatically on joining the co-operative societies. Secondly, trade unionists

[1] This and the subsequent figures in this section refer only to England and Wales, as the parties are organized separately in Scotland and Northern Ireland and it is not easy to secure comparable figures.

belonging to unions which are affiliated to the Labour Party pay the political levy unless they 'contract out' of doing so; and figures for the period 1927–46, when they had to 'contract in', suggest that between a third and a half of the present affiliated members subscribe because of inertia rather than from conviction. If allowance is made for these two factors the number of party members who subscribe by deliberate choice is reduced to between 7 and 8 million. A third point is that many people regard membership as primarily a social activity and turn their attention to politics only at election time. In two surveys in periods between elections people have been asked how interested they are in politics, and in both cases only 11 per cent of the respondents claimed to be very interested.[1] Finally, only a very small proportion of party members are willing to do more than pay a subscription and attend meetings. The same two studies indicate that about 1 per cent of the electorate can be relied on to go canvassing or to do other voluntary work during election campaigns. However, if this is general throughout the country it means that in the average constituency between 500 and 600 volunteers will be available. This is normally sufficient to run the parties' campaigns and the existence of these volunteers has the very important effect of enabling the candidates to do without paid help, thus keeping down the costs of the election.

The scale of participation in party politics can thus be summed up as follows: 45–50 per cent of the electorate subscribe to a political party; 23–27 per cent of the electorate *deliberately* subscribe to a political party; 10–12 per cent of the electorate claim to be keenly interested in politics; 1 per cent of the electorate do unpaid work for the parties. In addition, 0·15 per cent of the electorate hold elective office as Member of Parliament or local councillor.[2]

These figures indicate that large numbers of people participate, in various ways, in party politics. By doing so they acquire access, in varying degrees, to a channel of communication other than the electoral system. All the political parties in Britain are democratically organized in the sense that the members have the opportunity, through regional and national conferences and other means, to communicate their views on policy matters to the party leaders. The powers of the Labour Party Annual Conference in regard to party policy have been discussed in Chapter 9. The Annual Conference of the National Union of Conservative and Unionist Associations enjoys no formal power over policy, but party leaders can hardly avoid taking account of the views expressed there. On one memorable

---

[1] See *How People Vote*, p. 47, and *Small Town Politics*, p. 95.
[2] This figure includes aldermen but excludes parish councillors, whose powers are now negligible.

occasion in 1950 the Conference asked the Party to commit itself to the aim of building 300,000 houses a year when it was returned to power, and the Leader of the Party agreed to do so.[1] Normally the Conference avoids making specific demands of this kind, but it leaves the party leaders in no doubt as to the views of the membership. R. A. Butler, as a reforming Home Secretary, had to tread very gingerly on account of the attitude of the membership to questions of crime and punishment; and the attachment of the membership to Commonwealth ties is one of the factors that had to be weighed in the balance in the discussions on the Common Market. In the Liberal Party the Annual Conference has more formal powers than the Conservative Conference, and the influence of Liberal members on party policy is certainly not less than that of Conservative members.

The parties provide for the expression of members' opinions not only at conferences but also at local meetings which send resolutions or requests to their Member of Parliament, at week-end schools, and by correspondence. Local parties vary a great deal in the degree and type of pressure which they put on their M.P., and the requests which they direct to him. Some content themselves with requests and are willing to accept any reasonable explanation of why the Member is unable to act on the requests, even of the kind: 'It is not appropriate to press this matter at the moment, but I will certainly bear it in mind and raise it when a suitable opportunity presents itself'. Others expect more of their Member, and may even invoke the threat, implicitly or explicitly, that if he does not do as they wish he may be in danger of not being renominated. The cases that occurred at the time of the Suez crisis have doubtless impressed Members with the reality of this threat.

British parties engage in educational activities to an extent which is not paralleled in other western democracies. They produce a vast number of pamphlets and journals concerned with questions of party policy. They organize week-end schools, summer schools, and residential courses. They invite members, particularly young members, to produce ideas, to write essays, and to contribute articles to the journals. For instance, the Conservative Political Centre runs a series entitled 'Two-way Topics'. Each month it produces a short pamphlet setting out the arguments relating to a question of current political interest, and invites party meetings and discussion groups all over the country to submit their comments. In 1958 no fewer than 525 discussion groups took part in this programme, and '1,241 reports were sent in to be summarized and passed on to the Research Department, the chairman of the Advisory Committee on Policy,

[1] See *Official Report of the 71st Annual Conference of the National Union of Conservative and Unionist Associations* (1950), pp. 20, 56–65, 112–3.

and the Chairman of the Party Organization for consideration'.[1] As an example of the kind of questions discussed, in January 1961 the topic was juvenile delinquency, and meetings were asked to name, in order of priority, the three measures for checking juvenile crime that they thought would be most helpful. In February 1961 the topic was the future of broadcasting, which was then under consideration by the Pilkington Committee. On this local meetings were asked the following questions:

1. Are you in favour of a third television service? If so, who should run it?
2. Do you think there should be local radio stations? If so, who should run them?

A recent Chairman of the Conservative Party has said that 'political parties must do everything they can to interest and educate the electorate, not only in their own policies but in the basis of democratic government'.[2] All the British parties appear to accept this principle, and party members certainly cannot complain that they lack opportunities to make their views known.

The parties form a channel of communication not only for the views of their individual members but also, to a varying extent, for the views of pressure groups. The relations between the trade unions and the Labour Patry in this respect are well known: as the political wing of the Labour Movement, the Party is bound to take account of union views. The unions have a large majority of the votes at the Annual Conference, they elect 12 of the 28 members of the National Executive Committee, and through their votes at the Conference they can, if they act together, control the election of five other members of the Executive. Quite apart from this, Labour leaders in Parliament are in frequent consultation with union leaders, and many Labour M.P.'s are of course sponsored candidates of their unions. To some extent the political views of the co-operative movement are also expressed through the Labour Party, partly by the Co-operative–Labour M.P.'s and partly as a result of consultations between co-operative and Labour leaders. In addition the co-operative movement has its own Co-operative Party, with a large nominal membership but with little direct influence.

The Conservative Party has no organic links with trade associations to compare with the relations between Labour and the trade unions, but it is often said that the large donations given to the Party

[1] D. Hennesy, 'The Communication of Conservative Policy: 1957–59' in *Political Quarterly*, vol. 32 (1961), p. 254.
[2] R. A. Butler in Foreword to Milne and Mackenzie, op. cit., p. viii.

by industrialists make the Party leaders particularly receptive to the views of industry. This probably puts the emphasis in the wrong place. In so far as the Party stands for the preservation of free enterprise there is a natural coincidence between its policies and the interests of industry and commerce, and this is undoubtedly strengthened by the close personal relations between prominent Conservatives and the business world. But industrialists need the Conservative Party a good deal more than the Party needs the industrialists and their contributions, and the influence of the business lobby almost certainly owes more to the numerous personal connections between business and the Party than it does to the financial connections. That this influence is considerable cannot be doubted. One student of these matters has said that Conservative policy between 1945 and 1951 'was moulded by close contact between the Party's Central Office and various business interests';[1] another has shown how the quite small group in favour of commercial television was able to dominate the committee of Conservative back-benchers which dealt with broadcasting and to persuade the professional publicists of Central Office to campaign for this innovation even before the cabinet had agreed to it.[2] However, the influence clearly has limits, as has been shown in recent years by the actions of the Government in relation to profits tax, the continuing control of industrial location, and the refusal of the Air Minister (in November 1961) to allow a private airline to compete with BOAC in the provision of transatlantic services.

Promotional groups as well as interest groups work through the parties. Some of these, like the Keep Left group and the Victory for Socialism group, are really factions within the parties made up entirely of active party members. Others, like the Fabian Society and the Bow Group, are composed of sympathizers with a party, not all of whom are party members, whose object is to conduct research into political problems and suggest lines of policy which the party might follow. Others again are completely independent groups which choose to exert influence through the party organization rather than (or as well as) by means of direct contacts with M.P.'s and government departments. The Campaign for Nuclear Disarmament, for instance, has devoted a good part of its energies to the attempt to win a majority for its cause at Labour's Annual Conference.

## MEMBERS OF PARLIAMENT

A citizen who has a grievance against the government has the right to take the matter up with his Member of Parliament and can expect

[1] Finer, op. cit., p. 49.
[2] See H. H. Wilson, *Pressure Group* (London, 1961).

that the M.P. will do something about it unless the grievance is clearly unjustified. The M.P. will normally write or speak to the minister concerned: he may in some circumstances take the matter up at Question Time. In this way complaints which would otherwise have got no further than a junior official are brought to the attention of those in positions of higher authority. Moreover, by acting constantly on behalf of their constituents in this fashion M.P.'s come to know better than most people what aspects of government policy or administration are becoming unpopular or causing hardship. They pass this information on to the party whips if they are on the government side; they exploit it in speeches and debates if they are in opposition. In this way M.P.'s play an important part in the process by which those in power are made aware of the impact of their decisions on the man-in-the-street.

Such action by M.P.'s sometimes has a direct effect on government policy. In 1957, for instance, the debates on the proposed Rent Act were marked by confident and mutually incompatible generalizations by politicians about the degree of hardship that the Act was likely to cause. After the first stages of the Act came into effect M.P.'s were able to assess the hardship directly by considering the specific cases put to them by constituents. It quickly became clear that in many areas the Act would make little difference, in some it would work fairly smoothly, but in some (mainly in Greater London) it would cause appreciable hardship to tenants unless its full implementation were delayed. After hearing representations by M.P.'s the Minister concerned introduced an amending bill[1] which enabled tenants threatened with eviction orders to appeal to the courts for a suspension of the orders.

In cases like this the M.P.'s behaviour is not greatly affected by party politics: his political allegiance may determine to whom he passes on the information but it is not likely to distort the message appreciably. When it is a matter of transmitting opinions rather than one of reporting grievances the allegiance and personal attitudes of the M.P. are apt to be more important. A Conservative Member possessing a large majority in an agricultural constituency is unlikely to pay much attention to the opposition of some of his constituents to the system of tied cottages. A Nonconformist Member is more likely than a Roman Catholic to take serious notice of complaints about the establishment of betting shops. And if a Labour Member from an industrial town tells the House that his constituents are all up in arms about a proposal to charge differential rents for municipal houses, it is fair to assume that he has given more weight to the views of the tenants than to the views of the owner-occupiers in the area.

[1] *The Landlord and Tenants* (*Temporary Provisions*) *Bill* of April 1958.

Since Members normally feel that they have to take note of letters from constituents, pressure groups often urge members and sympathizers to write to their local M.P. Uniform letters are generally discounted by M.P.'s, but if constituents write in their own words and are clearly expressing their personal feelings M.P.'s are inclined to take notice of the correspondence, even though its timing may indicate that it has been stimulated by a pressure group. In 1956 a barrage of letters from schoolteachers to M.P.'s formed part of the successful campaign waged by the National Union of Teachers to prevent the immediate increase in the rate of teachers' superannuation contributions that was provided for in the Bill then before Parliament.[1] In 1961 a large number of letters from motor cyclists to M.P.'s apparently helped to persuade back-benchers not to support the Private Member's Bill which proposed that motor cyclists should be compelled to take out insurance to cover injuries to passengers.[2] This correspondence appears to have been stimulated not by one of the motoring organizations but simply by articles in the motorcycling press.

These are two cases in which the lobbying of M.P.'s appears to have had clear results, and it would not be very difficult to find other examples. But the effect of lobbying is not to be assessed simply on the basis of such cases, for it is a continuous process which has a continuous influence, in a variety of ways, on Parliamentary opinion. There are spontaneous letters from individuals to M.P.'s; there are letters organized or stimulated by others, whether they be established pressure groups or not;[3] there are interviews with M.P.'s in their constituencies or in the lobby at Westminster; there are petitions which M.P.'s are asked to present to Parliament or to a minister; there are direct approaches by pressure groups to M.P.'s, both by post and by personal contact.[4] The Political Correspondent of *The Times* estimates that in each day's mail the average M.P. is 'pursued by at least fifteen different causes, campaigns, companies, or cliques'.[5] Many or most of these appeals go straight into the wastepaper basket, but some of them must have some effect on Members' attitudes. And, of course, most pressure groups try to develop and maintain personal contacts with Members. All the more important groups have regular Parliamentary spokesmen, while the great majority of

[1] See Finer, op. cit., pp. 89–91.
[2] See *The Times*, July 17, 1961.
[3] Ministers of religion sometimes urge their parishioners to write to their M.P., as happened in 1961 when Baptist and other Free Church ministers asked people to write expressing their concern over events in Angola.
[4] A large number of examples are cited in Potter, op. cit., Chap. 14.
[5] *The Times*, July 17, 1961.

M.P.'s have one or two interests and causes on whose behalf they are prepared to speak.[1]

Although back-benchers have less power now than in the nineteenth century, they are by no means without influence. Their support is a necessary, though not a sufficient, condition for the success of Private Members' Bills: such a bill will die a speedy death unless it gets a good measure of back-bench support, but if it does there is some chance that the government of the day will find time for it.[2] Back-benchers often persuade the government to accept amendments to bills at the committee stage, which, indeed, 'is rarely effective except when there is a discussion between one set of experts speaking through the Minister and other experts speaking through various back-bench M.P.'s.[3] Very occasionally back-benchers secure amendments at the committee stage despite the government's opposition. In 1959, for instance, the Obscene Publications Bill was transformed in committee by the addition of a section which enabled publishers to establish literary merit as at least a partial defence against the allegation of obscenity. And questions and debates on the floor of the House clearly influence ministers on occasions, even though the government's majority is not in danger.

These forms of influence are visible to the casual observer. More important still are the constant contacts of back-benchers with whips and ministers 'upstairs', and the work of the Parliamentary committees of the parties. On occasion back-bench influence upstairs is clearly discernible, as when the Labour Government of 1945-51 was under pressure from its left-wing supporters, or when Sir Thomas Dugdale decided to resign after criticism in the Conservative Party's Agricultural Committee.[4] More recently, in 1961 it was evident that a group of Conservative back-benchers who were worried about the pace of developments in Northern Rhodesia, and who had doubtless been briefed by Sir Roy Welensky's supporters, were doing all they could to persuade the Government not to accede to African demands. In February 1961, while talks on constitutional reform in Northern Rhodesia were in progress, the Colonial Secretary was questioned by the Conservative Colonial Committee. He was pressed to give an assurance that any new constitution would ensure the continuance of a European majority on the Legislative Council, and he was apparently indefinite on this point.[5] On the

[1] The representation of organized groups in Parliament is fully dealt with in Potter, op. cit., Chap. 15.

[2] Readers are referred to P. A. Bromhead, *Private Members' Bills in the British Parliament* (London, 1956) for a discussion of this topic.

[3] W. J. M. Mackenzie, 'Pressure Groups in British Government', in *British Journal of Sociology*, vol. VI (1955), p. 142.          [4] See above, pp. 144-5.

[5] See *The Times*, Feb. 11, 1961.

following day his critics tabled a motion in the House calling on the Government to adhere to the principles of the 1958 White Paper on Northern Rhodesia, and by that evening 65 Conservative back-benchers had signed it. No debate on this motion was held or intended; it was tabled simply as a demonstration of back-bench opinion. A similar step was taken in July 1961 by a group of Conservative Members who wished to warn the Prime Minister of the scale of back-bench opposition to the proposal that Britain should enter the Common Market before securing acceptable guarantees about agricultural protection and Commonwealth trade: on this occasion the motion was signed by 32 back-benchers.[1]

It is unnecessary to multiply examples. There is a continuous process by which party leaders are made aware of the views of their Parliamentary supporters, and it is fair to assume that the influence of the latter is also continuous. It is this, rather than the ritual of Parliamentary debates, which makes the Member of Parliament so important a channel of communication between the public and the Government.

THE PRESS

The evidence discussed in the last chapter suggests that, in the short run at least, the public are largely immune to press propaganda, If this is true it follows that the press can have little direct influence on public opinion about the political parties or about major issues of policy, except possibly about issues of which people have no personal experience and about which they have no other source of information. Other evidence confirms this view. Lord Beaverbrook told the Royal Commission on the press that although his primary aim as a newspaper proprietor had been to influence public opinion, he had never had any success whatever.[2]

Apparently the press does not mould public opinion: does it reflect it? This is at first sight more plausible because it is clear that the aim of many popular papers is to give their readers what they want. Indeed, the post-war struggle for survival in the newspaper world makes this almost essential. The *Daily Mirror* appears to be ready to change its political stance in accordance with its estimate of its readers' views, having changed from pro-Conservative to pro-Labour during the war, and having shown signs of retreating from

[1] For an analysis of motions and the Members who sign them, see S. E. Finer, H. D. Berrington, and D. J. Bartholomew, *Backbench Opinion in the House of Commons, 1955–59* (Oxford, 1961).
[2] See *Minutes of Evidence of Royal Commission on the Press, 1947–1949* Q 8656–9.

this position immediately after the Labour Party was defeated for the third time in succession in a general election.[1] The other popular papers are less flexible in their attitudes to the political parties, but it is evident that both in their broad policy and in their daily make-up they try to appeal to the prejudices of their readers. This leads some papers to feature stories about juvenile delinquency and crimes of violence, others to give space to the activities of film stars, and others to write about wage claims and unofficial strikes. The emphasis is different but the principle is the same.

However, the mirror which the press holds up to public opinion is almost certainly a distorting mirror. It reflects opinions and interests which people like to read about to the exclusion of others, equally or more strongly held, which are less interesting. Moreover, it often imparts an unduly moralistic tone to those opinions which it reflects. For instance, a foreign observer reading the British popular press during 1960 and 1961 would have gained the impression that public opinion was strongly in favour of sterner penalties for driving under the influence of alcohol. The behaviour of juries concerned with such cases indicated that, on the contrary, most people were rather tolerant about this offence.

The press would appear to be important as a channel of communication in two quite different ways. In the first place, the press draws attention to individual incidents that might otherwise pass unnoticed. The immigration laws are applied harshly to a Hungarian refugee; an elderly widow is evicted from her cottage; a boy is struck by a policeman. Cases like this are often taken up by the press, and political action sometimes results from the publicity. In such cases the press does not mould public opinion, but it focuses an existing opinion upon a particular instance. There is a fairly narrow belt within which press publicity of this kind can be important. Landowners, business firms, and trade unions scarcely need publicity for their grievances, for they are well able to take care of themselves. At the other extreme, the sufferings of Irish horses on their travels from Dublin to Belgium two or three years ago would have passed unnoticed had it not been for the *Manchester Guardian*, but the horses had no rights under the British constitution and it was not clear what could be done to help them. Between these extremes are cases of people who have rights but do not know how to exercise them, and the press may fairly claim that it sometimes helps to protect the poor, the ignorant, and the unorganized from harsh treatment.

In the second place, the less popular papers act as a forum for the

[1] For instance, the slogan 'Forward with the People' was removed from the front page.

201

expression of informed opinions. *The Times* opens its correspondence columns to letters from influential people on topics of current importance. The *Guardian* prints informative articles by a variety of special contributors. The weekly journals air opinions about issues which correspondents think ought to be receiving more attention than they are getting. It is not easy to say how much influence all this has. It is clear that in the past some rather exaggerated claims have been made regarding the direct influence of *The Times*, and it is now known that at least one former editor made a habit of discovering what the government was going to propose a day or two before this was made public, and then recommending that course of action. But these papers and journals certainly form an excellent medium for the circulation of ideas among the educated minority, and it is difficult to read them regularly without gaining the impression that they play an appreciable part in the process by which the arguments for various lines of policy are canvassed and assessed. Possibly the same ideas would circulate by other channels if these papers did not exist; in this sense one cannot identify the influence of the papers; but they undoubtedly constitute a convenient medium for the exchange of opinions among influential people.

## THE ADMINISTRATION AND OFFICIAL ADVISORY COMMITTEES

The departments that administer public services are in a better position than anyone else to form a general picture of the ways in which their activities affect the public. Their picture is sometimes one-sided and needs to be supplemented by unofficial sources, but officials who are in constant contact with the public are normally well aware of the aspects of their work which cause tension or hardship. If the Minister of Pensions and National Insurance wants to know how hardly the means test for national assistance is bearing on various types of applicant, his first source of information is his own local officials. If the Home Secretary wants to know about the probable effects of changes in the licensing laws, the police are the best people to tell him.

The departments naturally make it their business to keep themselves informed about the bearing of their activities upon the public: they could not be efficient unless they did so. To assist the departments in this respect there exist a large number of permanent advisory committees, whose constitution varies a great deal. Some are statutory and others are non-statutory; some are composed largely of representatives of organized groups while others are composed of individuals chosen for their personal knowledge and experience; the reports of some are published while those of others are used only within the department concerned.[1] In November 1958, the Financial Secretary to the Treasury said that there were about 850 such committees advising the central government.[2]

This is a very large number, and there are even more local advisory committees. In each area local citizens serve in a voluntary capacity on committees whose function is to advise the local branch of the Ministry of Labour about the employment problems of the area, to advise the Post Office about the needs of local telephone users, to advise the regional Electricity Board about the needs and complaints of consumers, and so on. In one small town[3] in 1954 there were 17 officials of the central government and the nationalized public utilities (excluding clerks and typists) and no fewer than 26 members of advisory committees concerned with the work of these officials.

In addition to gaining advice and information from these permanent committees, the British Government makes considerable use of special committees which are established to enquire into particular problems. These may be constituted as Royal Commissions, as special committees of enquiry, or as inter-departmental committees. Some of them are composed mainly of representatives of the departments and interests concerned; others are composed mainly or entirely of independent members. All of them hear evidence from officials and affected groups, and some also hear evidence from members of the general public who wish to give it. Some make special efforts to secure the views of members of the public: thus the Wolfenden Committee invited a number of homosexuals to give evidence to it (in strict confidence), while the Robbins Committee on Higher Education has employed an agency to poll a random sample of undergraduates in order to secure their views on the education they are getting at university. The functions of these special advisory committees are to collect information about an existing situation, to sift evidence and views about the probable consequences of any proposed changes, and to make recommendations to Parliament or to the government. Their importance can hardly be exaggerated, since most major legislative changes are preceded by this kind of enquiry.

### THE ADMINISTRATION AND ORGANIZED GROUPS

One of the features of British political life in the present century has been the growth and proliferation of organizations concerned

[1] Readers are referred to K. C. Wheare, *Government by Committee* (Oxford, 1955) for an account of the place of these (and other) committees in the British system of government.
[2] See *House of Commons Debates* 5th s., v. 595, c. 1305.
[3] Glossop, Derbyshire.

to defend and advance the interests of groups whose activities are affected by government action. Such organizations naturally make it their business to be as well informed as they can about the needs and problems of their members, and in as far as they are successful in this aim they make themselves useful not only to their members but also to Whitehall. The system of recruitment and training in the British civil service does not ensure that senior officials have any technical qualifications that are relevant to the trade or industry or social service with which they are concerned, and in consequence they welcome the assistance of organized groups who can provide the officials with the technical information they need for their work. The Board of Trade is helped in this way by trade associations; the Ministry of Labour, by trade unions; the Ministry of Agriculture, Fisheries and Food, by organizations representing the farmers and the fishing industry; other departments, by a variety of other organizations.

Organized groups help the administration not only by providing specialized information but also in other ways. In the first place, they act as a funnel for public responses to the work of the departments and so save civil servants a good deal of correspondence with individuals that would otherwise be necessary. Secondly, trade associations and other interest groups can often provide the departments with an assurance that the latter's decisions will be accepted by the trade or profession concerned. Thirdly, and in some fields this is most important, organized groups sometimes act as a buffer between Whitehall and the various interests, authorities and firms represented by the group. For instance, in the cotton industry there is a fairly sharp conflict of interest between the majority of firms, who dislike the importation of cheap grey cloth from the Far East, and the minority of firms (engaged in making-up) who welcome such imports. All these firms are compelled by an Act passed in 1946 to subscribe to the Cotton Board, and the views of the Cotton Board are accepted by the government as being the views of the industry. In this way the government has to some extent been able to avoid the awkward task of arbitrating between conflicting interests within the cotton industry.

This is an interesting example because it illustrates fairly clearly one of the prices that may have to be paid (at any rate by a minority within an industry) for the advantage of having a trade association which is recognized and consulted by Whitehall. It may be said as a generalization that whenever a channel of communication becomes 'the established channel' it is on the way towards being a bottleneck. In this sense (though not, of course, in others) a parallel may be drawn between the position of trade associations like the Cotton

Board and the position of a minister, who also acts as a channel, bottleneck, and buffer between Whitehall and outside persons (in this case M.P.'s) seeking to influence Whitehall.

During the past thirty years the contacts between organized groups and Whitehall have become very close. In the 1930's the government's measures to help industry and agriculture recover from the depression involved it in negotiations with groups representing the producers concerned, and in some cases the government encouraged or even sponsored the formation of trade organizations to make its work easier: examples are the Potato Marketing Board and the British Iron and Steel Federation. The control of industry during the war and in the immediate post-war years tightened the bonds of mutual dependence between the government and trade associations. Many officials of the associations were temporary civil servants during the war and established personal contacts in Whitehall which they kept up after the war. And while, on the one hand, the associations help government departments in the ways enumerated, on the other, the associations have acquired a conventional right to be consulted by the departments before administrative or legislative changes are introduced affecting their industries. Trade unions enjoy a similar position.

Direct access to Whitehall is not confined to trade associations and trade unions, but is also enjoyed by a variety of promotional groups and groups representing other interests. The motoring organizations are consulted about road traffic problems; the local government associations are consulted about legislation affecting local authorities; the Howard League for Penal Reform is in frequent contact with the Home Office about the treatment of offenders.[1]

Groups that enjoy direct access to Whitehall have a channel of communication to those who make decisions which, in some fields, is more effective than any other. It is better to be consulted by those who draft legislation than to have to campaign for the amendment of a bill after it has been presented to Parliament. There are, of course, degrees of access and of influence. Organizations like the Trades Union Congress and the Federation of British Industries enjoy both to a high degree. 'The days of lobbying are . . . past,' states a TUC publication: 'The General Council have now established their right to consult or to be consulted on all ministerial moves, bills, regulations and administrative actions which are likely to have an effect on the interests of the workers and their organizations'.[2] Here is power undreamt of by the delegates who

[1] Readers are referred to Potter, op. cit., Parts 2 and 3, for an enumeration and classification of promotional and interest groups.

[2] *A.B.C. of the T.U.C.* (London, 1954), p. 11, quoted in Potter, op. cit., p. 205.

founded the Labour Representation Committee some sixty years ago. And direct access of this kind naturally makes the work of trade union M.P.'s less important, and the success of the Labour Party less vital to the unions.

Other organizations, while more restricted in their interests and therefore in the range of affairs on which they are consulted, have an equally privileged position in that they are in constant touch with the government department concerned with their affairs. The National Farmers' Union, for example, enjoys very close relations with the Ministry of Argiculture, Fisheries and Food. Each year elaborate negotiations take place between representatives of the Union and officials of the Ministry regarding the level of government price support for agricultural products in the following year. When Parliament is informed of the government's policy the ensuing debate is apt to be somewhat perfunctory simply because the important arguments have already been conducted.

Another group of associations which are in constant touch with Whitehall consists of the associations of local authorities. Finer reports that at a single meeting the Executive Council of the County Councils' Association dealt with five draft statutory orders on which the Ministry of Transport had asked for its comments, a draft circular to local authorities from the same Ministry, and two memoranda on which the Ministry of Housing and Local Government had sought its views.[1] It seems fair to assume that this is typical.

A different example again is provided by university finance. Policy in this field is determined largely by a process of consultation between Treasury officials, the University Grants Committee, and the Committee of Vice-Chancellors and Principals, with occasional interventions by the Association of University Teachers. Parliament sometimes holds debates on policy for higher education, but until very recently the universities have not thought of using the House of Commons as a channel for the expression of their views. They have direct access to Whitehall and have assumed that this is a much more effective channel than Parliament. It is supplemented by another channel which academics are particularly well equipped to use, namely the press. Letters to *The Times*, articles in the journals of opinion, talks on the radio, and speeches which the papers are likely to report are the main public ways in which academics canvass their opinions about the future of universities.

The majority of interest groups have relations with Whitehall which are less intimate than those of the FBI, the NFU, or the local authorities' associations, but are close enough for a direct approach

[1] Finer, op. cit., p. 33.

to the departments to be the first step that the groups take when they want a concession or reform. Equally, such groups are normally consulted by the departments before decisions are taken affecting the interests which the groups represent. When legislation affecting particular trades or professions is introduced into Parliament it is now usual for the minister to explain that he has consulted representatives of the affected interests and it is helpful if he can say that he has secured their agreement to the proposed changes. If the minister had not consulted them this would be regarded as a serious ground for criticism in Parliament.

Of course, not all organized groups enjoy ready access to the departments. There are a large number of promotional groups which are not recognized as representing any affected interest. Obvious examples are the Anti-Vivisection Society, the Lord's Day Observance Society, the League Against Cruel Sports, the Campaign for Nuclear Disarmament, the Electoral Reform Society, the Peace Pledge Union. Such groups have to propagate their causes through other channels. But there can be no doubt that a promotional group which has direct access to the administration, such as the Royal Society for the Prevention of Cruelty to Animals, is in a much stronger position to exert influence on government decisions than one which lacks such access.

At the beginning of this chapter it was noted that the network of political communication is extremely complex. It may be appropriate to end this brief section on the position of organized groups by emphasizing this elementary fact. No short discussion can possibly do justice to the variety of ways in which organized groups create, reflect, and express opinions on political topics. Some groups have a clear aim to which all their members subscribe (for example, the League Against Blood Sports); others have such heterogeneous memberships that their position is essentially that of a channel through which the members express their own opinions. Some groups are almost wholly oriented towards political action (for instance, the National Campaign for the Abolition of Capital Punishment); others are mainly concerned with the provision of services to members, and only occasionally turn their attention to political matters. Some groups enjoy such close relations with Whitehall that they are almost part of the machinery of government, others are regularly consulted, others again are listened to but not consulted, while some are politely ignored. The range of variation is immense, but all the groups play some part in the process by which political opinions are conveyed to those in positions of authority.

## THE TWO-WAY FLOW

All the channels mentioned in this chapter carry information, opinions, and demands from the public at large to the people who take political decisions. But communications flow in both directions, and the same channels are used by politicians and civil servants as a way of spreading information about their policies and securing public consent to them.

That election campaigns are used in this way by political leaders is obvious. Much of their effort is apparently in vain, but at the last general election the television broadcasts at least proved effective in disseminating information about issues and policies. Between elections political leaders make speeches, make political broadcasts, and use the party machines as media of political education and propaganda. The constant flow of party pamphlets presumably helps to inform party members about policies, even if it does not secure their agreement to them. The Conservative Party's 'Two-way Topics' must be at least as effective in presenting facts and arguments to local Party meetings as they are in eliciting opinions from these meetings. On the Labour side Fabian pamphlets are sometimes used by Party leaders to try out new ideas: it was notable that several of the most important policy statements put out by the Party between 1956 and 1958 (during the period of 're-thinking') were presaged by Fabian pamphlets written by individual leaders.[1]

Members of Parliament also play a part in the two-way flow of ideas. The letters they receive are full of requests; their replies are full of explanations of why existing legislation or policy makes it impossible for the government to accede to the requests. Their weekend speeches expound the policies of government or opposition. At their meetings with their constituency parties they explain that the demand for a new bridge or hospital, however well justified, must wait until the economic situation is easier or a new overall plan has been prepared.

The role of the press is perhaps less easy to assess. Most people get most of their political news through the newspapers. British Parliamentary debates are reported regularly and are given very much more prominence than are Congressional debates in American newspapers or French Parliamentary debates in French newspapers. It often seems, indeed, that the main purpose of the set debates on major issues in Parliament is to provide headlines for the following day's papers. In this sense the press plays a vital part in spreading information about government policies.

[1] For instance, the very important statement on *Public Ownership* was presaged by Hugh Gaitskell's pamphlet on *Socialism and Nationalisation* (London, 1956).

Beyond this, it is sometimes said that the British press tends to act as the mouthpiece of the government of the day. Foreign observers have suggested that British newspapers (and particularly *The Times*) rely on official sources to such an extent that legitimate criticism of government activities is stifled for lack of independent information about them. Nobody who is familiar with the American and French press can deny that there may be an element of truth in this suggestion, particularly in relation to foreign affairs. Certainly there are many issues on which the press maintains a discreet silence which works to the advantage of the government. But it may be that in this respect the press simply reflects the consensus that normally exists in Britain about foreign policy, and the widespread willingness to give the government of the day the benefit of the doubt in practically all fields of activity. When this consensus breaks down, as at the time of the Suez expedition, there is certainly no sign that the opposition papers are inhibited in their criticisms of the government. There is a sense, therefore, in which people who criticize the British press on these lines are really regretting the normally equable tone of British politics.

Advisory committees do not always act as two-way channels of communication. Many of the committees described by Wheare as 'committees to advise' are set up simply to collect and assess information about a problem for the benefit of the government. Their reports may give a good deal of weight to official evidence and so have the incidental effect of publicizing official arguments. But in many cases they do not. The Wolfenden Report[1] did not do so; neither did the Herbert Report[2] on London Government.

On the other hand, some special committees are established partly with the object of publicizing evidence in favour of reforms which the government wishes to introduce. Thus, the appointment of the Royal Commission on Betting, Lotteries and Gaming was a sign that the government was prepared to reform the laws relating to gambling. It was predictable that the Commission would find evidence that the law banning off-the-course betting in cash was unenforceable, and that the attempts the police made to enforce it tended to damage relations between police and public. This was not news to the Home Office, because Chief Constables had been saying as much for years. But when the evidence was formally given to and accepted by the Royal Commission it made headlines in the press

[1] *Report of the Committee on Homosexual Offences and Prostitution*, Cmnd. 247 of 1957.
[2] *Report of the Royal Commission on Local Government in Greater London*, Cmnd. 1164 of 1960.

and so helped to prepare public opinion for the reforms which the government subsequently introduced. Equally, the appointment of the Beaver Committee on Air Pollution was a sign that the Government was ready to consider legislation on this subject, and one of the functions that the Committee served was to collect and publish evidence of the evil effects of air pollution for the education of the public.[1] If the government were to appoint a committee to examine the Sunday Observance laws, as has been suggested, the committee would undoubtedly collect evidence of the inconsistency of these laws. No government would be likely to appoint such a committee unless it were prepared to reform the laws, and if it did appoint such a committee one of the objects of this move would be to prepare public opinion for reform.[2]

Standing advisory committees almost always act as two-way channels, and some of them are probably more effective in disseminating official views than they are in bringing the views of the public to the notice of the authorities. This was certainly true of some of the local advisory committees whose work we examined in the survey of Glossop. The quarterly meetings of the local Employment Committee, for instance, were devoted to a brief report of the employment situation in the town followed by a discussion on some general topic relating to the work of the Ministry of Labour. These discussions were generally opened by a Ministry official, and they frequently dealt with the subject of a current White Paper or other government pronouncement.[3] It seemed clear that the advisory function of this committee was less important than its function of spreading knowledge about developments in Ministry policy. This was even more true of the consultative councils set up to bring public complaints and public views to the attention of the authorities in charge of nationalized industries. It was evident that these councils were more effective in bringing the excuses of the authorities to the attention of the public than in bringing the complaints of the public to the attention of the authorities.[4] This judgement could not be applied to some of the other local committees, which were advisory in fact as well as in form. But they all acted as two-way channels of communication, as it is clearly desirable that they should.

The standing committees which advise the government at the national level are in a somewhat similar position. Their composition

[1] See *Report of the Committee on Air Pollution*, Cmnd. 9322 of 1954.

[2] Not the only object, of course: such a committee would also have the advisory function of suggesting specific changes, as did the Beaver Committee and the Royal Commission on Betting, Lotteries and Gaming.

[3] See *Small-Town Politics*, p. 160.      [4] Ibid., p. 162.

varies, but they nearly all include at least one official and some include several. Most of them also include some of the experts and representatives of interested parties who are in the best position to criticize the work of the administration. Since membership of an official advisory committee inhibits such people from voicing their criticisms in public, there is a risk that 'all those who might influence and guide public opinion may be captured by the departments, placed on their advisory committees, and so won over to the official side from the start'.[1] Perhaps this is no more than a risk, but it is clear that these committees are useful to the administration in more ways than those set out in their terms of reference.

To say that the administration disseminates information about its own activities is of course a platitude. Government departments are well aware of the need for good public relations, and are constantly developing ways of informing the public about their work. But it needs to be noted that when organized groups acquire direct access to the administration in the ways described above, they also become channels through which the administration informs the relevant sections of the public about policy. A group which enjoys the privilege of access and consultation acquires the responsibility of explaining the difficulties of the administration (in so far as they are not confidential) to its members. The Committee on Intermediaries pointed out that trade associations and similar bodies know 'far more of government policy over a wide field than any individual', and suggested that their main function was that of advising their members on questions of policy.[2]

Pressure groups having access to Whitehall not only propagate information about government policy but also frequently persuade their members to comply with that policy. Often this is a matter of persuading them to do something which is 'for the benefit of the industry', such as making accurate returns of production to the Board of Trade or adopting codes for the prevention of industrial accidents. Sometimes the appeal is to the national interest, as when trade associations urge their members to increase exports. In the period of severe economic difficulty after the last war the Government appealed to both sides of industry for help in the attempt to prevent inflation. The TUC responded by urging its members to forego or to moderate their wage claims. The FBI responded by introducing a voluntary scheme for the limitation of advertising. And in 1948 and 1949 the FBI, the National Union of Manufacturers, and the Association of British Chambers of Commerce jointly

[1] Wheare, op. cit., p. 66.
[2] See *Report of the Committee on Intermediaries*, Cmd. 7904 of 1950.

urged their members to limit dividends.[1] Broadly speaking, the closer a group's relations are with the government, the easier it is for the latter to ask for the group's assistance in implementing government policy. Here as elsewhere, the channels of communication are invariably two-way.

[1] See Finer, in *Political Studies*, vol. IV, p. 80.

# CHAPTER 16

## Opinions and Policies

In the previous chapter an attempt was made to outline the main channels through which public opinions and demands are communicated to those who have authority to make political decisions at the national level, and, conversely, official views and information are communicated to the public. In this chapter, which is of necessity more speculative, an attempt will be made to illustrate this process by a number of recent examples.

The factors which determine the probable influence of public claims and opinions have been discussed by many writers, from Jeremy Bentham onwards. These factors include the number of people who hold the opinion, the intensity with which it is held, the extent to which it is in line with general public sentiments, the channels through which it is communicated to those in authority, and the way in which it fits in or conflicts with the tendencies and programme of the government of the day.

It would be absurd to try to put these factors in order of importance. It may be said, however, that the one which is least easy to analyse, namely public sentiment, is also the one which can least easily be manipulated, changed, or disregarded. Jefferson once observed that 'there is a snail-paced gate for the advance of new ideas on the general mind, under which we must acquiesce'.[1] The wise politician understands this, and acts accordingly, whether he be in a position of authority or acting as spokesman for an interest or promotional group. Trotsky took a different view when he said that 'the virtue of an extreme proposal is that it makes all those that fall short of it seem moderate'. But while this is often true in negotiations between groups (or nations) of comparable strength, it is not applicable to a minority wishing to advance its claims in a democracy. In these circumstances a condition of success is that the general public shall tolerate the claims as being legitimate ones for the minority to put forward. General support is not usually necessary, but a widespread feeling that the claims are contrary to the public interest is apt to be fatal to their chances.[2] Progress can occasionally be made by taking advantage of a temporary current running against

[1] In a letter to Barlow, 1807.
[2] See John Plamenatz, 'Interests', in *Political Studies*, vol. 2 (1954).

the tide of opinion, but in the long run it is often better to wait for the tide to change. To mention only one simple example of the way that this happens, the claim that rent restriction is unfair to landlords was regarded as an outrageous piece of special pleading in the 'forties, but is now accepted as reasonable even by those who want some kinds of rent restriction to continue.

Much also depends on the channel through which the particular opinions or claims are advanced. If large numbers of voters hold an opinion with some intensity, or share an interest which they regard as important, they may be able to persuade M.P.'s and party organizers that flouting their views would lead to a loss of support for the governing party at the next election. In these circumstances letters to M.P.'s and contacts with party organizers may be an extremely effective way of securing influence. But this kind of influence is more likely to be negative than positive. In the last few years the fear of losing votes has probably helped to deter the Government from abolishing rent restriction, increasing the price of school meals, and reducing certain welfare payments.[1] But it is not so easy to find examples of positive influence exerted in this way, apart from the moderate degree of success which old people have had in securing increases in the old-age pension.

The reason for this is that, although there are many issues which affect large numbers of voters, there are very few about which people feel strongly enough to consider changing their voting habits. An interesting example is the case of expenditure on roads during the past twelve years, which seems to have been affected very little by the claims of private motorists.

This is interesting because at first sight it would seem that the conditions have favoured a great deal of influence. There are several million private motorists, all with personal and financial interests in better roads and facilities. The fact that for many years car owners have been paying an annual licence fee which is labelled 'road fund', but of which only a small fraction has ever been used for the roads, has given motorists a grievance which could easily have been exploited. This grievance has been aggravated by the contrast between the vast scale on which motorists contribute to the exchequer and the vast scale on which the railways are subsidized by the exchequer. British roads are the most congested in the world, and expenditure on them has for many years been smaller, as a proportion of the national income, than expenditure on roads in other western countries. Better roads would not only benefit motorists, but would

---

[1] It is not suggested that otherwise the Government would have done all these things, merely that the fear of losing votes must have weighed appreciably in the scales when these issues were discussed.

also save the lives of pedestrians and benefit the national economy by speeding communications. The list of arguments could be extended, and would seem to have put motorists in a position of impressive strength. A broadly similar situation in the United States has resulted in the general acceptance by politicians of the view that road construction must have top priority when government expenditure (other than on defence) is planned. But in Britain motorists have been so unsuccessful in pressing their claims that it is only in the last three or four years that an extensive programme of road construction has been adopted, and this clearly owes more to the influence of road hauliers and industrial interests than it does to the influence of private motorists.

There seem to be two main reasons for this difference between the United States and Britain. One is that the general climate of opinion about motoring is different: in America it is accepted as an essential part of modern life, while in Britain it is still regarded in some quarters as a luxury which should not necessarily be encouraged. This attitude is losing strength as more and more people acquire cars, but it is taking a long time to evaporate and its existence means that private motorists have to back their claims with more than arguments if they are to secure influence. The other reason is that an appreciable number of American motorists would be willing to consider switching their votes if an existing administration failed to build adequate roads, whereas in Britain (because of the nature of party loyalties) hardly any motorists would be willing to take such a step. The consequence of these factors is that the large size of the motoring lobby in Britain has had little effect on road expenditure, and the only effective campaign for better roads has been conducted not through the constituencies but through the work of industrial pressure groups enjoying direct access to Whitehall. The most important of these groups are the Roads Campaign Council (financed largely by motor manufacturers) and the National Production Advisory Council on Industry, which took up the question of road construction between 1954 and 1958.[1]

## PENAL REFORM

Motorists are a large minority who have not exerted much influence on government policy. Penal reformers, on the other hand, are a very small minority who have had a good deal of influence on policy. In part this is because they have been (and are) well organized, and have chosen the right channels of communication for their views.

[1] See S. E. Finer, 'Transport Interests and the Roads Lobby', in *Politica Quarterly*, vol. 29 (1958).

Their main organization is the Howard League for Penal Reform, whose officers and members are well informed about penal matters. The Howard League avoids public campaigns, partly because it recognizes that 'the chief resistance to penal reform comes from general public opinion'.[1] Instead, the League relies partly on the direct influence it can bring to bear on the Prison Commissioners and the Home Office, with whom it enjoys close relations, and partly on letters to the better papers, articles in the weekly journals, and books written by its members. There can be no doubt that, over the years, the League has helped to educate informed opinion and has had a good deal of quiet influence on the administration.[2]

The limitations of the Howard League's approach became apparent during the controversy over capital punishment a few years ago. The League had played its part in persuading the Government to appoint the Royal Commission on Capital Punishment in 1949. One of the League's officers was made a member of the Commission and the League gave evidence to the Commission. The terms of reference of the Commission prevented it from recommending the abolition of the death penalty, but the evidence it collected pointed to this solution and it was clear that by the time the Commission had finished its work most of its members were in favour of abolition. The Government was opposed to abolition, partly because of the views of the police, partly because of the assumed hostility of the general public. The time was ripe for a public campaign on the subject, but the League was unwilling to make such a radical departure from its normal methods, perhaps thinking that such a step might endanger its relations with the administration.

In this situation a new organization was created called the National Campaign for the Abolition of Capital Punishment. Between 1955 and 1957 it published pamphlets, held mass meetings, and lobbied Members of Parliament. Its efforts met with striking success and resulted in a swing of back-bench opinion, a change of Government policy, and the abolition of the death penalty for most kinds of murder. The Campaign's success rested partly on the earlier work done by the League, partly on the mass of evidence sifted and published by the Royal Commission, and partly on good timing and clever propaganda. Five years earlier, few people would have predicted that such a campaign could be successful, and the episode shows how quickly opinions and policies can change if the right kind of pressure is applied at the right moment.

[1] Potter, op. cit., p. 195.
[2] For details, see Gordon Rose, *The Struggle for Penal Reform* (London, 1961).

## EDUCATIONAL POLICIES

Between the wars it was sometimes said that Socialists were un-interested in defence, while Conservatives did not care about educa-tion. Neither allegation could be made today. Labour's concern about defence is evident, and since the Conservatives returned to power in 1951 they have developed an interest in the improvement of the educational system which was previously noticeable in only one or two of their leaders. The main swing of Conservative opinion appears to have taken place between 1954 and 1958, and to have been based largely on the realization that investment in education, particularly technical education, was necessary to prevent British industry falling behind that of other countries. The Prime Minister summed up the new Conservative attitude in a speech in November 1958:

'Our continued prosperity depends more than ever on our being able to develop and use to the full the brains and skill of our people, and in the adjustment and change of industry to new conditions. That is why we regard education as the most fundamental productive investment we can make.'[1]

This change in Conservative attitudes has been matched by a change in the general tone of public opinion. There is now general acceptance, as there was not ten years ago, of the need for a rapid expansion of all forms of technical and higher education, the need for an improve-ment in the status and rewards of the teaching profession, and the need for an improvement in teachers' training. At the same time there is continuing and perhaps increasing concern about the training of young workers in industry, about the eleven-plus examination, about the tripartite system of secondary school education established by the 1944 Act, about the degree of specialization common in grammar schools, and about the problem of selection for university entrance. Virtually all aspects of the educational system have been the subject of debate, criticism, and attempted reform in the past few years, and the overall picture is complex and confusing. In the following paragraphs we shall therefore deal not with the whole range of educational policies but merely with three particular stories, which have been selected for the contrasts they provide. These stories relate to the expansion of higher education, where

[1] *House of Commons Debates*, 5th ser., v. 594, c. 33. The changes in Con-servative attitudes and policies have been analysed in an unpublished dissertation at Manchester University by Valerie P. M. Nicholls: 'The Conservative Party's Attitude Towards Educational Policy: 1951–59'.

the reformers have won most of their battles; the reform of technical training in industry, where progress has been very slow despite widespread agreement that changes are needed; and the campaign for comprehensive schools, which has become the subject of party-political dispute.

In university education the expansionists have won a substantial victory. The arguments they have canvassed in speeches, articles, radio talks, and group reports[1] have been widely accepted, and the Government has committed itself to rapid expansion. Some of the more radical reformers are dissatisfied, and the debate about expansion will undoubtedly continue. But the present programme for the enlargement of existing universities and the development of new ones is as ambitious as most informed people think practicable, and much more radical than anyone predicted ten years ago. The development of the Colleges of Advanced Technology has involved greater difficulties, because the Government has felt it necessary to secure the agreement and co-operation of industry, the local authorities concerned, and the universities. As a result of the claims of industry, most students at the colleges are taking 'sandwich courses', half their time being spent at college and the remainder at a local factory. This naturally makes their training rather more practical than that given to students at the American and German institutes of technology which many people thought would be the appropriate models for Britain to copy. As a result of the claims of local authorities, the colleges were developed under local government auspices, though in 1961 the Government announced that they would henceforth be independent of municipal control. As a result of the claims of universities, the colleges are not allowed to award degrees. The courses they give are of degree standard, but the award given to successful students is called a diploma.

The improvement of technical training at a lower level has been less rapid. Many people have been concerned because British schemes of apprenticeship date from an earlier industrial era, and some think that the apprenticeship schemes which have been developed in France and Germany give young people a more thorough training in a shorter period than is possible in this country. However, the reformers in this field have made less impact on public opinion than the reformers of higher education. Some of them, such as Youth Employment Officers, hold official positions which prevent them from entering into public debate. Others are less

[1] For instance, the A.U.T. report on 'A Policy for University Expansion' (May 1958) and the particularly prescient article, 'A Policy for Higher Education', which was written by a group of dons and published in *Socialist Commentary*, September, 1959.

articulate or have less ready access to the media of communication than university teachers. On the other hand, the vested interests in this field are more powerful than those in higher education, as they include both industry and the trade unions. The combination of these factors has tipped the balance against radical reform.

Between 1945 and 1956 the Government asked industry to improve the arrangements for the training of young workers, but the arrangements that were made followed traditional lines. In January 1956, following suggestions that changes were needed, the Minister of Labour and National Service invited the National Joint Advisory Council[1] to appoint a sub-committee to look into the matter. The sub-committee reported in 1958 and Government policy since then has been based on its recommendations, which were themselves based on a view of the situation which many people regard as complacent. The sub-committee agreed that 'at its best the British apprenticeship system is at present turning out skilled workers who are the equal of any in the world'[2]; it rejected the suggestion that the Government should build apprenticeship training centres as 'not very practical,'[3] without saying why; and it recommended that 'the responsibility for the industrial training of apprentices should rest firmly with industry',[4] not with the government. One technical journal saw this report as 'proof that Britain is not even now taking technical education seriously enough'[5]; another has published even stronger criticisms of it.[6]

That the sub-committee would produce a slightly complacent report was almost inevitable in view of its composition. It was composed (like its parent body) of representatives of the British Employers' Confederation, the General Council of the Trades Union Congress, and the boards of nationalized industries, with the Parliamentary Secretary to the Ministry of Labour and National Service as chairman. It contained no independent members, no representatives of schools or technical colleges, and nobody from the youth employment service. As has been said, 'it was natural that the employers and the unions should report that the matter was one which could be safely left in their own hands.'[7]

The main development since the report was published is that in July 1958 an Industrial Training Council was established. This was done on the initiative of the British Employers' Confederation,

[1] Comprised of representatives of both sides of industry, meeting under the chairmanship of the Minister of Labour, and charged with the responsibility of advising the Government on matters in which employers and workers both have a direct interest.     [2] *Training for Skill* (H.M.S.O., 1958), p. 6.
[3] Ibid.          [4] Ibid.          [5] *Technology* March 1958.
[6] See *Technical Education*, Nov./Dec. 1959 and June 1960.
[7] *Technical Education*, Nov./Dec. 1959.

which invited the unions and the nationalized industries to nominate representatives, and which at first provided both the offices and the secretarial services for the Council. The Government has acknowledged that the Council is responsible for reinvigorating apprenticeship, even though (in the words of a Special Correspondent of *The Times*) the Council 'is perfectly framed to preserve the entrenched interests of the B.E.C. and the T.U.C.'.[1] In fact a smaller proportion of boy school leavers were apprenticed in 1960 than in 1955, 1956 and 1957, and this is only one of several indications that little progress is being made. The Government is clearly aware of this, but in the absence of any effective pressure of public opinion ministers are reluctant to do more than issue warnings and exhortations.

The latest warning came from the mouth of the Minister of Labour early in 1961. He said:

'If when the bulge comes it is seen that enough young people are not getting the opportunity of skilled training I foresee that there will be such a demand for government action of one sort or another that the basic doctrine that the responsibility for training rests with industry may be subject to pressure that will be very hard to resist.'[2]

It is difficult to see where the Minister thought this demand would come from. The general public do not appear to be concerned about the matter, for their children can earn higher wages by taking up other employment than they can by entering apprenticeship. The Minister was apparently hoping that a breeze would spring up which would get his ship out of the doldrums, but in fact it is likely to remain becalmed until he or his successor decides to start the engine. This is, of course, only one of a large class of cases in which agreement among the affected interests tends to settle the issue unless the Government is resolute in a desire for change.

If the training of young workers is an issue on which most effective opinion is on one side, the question of comprehensive schools is one which created a lively and well-balanced controversy. The advocates of these schools have a number of powerful arguments at their disposal, and in addition they can appeal to the widespread dislike among parents of the eleven-plus examination. There was a time in the early 1950's when the campaign for comprehensive schools was gathering momentum and seemed to have a good chance of success, even though the opponents of this innovation had entered the debate with a vigorous defence of the tripartite system.

It is now clear that this campaign took a wrong turning which was fatal to its immediate chances. The mistake was made in 1953,

[1] *The Times*, 3 August 1961.  [2] Quoted in ibid.

when the National Association of Labour Teachers (one of the groups who were leading the campaign) decided to try to persuade the Labour Party to incorporate the reform in its official policy. At the Party's Annual Conference of that year the Association successfully moved a resolution declaring that the Party stood for the abolition of the eleven-plus examination and the establishment of comprehensive schools which all children (other than those at private schools) would attend.

This move must have been based on a number of miscalculations. One was (presumably) that the Labour Party would shortly return to power. Another must have been that the passage of the resolution at an Annual Conference would commit the next Labour Government to implementing the policy, which experience suggests is very far from certain. In fact the party did not mention schools in its election manifesto of 1955. A third miscalculation must have been that there was no chance of a Conservative Government allowing local authorities to go ahead with this reform. There was scant evidence for this view, since the Government had already permitted some authorities to build comprehensive schools and the Conservative Party had no official policy on the subject. But the adoption of this policy by the Labour Party Conference made the issue a party-political one and virtually pushed the Conservatives into defence of the tripartite system.

All experience suggests that reforms of this kind, which involve rather complicated arguments and are not naturally party-political issues, can be advocated more successfully if they are kept out of party politics. The best way to propagate the idea of comprehensive schools would have been to convert informed opinion by articles in the weekly journals, by lectures and talks, and by successful local experiments. The decision to make it a matter of Labour Party policy was a classical case of a group of reformers using an inappropriate channel for the communication of their ideas.

### THE LAW REGARDING HOMOSEXUAL OFFENCES

Education is a field which is dominated by experts and by the demands of interested parties. General opinion is important, but the general public have fairly malleable views about education and are usually willing to take the advice of those qualified to give it. Homosexual behaviour provides a complete contrast to this. Very few people have acceptable qualifications as experts, the only group which is directly interested is silent, and the general public are thought to have deeply-rooted prejudices on the subject.

In this situation it is not easy to trace the relations between opinions and policies. The Labouchere Amendment of 1883, which made homosexual behaviour illegal, was passed almost by accident and without debate. Parliament did not discuss the subject, except incidentally, until the debate on the Wolfenden Report in 1958. This Report[1] was the result of the first official enquiry ever to be held on the subject.

The Wolfenden Committee, faced with the problem of finding expert witnesses and groups with a genuine claim to be interested, took evidence from representatives of the Magistrates' Association, the churches, the police, the British Medical Association, the Law Society, and a number of organizations concerned with moral welfare. During the course of the Committee's enquiries and the subsequent controversy over its findings, it became clear that the main division of opinion was between people at 'the centre' and people at 'the grass roots'. This is a deliberately vague form of categorization because it is not clear whether the division was related to education, to specialized knowledge, to place of residence, or to a combination of these and other factors. The division appeared sharply in the proceedings of the Magistrates' Association. The Council of the Association recommended in its written evidence to the Committee that the law should be changed so that private homosexual acts between consenting adults aged thirty or over should no longer be regarded as criminal. The annual meeting of the Association in 1955 voted by a large majority to reverse this recommendation when oral evidence was given. A similar division of opinion was evident in the Church of Scotland and in several of the other organizations which gave evidence or which subsequently discussed the Committee's report.

The Wolfenden Committee recommended that private homosexual behaviour between consenting adults should cease to be a criminal offence. This recommendation was welcomed by the weekly journals of opinion but criticized by some of the popular newspapers. The Conservative Party was divided on the issue. The Home Secretary was thought to be personally in favour of reform but was clearly aware of the possible unpopularity of such a measure among backbenchers and in the electorate at large. In the event he announced that the Government would not accept the Committee's recommendation because public opinion was not yet ready for such a change. He might appropriately have quoted Jefferson's remark: 'He who would do his country the most good he can, must go quietly with the prejudices of the majority till he can lead them into reason.'[2]

[1] *Report of the Committee on Homosexual Offences and Prostitution*, Cmnd· 247 of 1957.

[2] From a letter to Caesar Rodney, 1805.

## NUCLEAR DISARMAMENT

The Campaign for Nuclear Disarmament is an interesting example of a pressure group that is supported by great intensity of conviction and great enthusiasm, but which lacks access to any of the more effective channels of communication with those in authority. Unlike groups which represent accepted interests, it has no claim to be consulted by the government and no right to demand access to the government. Unlike many promotional groups, such as the RSPCA and the National Council of Social Service, it has no specialized information which would be of use to government departments or politicians. In this it is unusual, for most promotional groups have either some claim to represent an interest or some degree of specialized knowledge, one or the other of which gives them access to Whitehall or Westminster.[1]

There are of course other groups in a similar position to the Campaign for Nuclear Disarmament (henceforth CND); for instance the Peace Pledge Union. But the CND differs from them in that it is both ambitious and impatient. Accordingly, it has resorted to public demonstrations, which bring it a great deal of free publicity, and to a campaign within the trade union movement and the Labour Party. It is doubtful whether either tactic has advanced its cause.

The demonstrations have tended to create an unfavourable public image of the Campaign, and they suffer from the disadvantage that if they are not to lose their press they must become progressively more sensational. Supporters of nuclear disarmament are already split on this question, and the activities of the 'direct action' groups almost certainly tend to alienate public opinion. Nuclear disarmers are not bound by the 'rules of the game' which prevent groups which are granted privileges by the government from doing anything likely to cause the government serious embarrassment. But there is a widespread (if generally unspoken) belief that all citizens enjoying normal political rights should refrain from direct obstruction of government activities. While the CND as such has not endorsed the campaigns of civil disobedience organized by groups of its members, it has naturally tended to reap both the gains and losses consequent upon the ensuing publicity.[2] Public opinion polls suggest that the net effect

[1] This is true of nearly all groups concerned with education, the social services, health and amenities, and animal welfare. Even an 'off-beat' group like the Simplified Spelling Society possesses specialized information which will ensure that it is consulted if opinion moves in favour of its cause.

[2] Not surprisingly, the general public find it difficult to distinguish between the campaign for nuclear disarmament, which is promoted by several groups, and the Campaign for Nuclear Disarmament which is the largest group involved.

of the public demonstrations has been to convert a fair number of people who previously had no opinion on the subject into opponents of nuclear disarmament.

The campaign within the unions and the Labour Party, although successful in 1960, had the effect of mobilizing the opponents of the CND into a counter-campaign which reversed the decision at the Labour Party Conference of 1961. Since the opponents of the CND are clearly in a majority, the long-term effects of the CND's efforts in this sphere may also be to its disadvantage. To say this is not, of course, to criticize the CND. A group of reformers who lack access to all the direct channels of communication with those in authority are in a difficult position. They may, like the pacifists, be content to help those who share their views, and give up the attempt to change official policy. They may bide their time until a particular combination of circumstances creates a situation favourable to their chances, like the opponents of capital punishment. But if they are both ambitious and impatient, they have no choice but to pursue unpromising paths to political influence, in the hope that fortune or the general public may reward them with unexpected favours.

## GOVERNMENT LEADERSHIP

In a discussion of the relations between opinions and policies it is important not to under-rate the role of government leadership. It is true that there are some issues on which the government is reluctant to take the lead, and prefers to wait until the groups and organizations concerned suggest a change of policy. It would, for instance, be difficult for the present Government to reform the arrangements for apprenticeship against the opposition of both sides of industry. It would not be impossible and it may yet be done, but the Minister of Labour would clearly be happier if suggestions for reform came from within industry. But there are other issues on which the government takes the lead in an inconspicuous way, perhaps suggesting to independent organizations that they should make claims which the government subsequently recognizes. And there are other issues again, and they include some of the most important, on which leadership is openly exercised by individual ministers or by the cabinet.

In 1960, for instance, members of the Government made a deliberate effort to prepare public opinion for a modification of policy towards the political rights of Africans in East and Central Africa. The Prime Minister spoke of 'the wind of change', not only in South Africa but in a television broadcast in Britain. The Colonial Secretary gave a lecture to 6,000 school-children in which he warned them that many accepted views about Africa were illusions. It was, he said, an illusion that economic and social progress was a substitute for political progress, an illusion that a tiny minority could govern a country more efficiently than the great majority of its inhabitants, and an illusion that a new self-governing régime could only be democratic if it were modelled on the British Constitution.[1]

Again, in 1961, the Government made up its own mind about Britain's application to join the Common Market. There was a great deal of lobbying about this and a great deal of consultation with interest groups, but in the end the cabinet took the decision and its members then set out to persuade the country that the decision was correct. To do so, they used the same channels of communication with the public that were simultaneously being used by citizens and by organized groups to communicate their views to the Government. As was pointed out in the previous chapter, ideas and information constantly flow in both directions.

## SUMMARY

This brief discussion of a few recent issues serves to reinforce the conclusions of the previous chapter, both about the two-way flow of ideas and about the complexity of the network of political communication. In British politics there is no single channel of communication which dominates the rest, but a great variety of channels which are appropriate in differing circumstances. To recognize which is the most appropriate in any particular situation is an art which good politicians possess in fairly high degree. Some generalization about it is possible but, as with all arts, its essence is that it cannot be reduced to rules and precepts.

The examples quoted in the past two chapters indicate some of the generalizations that can be made. First, there are situations in which large numbers of people feel so strongly about a political issue that contact with M.P.'s and party organizers (backed by the threat of withholding electoral support) is the most effective channel through which to secure or prevent a change. Second, there are situations in which the number of people who feel strongly about an issue is relatively small, but their cause has such a good reputation that few politicians would wish to go on record as opposing it. Animal welfare and Sunday observance are examples, and in cases of this kind pressure through back-bench M.P.'s may be the best way of getting things done. Third, there are situations in which the arguments are complicated and public passions have not been aroused. In these cases the best tactic for reformers is to try to convert

[1] Reported in *Daily Mail*, January 4, 1960.

informed opinion without making the issue a party-political one. The success of the clean-air movement and the movement to expand technological education are examples of this, and the failure of the campaign for comprehensive schools is also illuminating. Fourth, there are situations in which party passions are inevitably involved, when reformers have no choice but to concentrate their efforts on an attempt to gain the active support of the leaders of the party which is predisposed to favour their cause. The campaign for commercial television illustrates how this may be done.[1] Fifth, there are situations in which agreement among the interests concerned is more important than anything else, as in the case of apprenticeship schemes or, to take an example which has not been mentioned before, the registration of professions. In these cases decisions are normally made by a process of consultation between the affected interests and the government department concerned. Sixth, there are situations in which the government itself takes the lead, as in the decision to apply for entry to the Common Market and the associated decisions to go over to a decimal coinage and to the centigrade scale.

This list could easily be extended. There is no particular difficulty about classifying political situations and framing tentative generalizations about the appropriate channels of communication on the basis of such a classification. Up to a point, this activity may extend our understanding of the British political system. On the other hand, it would be seriously misleading if it gave the impression that a body of generalizations could constitute an adequate guide to political practice. To almost every generalization, exceptions may be found. For instance, as a generalization it is clearly true that penal reform is best secured by the quiet pressure of informed opinion, but the National Campaign for the Abolition of Capital Punishment achieved a large measure of success by ignoring this rule. A body of rules about the channels of political communication would be rather like a sketch-map of navigable channels in an estuary which is affected by strong tides, shifting sandbanks, and constantly changing currents. It would be a considerable help, particularly to the inexperienced politician or navigator, but it would not be an adequate guide to the complexities of the situation.

[1] On this, see H. H. Wilson, *Pressure Group* (London, 1961).

# PART VI
# CONCLUSIONS

---

## CHAPTER 17

# Representative and Responsible Government in Britain

It is evident from the discussion in Parts II and III of this book that there is no single theory of political representation in Britain which commands general acceptance. Instead there is a continuing debate in which a variety of theories are invoked, some of them being variations on a theme and others being logically incompatible with one another. Each of these theories originated in a particular period as a reaction to a particular set of circumstances. As circumstances changed, so fresh theories were formulated to meet them, but it cannot be said that the fresh theories have generally replaced the older ones. To some extent this has happened over the years, but the more usual development has been for the fresh theory to take its place alongside the older ones as an additional strand in the British political tradition.

Although the debate encompasses a wide variety of attitudes, it is nevertheless a debate within limits which can be defined. Some doctrines about political representation which are current in other countries have never been seriously canvassed in Britain. Thus, there has been no support in this country for the Populist doctrine that representation is an inferior alternative to direct democracy which is made necessary only by the fact that the population is too large for all citizens to meet in person. No serious politician has suggested that representatives should be bound by specific instructions from their constituents and subject to recall if they do not follow these instructions. It has occasionally been proposed that a referendum might be held on a particular issue, but the proposals do not ever appear to have been taken seriously. And there has been no support at all for the idea that the initiative and the referendum should be adopted as permanent institutions of government, as in Switzerland, so that the representatives could be by-passed. Views of this kind have found favour among people of British extraction in both Australia and the United States, but in Britain itself they have never acquired any kind of influence.

Secondly, and at the other extreme, nobody has ever suggested that the Parliamentary system should be replaced by a system which would concentrate power permanently in the hands of a single party or a single political leader. Communist and Fascist groups have been of negligible importance in Britain, and in point of fact neither of them has openly advocated this kind of change. Nor has this country ever produced a charismatic leader who has claimed, like Louis Napoleon, that 'it is in the nature of democracy to personify itself in one man'.

In the third place, there is a whole area of controversy about the registration and regulation of political parties which has been avoided in Britain because it has never been seriously suggested that the electoral laws should take cognisance of the existence of political parties. There has been no British equivalent of the debate which has waged in many American states about the requirements that a party ought to satisfy before it is given a place on the ballot.[1] There has been no debate about the advantages of primary elections or about the desirability of laws regulating the organization of political parties and the elections to office within a party. There has been no debate about the advantages of a system of *scrutin de liste*, popular in several continental democracies, whereby votes are cast not for individuals but for party lists in multi-member constituencies, with or without provision for the voters to change the order in which candidates are placed in the lists.

In Britain, to repeat, none of these complicated and controversial issues has ever been brought into the debate. Here it has simply been taken for granted that groups of electors should be free to form parties in any way they pleased, that any elector should be free to stand for Parliament, and that the electoral arrangements should be based on the assumption that voters would choose between candidates who in a formal sense were standing as individuals, not as party representatives.[2]

In the fourth place, there is another area of controversy that Britain has avoided as a result of the homogeneity of the population.

[1] For instance, that it should have secured a certain proportion of votes at a previous election or be supported by a petition signed by a certain proportion of the registered electors.

[2] The assumptions and conventions on which the British electoral system is based are delineated in W. J. M. Mackenzie, *Free Elections* (London, 1958).

This is the controversy about communal representation which played such a prominent part in Indian politics before the war and has caused such difficulty in Central and East Africa since the war.

If these exclusions are considered together, it becomes clear that, apart from the question of the franchise, Britain has avoided all the more explosive issues connected with representation. In the context of the British political tradition, the debate on representation appears to have been lively and to have been marked by the expression of a fairly wide variety of political attitudes: in the context of world politics, the British debate appears to have been confined to a fairly narrow range of issues and to have excluded the conflicts which have recently caused most trouble elsewhere.

In addition to the views that have never been seriously advanced in Britain, there are a number of views which have gained temporary acceptance among some groups but have now faded into insignificance. The most important of these is the eighteenth-century Tory view discussed in Chapter 2, that the prime responsibility for assessing the national interest should rest with the monarch, who would thereby act as the representative of the whole nation while Members of Parliament acted merely as representatives of particular interests and communities. The decline in the personal powers of the monarch since the eighteenth century has made this view untenable.

At the other end of the political spectrum, another view which has faded from the scene is the Marxist view discussed in Chapter 6. To be sure, class rivalries still have their place in British politics, but the post-war growth in the prosperity of industrial workers has blurred the economic conflict between classes while the acceptance of the policies of the welfare state by all parties has blurred the political conflict. Few people now regard the Parliamentary system as a façade of which the main function is to disguise the real struggle between capitalists and proletariat, and nobody now thinks, as Laski and Cripps did in the 'thirties, that the system might be drastically amended if the Labour Party were to win the next general election.

Two other kinds of view which have passed from general currency are the Idealist approach to politics discussed in Chapter 7 and the doctrines of group representation discussed in Chapter 8. In academic circles the development of linguistic analysis has made Idealism seem outmoded, and though it is possible to discern echoes of the Idealist attitude in a good deal of general political discussion it would now be difficult to find anyone who consistently viewed politics in Idealist terms. The doctrines of group representation have disappeared so completely that it is not easy for members of a younger generation to realize that less than fifty years ago these views were widely regarded as progressive and advanced.

There remain current a number of attitudes to the representative process that must now be listed and briefly discussed. These include attitudes based on the Whig view of the constitution, attitudes derived from the theories of Jeremy Bentham, attitudes similar to those of mid-Victorian liberals, and attitudes based on a belief in the doctrine of the electoral mandate.

What chiefly remains of the Whig view of the constitution is a concern for the independence of Members of Parliament. This is seen in the jealousy with which the House protects Members from any threat to their independence of action. In one well-known case an M.P. who received a considerable salary as 'Parliamentary General Secretary' to a trade union complained to the House when the union attempted to terminate this arrangement because the M.P. was no longer advancing the views that the union expected him to advance. The House found that this attempt constituted a *prima facie* case of breach of privilege and referred the matter to the Committee of Privileges. In the event the Committee found that no breach of privilege had occurred, but the House subsequently passed a resolution stating that it would be wrong for a Member 'to enter into any contractual agreement with an outside body, controlling or limiting the Member's complete independence and freedom of action in Parliament . . . the duty of a Member being to his constituents and to the country as a whole, rather than to any particular section thereof'.[1] On another occasion the Committee of Privileges found that a serious breach of privilege had been committed by a newspaper editor who advised those of his readers who disagreed with the views of a particular Member to telephone this Member and say so. The Committee insisted that Members must be free to say what they pleased in the House without the fear that it might lead to their being pestered in this way.[2]

This concern for the independence of Members was also reflected in the debate on the proposal to abolish University representation in 1948, in the regret expressed in *The Times* and other newspapers over the virtual disappearance of non-party M.P.'s after the general election of 1950, and in public reactions to those constituency Conservative parties which penalized their Members for failing to support the Government at the time of the Suez crisis. As noted above, one of these Members subsequently wrote a book

[1] *House of Commons Debates*, 5th s., v. 440, c. 365.
[2] This and other cases involving privileges are discussed in G. Marshall and G. C. Moodie, *Some Problems of the Constitution* (London, 1959), chap. VII.

about the incident which contains an excellent statement of Whig principles.[1]

Another attitude which survives from the eighteenth century is the desire that the Boundary Commissioners should not forget the old principle that the function of M.P.'s is to represent local communities. The very existence of the Boundary Commissioners indicates the victory of the contrary principle crystallized in the slogan 'One vote, one value', and the Representation of the People Act does not permit variations in the population of constituencies to be too great. But in practice the Commissioners are very careful not to alter constituencies more often than is necessary and not to cut across local government boundaries except where this is unavoidable. In this way we have a system of boundary delimitation which is influenced by both Whig and Radical principles, each of which would exclude the other if taken to its logical conclusion.

The attitude which derives from Jeremy Bentham is the enduring fear that the political process will be dominated by 'sinister interests'. Bentham's proposed remedy for this was the concentration of power in the House of Commons and an electoral system which would secure that all interests in the country were fairly represented in the House. One or two modern writers have taken this view to its extreme and suggested that the House ought actually to be a microcosm of the electorate in respect of such factors as age, education, and occupation. This is, of course, a situation which is never likely to result from a process of free election. The average man does not wish to devote his life to politics, and the process by which a few hundred are selected from among those who do have this ambition is likely to distort the sample still further. Nevertheless, a certain amount of critical comment is based on the belief that the House ought to be a social microcosm of the nation.

One writer who apparently held this belief made a detailed examination of the composition of the House between the wars in order to establish his point. In his book on *Parliamentary Representation* J. F. S. Ross presented statistics relating to the ages, education, and occupations of M.P.'s in this period. Commenting on their age distribution, he said that people under 40 were 'severely underrepresented';[2] of their education, he said that 'elementary schools have less than a quarter of their proportionate representation . . . while public schools have no less than twenty-eight times as many Members as their strength in the population would entitle them to have';[3] of their occupations, he said that 'rank-and-file workers have

---

[1] See Nigel Nicolson, *People and Parliament* (London, 1958).
[2] *Parliamentary Representation* (2nd edn. London, 1948), p. 106.
[3] Ibid., p. 109.

little more than one third of their proportionate share of the membership, while the unoccupied have three times, the employers and managers five or six times, and the professional workers more than twelve times as many Members as their respective numbers in the community would justify'.[1] In a later book Ross published an analysis of the composition of the post-war House of Commons which was based on similar assumptions.[2]

Used in this way, the concept of the House as a social microcosm of the nation has radical implications. Occasionally, however, the same concept is used to defend the *status quo*. Thus when it was suggested in 1958 that M.P.'s salaries should be increased, *The Times* commented in a leading article that 'the House of Commons should be the microcosm of the nation, and this it can never be if the great bulk of its members are professional politicians'.[3] And in 1960 Lord Boothby observed in an unscripted radio programme that: 'Ideally, the House of Commons should be a social microcosm of the nation. The nation includes a great many people who are rather stupid, and so should the House.'[4]

The fear of sinister interests is reflected not only in comments on the House of Commons but also in criticisms that are sometimes levelled at the civil service. Thus Herman Finer thought it unfortunate that in the selection process for the administrative class a good deal of weight was attached to an interview in which candidates from the upper-middle classes would be at an advantage compared with lower-middle and working-class candidates.[5] In the following year Harold Laski noted with regret that 'all the leading figures in the public services . . . come . . . from an extraordinarily narrow class within the community'.[6] He felt that as a consequence of this departmental policy was largely controlled by people whose experience was too limited for them to be able to appreciate the real problems of the society with which they were dealing: for instance, they were simply unable to understand what the fear of unemployment meant to the ordinary manual worker. In the same year H. R. G. Greaves said much the same thing in his textbook on British government,[7] and four years later Laski returned to the theme, saying that the most obvious reason for the inadequacy (as he saw it) of the civil service was that 'the predominant temper and

---

[1] *Parliamentary Representation* (2nd edn. London, 1948), p. 112.
[2] See *Elections and Electors* (London, 1955), Part VI.
[3] *The Times*, January 17, 1958.
[4] In a programme called 'Let's Find Out', broadcast on September 1, 1960.
[5] See H. Finer, *The British Civil Service* (London, 1937), pp. 100–8.
[6] H. J. Laski, *Parliamentary Government in England*, p. 321.
[7] *The British Constitution* (London, 1938).

outlook of the administrative class represent too narrow an area of public opinion'.[1]

Since the war this kind of criticism has continued. Journals like the *New Statesman* and *Political Quarterly* have on several occasions complained about the large proportion of people from the public schools and the predominance of people from Oxford and Cambridge among recruits to the administrative class. In 1955 R. K. Kelsall published an exhaustive study of the social origins and educational backgrounds of higher civil servants in which he proved conclusively that the middle classes were 'over-represented' and looked to a widening of the social strata from which higher civil servants are drawn as a remedy for the 'defects in temper and attitude of mind' that were 'widely held' to exist among them.[2]

Kenneth Robinson (a don who was formerly a civil servant) pointed out in a long review of Kelsall's book that these alleged defects were in fact held to exist by only a very small group of writers. He further suggested that it was more important that the 2,700 members of the administrative class should possess the intellectual and moral qualities they needed to do their work 'than that they should not have been to public schools, not have been to Oxford or Cambridge, and not, above all, had middle-class parents'.[3] To this Kelsall replied that he wanted more equal representation of the various social classes not for its own sake but because he thought that 'the efficiency of the service would probably be increased if those sources of talent hitherto under-represented were more fully utilized'.[4] But at no time did Kelsall produce any evidence of inefficiency in the civil service, and in the absence of this it is difficult to avoid the conclusion that his judgements were based on *a priori* assumptions of what may be called a neo-Benthamite kind.

Similar assumptions underlie the suggestion that is occasionally made that the boards of public corporations ought to be a social microcosm of the nation. Thus one writer, having analysed the membership of the British Transport Commission, complained that 'the Commission is not a typical or representative cross-section of British society'.[5] After broadening his study to include all the nationalized industries he noted that 'directors of public companies

[1] In the Introduction to J. P. W. Mallalieu, *Passed to You, Please* (London, 1942), p. 7.

[2] R. K. Kelsall, *Higher Civil Servants in Britain* (London, 1955), p. 191.

[3] K. Robinson, 'Selection and the Social Background of the Administrative Class', in *Public Administration*, vol. 33 (1955), p. 388.

[4] R. K. Kelsall, 'Selection and the Social Background of the Administrative Class: a Rejoinder', in ibid., vol. 34 (1956), p. 169.

[5] Clive Jenkins, 'The Labour Party and the Public Corporations', in *The Insiders*, a supplement to *Universities and Left Review* (London, 1957), p. 31.

constitute one of the smallest occupational groups in modern society. Yet they have by far the largest representation'.[1] His clear implication was that this was quite wrong.

The continued currency of views of this kind is perhaps not surprising in a society which is both democratic and deeply conscious of class divisions. The criticisms have been extended from Parliament to other institutions because people are increasingly aware that political power is divided between Parliament and these institutions. If in the future it appears that nuclear scientists are acquiring a large share of power there can be little doubt that critics will be heard to complain that an unduly large proportion of nuclear scientists have middle-class origins and to suggest that it would be better if they were drawn more equally from all levels of society.

It was noted earlier in this chapter that some current attitudes towards representation reflect the views of the Victorian Liberals. This is only to be expected. Even though political behaviour does not now conform to the Liberal model, our present representative institutions have been largely shaped by Liberal views. The fact that these institutions are rarely attacked indicates a widespread acceptance of Liberal attitudes towards the representative system. They have not featured prominently in political debate since plural voting was finally abolished in 1948, but they are always there. They are currently expressed in concern about the influence of advertising in elections, in concern about the declining numbers of independent newspapers and journals, in concern about the powers of pressure groups and the apparent weakness of Parliament in relation to Whitehall. The electoral system itself is no longer a bone of contention, but if the recent revival in the fortunes of the Liberal Party should grow to major proportions it is possible that the case for proportional representation would become a serious political issue, and the old Liberal arguments for this reform be aired once again in Parliament.

Another doctrine which is reflected in current political debate is the belief in the idea of the electoral mandate. Though younger Labour politicians appear to attach less importance to this idea than their predecessors, it is still commonly invoked in political debate by spokesmen for the left. A few years ago, for instance, Herbert Morrison said that 'if the electoral system is to be reformed there ought to be a mandate for it from the electors of the country'.[2] During the debate on the Common Market many Labour politicians confessed doubt as to whether it would be proper for the Govern-

[1] Clive Jenkins, 'The Labour Party and the Public Corporations', in *The Insiders*, a supplement to *Universities and Left Review* (London, 1957), p. 45.
[2] *House of Commons Debates*, 5th s., v. 472, c. 143 (1950).

ment to sign the Treaty of Rome without first securing a mandate for this step. In 1961 a group of nineteen prominent trade union officers wrote to *The Times* saying that they regarded it as 'unthinkable that a decision which might dissolve the Commonwealth should be taken administratively by a Government without a mandate'.[1]

The doctrine of the mandate is not generally endorsed by academic commentators but there are exceptions to this rule. The most notable is the constitutional historian C. S. Emden, who asserted in 1956 that 'the principle of the people's mandate has been recognized as operative by statesmen and by constitutional experts for the best part of a century'.[2] Emden acknowledged that in practice 'issues are bandied about in irresponsible fashion during election campaigns' and that in consequence there is often a degree of confusion about the issues on which an election is being fought. But the lesson he drew from this was that party leaders should 'agree prior to an election what are the issues to be put to the electorate, and . . . the form in which the issues should be published to the people'.[3] If this were done, he said, the people's mandate could be made fully operative and (as he put it in another publication) 'our frail democratic structure could be invigorated'.[4]

These current doctrines—Whig, neo-Benthamite, Victorian Liberal, and the doctrine of the mandate—are not consistent with one another and they clearly do not add up to a theory of representation. The present representative system, in which party management plays so important a role, does not have ideological origins and cannot easily be justified in terms of a theory about the proper functions of Members of Parliament. It can be argued that sufficient justification is to be found in the fact that the system is based on experience, has evolved slowly over the years, and is generally accepted by the public. If further justification is required, it is to be found in the function of the representative system in the whole pattern of relations between government and people.

If these relations are considered, it is apparent that the representative system has a number of vital functions. First, the fact that the government is made up of members of the party which wins in a general election has the effect of endowing the government with a special kind of legitimacy. Given the nature of British political values in the twentieth century, it is doubtful whether a government which acquired power in any other way would be accepted as having a legitimate claim to authority.

[1] *The Times*, July 21, 1961.

[2] C. S. Emden, *The People and the Constitution* (2nd edn., Oxford, 1956), p. 315.　　　　　　　　　　　　　　　　[3] Ibid., p. 315.

[4] 'Parties and the People's Mandate', in *Parliamentary Affairs*, vol. V (1951–52), p. 169.

Second, the election itself gives voters an opportunity to express their views on the behaviour of the retiring government and opposition. It is true that voting behaviour is not markedly affected by debates about policy and consideration of party programmes. But this does not mean that it is irrational or arbitrary, that it is determined by publicity campaigns, or that it hinges on the personalities of the candidates. Given that we must reject the idea that an election result indicates a collective preference for one party programme rather than another, it remains true that most voters choose between parties, not between men, and that their choice is influenced by their knowledge and experience of what the parties have done in the preceding years and their impressions, however hazy, of what the parties stand for. Party leaders are well aware of this, and adapt their behaviour accordingly. The fact that the next general election is never more than five years away is one of the more important of the factors that induce politicians to respect public opinion and adjust their policies to intimations of public need.

In the third place, the representative system provides a permanent channel for the communication of opinions and complaints from the people to their government. It is by no means the only channel and only in some circumstances is it the most effective, but there can be no doubt of its importance.

Finally, it is clear that to some extent the representative system provides a counterbalance to the influence of pressure groups. In Parliamentary debates the public need is nearly always accepted as the criterion by which actions should be judged, and relations between members of the government and organized groups are bound to be affected by the knowledge that government actions will have to be publicly defended in these terms. Moreover, the public vote in elections, and only a few organized groups can influence an appreciable number of votes. A government without an effective representative system would not necessarily ignore public opinion, but it would be likely to pay relatively more heed to the views of organized pressure groups and institutions like the civil service, the church and the armed forces, and relatively less to the views of the ordinary unorganized citizen.

It should be noted that the British representative system is not hindered from performing any of these four functions by the development of party discipline in the past eight or nine decades, and it can be argued that its performance of the second function mentioned is enhanced by this development. Discipline ensures that the lines of responsibility are clear, and those who see a general election as a time of judgement can argue that the prospect of an election is likely to have more effect on government policy in this situation than it would if the behaviour of M.P.'s were more fluid and the judgement of the electors therefore applied to individuals rather than to the governing party as a whole.

These seem to be the main functions of the representative system in the pattern of relations between government and people, but there are of course other elements in the pattern which must also be considered. These have been discussed in Parts IV and V of this book, and some of them are reflected in the perennial debate about political responsibility.

## THE DEBATE ABOUT RESPONSIBILITY

There are two general differences between the debate about representation and the debate about political responsibility. The first is a difference of date. While the debate about representation was at its height in the nineteenth century and has tailed off since 1918, concern about political responsibility did not become a prominent feature of constitutional debate until the twentieth century. The reason for this is that constitutional debate in the nineteenth century was generally initiated by reformers who wished to see the government made more responsive to public needs and opinions. Since, by 1832, the cabinet had become accountable to Parliament, most reformers assumed that they had only to ensure that Parliament represented the whole nation to secure a system in which the government would be responsive to the needs and opinions of the whole nation. The main focus of the debate was therefore on the question of reforming the representative system, and it was only after the more important aims of the reformers had been achieved that people began to question the significance of the convention of ministerial responsibility and the reality of Parliamentary control of the executive.

The second general difference relates to the range of the discussion. While the debate about representation has been and is marked by the expression of a wide variety of theories and attitudes, the debate about responsibility has been and is marked by the dominance of a single way of discussing the situation. To put the matter shortly, this is in terms of the Liberal view of the constitution, as outlined in Chapter 5. Not everybody accepts the Liberal view as either accurate or desirable, but even those who take a different view tend to use the Liberal terminology when discussing the nature of political responsibility. To a large extent, the Liberal view has provided the language in which this aspect of the constitution is debated; and the mythology of the constitution as a whole undoubtedly bears a Liberal stamp.

The most important terms in the Liberal language are the sovereignty of Parliament, ministerial responsibility, and Parliamentary control of the executive. This terminology is misleading in two rather different ways. In the first place, the terms are misleading because they are ambiguous. Each of them has both a formal and limited meaning which is correct and a wider and looser meaning which gives a false impression of the situation. Thus, the statement that Parliament is sovereign embodies an important truth: that legislation passed by Parliament cannot legally be challenged by any other authority. But the statement also carries the implication that Parliament is all-powerful, and this hardly corresponds with the facts of the matter. Equally, the statement that ministers are responsible to Parliament for the work of their departments conveys the important truth that ministers have to appear in Parliament and explain and if possible justify what their departments have done. But it also conveys the impression that ministers have to pay the penalty of resignation if departmental blunders are revealed, and this is hardly borne out by experience.

In the second place, this terminology is misleading because it focuses attention on some parts of the political process and omits all mention of other parts. Discussion of politics in these terms makes it appear as if the responsiveness of the administration to intimations of public needs and opinions depends entirely upon the efficiency of Parliament in criticizing and controlling ministers, a view which grossly under-estimates the complexity and flexibility of the political system. It is one result of the prevalence of the Liberal language that many critics have fallen into the trap of assuming that the activities of pressure groups, public campaigns and demonstrations, and the mass media of communication are outside the political process rather than part of it, and that political influence secured through these channels is less legitimate than influence through Parliamentary activity.

As has been noted in Chapter 13, there is another language, described there as the Whitehall language, which is also used in discussions of constitutional matters. In its account of the role of Parliament this language probably contains more of the truth than the Liberal language, though in fact the two complement each other and a balanced view of Parliament's position would need to draw on both kinds of terminology. But as a language for the analysis of the political system as a whole the Whitehall language is just as limited, though in a different way, as the Liberal language. Its limitation is that it gives the impression that the responsiveness of the administration to public wants depends simply upon the sense of duty of civil servants and ministers. Like the Liberal language, it seriously underrates the complexity and flexibility of the political system.

Of course, the inadequacies of the conventional ways of portraying the political system have causes other than the inadequacies of the languages which are used. One of these causes, it is suggested, is the prevailing (and long-standing) fashion of focusing attention on the role of institutions rather than on the nature of political processes. The Liberal propositions that Parliament is sovereign, that Parliament has supreme power over legislation, that Parliament controls the executive are obvious examples of this fashion. So is the proposition that the powers of Parliament are declining. These propositions are not exactly untrue, but they do not contribute very much to an understanding of the way Britain is governed.

One of their limitations is that they do not distinguish between the various groups of people who make up the entity known as Parliament. Formally, Parliament consists of the House of Commons, the House of Lords, and the monarch. The Lords and the monarch have lost so many of their powers in recent years that when people refer to the powers of Parliament they are normally thinking of the powers of the Commons. But the Commons consists of members of the government, back-benchers who belong to the governing party, and members of the opposition, and the positions of these groups vary considerably. When critics say that the powers of Parliament have declined in the past hundred years they do not mean that the powers of all Members of Parliament have declined. The main point they are trying to communicate is that the position of the ninety or more M.P.'s who are members of the government is stronger in relation to the 500 or so other M.P.'s than it used to be. And even this is a very crude statement which needs to be refined by discussing such factors as the changing position of the Prime Minister and the circumstances in which back-benchers of the governing body enjoy more or less influence in relation to the front bench.

Another weakness of the propositions cited above in their implication that political power can be clearly and precisely located. It is said, for instance, that Parliament controls the executive. But in practice it is only appropriate to talk of control when referring to hierarchical organizations. The commanding officer controls his troops and the permanent secretary of a Government department controls the staff of his department. But to say that a minister controls the work of his department is to give a somewhat exaggerated impression of the degree of influence which ministers enjoy, and to say that Parliament controls the minister is to use the same word to describe a quite different and much more tenuous relationship.

239

It is suggested, therefore, that the accepted ways of describing the British constitution not only have the effect of making the debate about responsible government somewhat artificial, but also give a misleading picture of the distribution of political power and influence. At the risk of digression, it is perhaps appropriate to indicate the elements out of which a more helpful picture might be constructed. These would appear to be three in number: an account of the various categories of people who take part in the political process, a description of the channels of communication between them, and an understanding of the traditions of behaviour which largely govern the way in which they act.

An account of the various categories of people who take part in the political process should deal with voters and candidates, party agents and party workers, M.P.'s and local councillors, ministers and civil servants, members of advisory committees and organizers of pressure groups, advertising agents and journalists. Ideally, the information given should include details about the kinds of people who come into these categories, the routes by which they reached the positions they now hold, their motives for doing so, their conception of their place in the political process, and the ways in which they behave.

These requirements have only to be listed for our considerable ignorance about the personnel of politics to become apparent. Until a few years ago practically nothing was known about these categories of people apart from the information about successful politicians and a handful of leading civil servants provided by historians. As a result of work done in the last ten years we now have one or two books about the civil service, one book about the personnel and role of committees in British government, two or three studies of the work of M.P.'s, two or three studies of pressure groups which say something about their members and organizers, and four or five studies of voting behaviour. But very little is known about the agents and active party workers who keep the party organizations alive in the constituencies; very little is known about the motives of local councillors and Parliamentary candidates, of how they took up politics and what they conceive to be their roles; very little is known about civil servants other than those in the administrative grade; very little is known about the journalists and advertising men whose business it is to present a picture of politics to the public. It is only necessary to think of the amount of information available about the personnel of American politics to realize the inadequacy of our knowledge about this aspect of British politics.

An account of the channels of communication in the British political system should include both those channels which have been established as part of a formal process for the transaction of business

240

and those which have developed by usage and convention. Our ignorance in this field is not so great as our ignorance about the personnel of politics, and an attempt has been made in Chapter 15 to say a little about the more important of these channels. A good deal more could be done to illuminate this aspect of politics simply by re-arranging and re-interpreting material which is already available. It remains true, however, that some very important channels are peculiarly difficult to illuminate, particularly those that are colloquially known as 'the old-boy network'.

This lack of published material about the personnel of politics and the channels of communication between them is undoubtedly one reason for the continued use of a rather formal language about institutions in accounts of the British political system. We simply do not know enough to give a more realistic account of how we are governed.[1] But even if much more information of this kind were available, it would not in itself provide the material for an adequate understanding of British politics. For the way in which people behave in political situations depends very much on the values and political traditions of their society. These values and traditions are to a large extent, though by no means entirely, embodied in the prescriptive theories about representation and responsibility that have been examined in some of the earlier chapters of this book.

As was noted at the beginning of this chapter, some values and traditions have not been formulated in theories or doctrines in this country for the good reason that they are so generally accepted that they need neither advocacy nor defence. Some of those which relate to the representative system have been examined above, and it is now appropriate to discuss some of those which relate to the British system of responsible government.

One of them is the general belief that civil servants and serving officers of the armed forces should be politically neutral in the sense that they should not openly take sides in party-political disputes. Nobody has seriously suggested that there should be political appointments to the civil service, as there are on a large scale in the United States and on a small scale in France. Hardly anybody objects to the rules which prevent civil servants and serving officers from standing for Parliament. But the rules would not of themselves establish the kind of political neutrality that exists. French army officers are not permitted to stand for the National Assembly, but this has not prevented a fair number of them from indicating where their political sympathies lie. There are many issues of British defence and domestic

[1] An American critic has suggested that a similar ignorance prevails about administrative law. See Kenneth Culp Davis, 'English Administrative Law—an American View', in *Public Law* (Summer 1962).

policy on which it would be very easy for officers and civil servants to express partisan opinions in public, were they not careful to avoid doing so. This tradition of public impartiality among public servants plays an important part in upholding the convention whereby the political head of a department takes the entire blame or credit for the policies of the department.

Another and equally important tradition is that which protects the anonymity of civil servants. This again is not and could not be established simply by rules and regulations. Civil servants sign letters with their own names, interview members of the public, and are listed in the Imperial Calendar. They normally remain anonymous in public controversy only because of a strongly-held tradition which governs the behaviour not only of civil servants but also of politicians, journalists, and members of the general public. To cite a simple example, if the manager of a Labour Exchange acts in a way which gives rise to grievances among local citizens, he could very easily be criticized by name at public meetings and in the Press and quickly become the centre of a public controversy. This does not happen only because everyone concerned, including the aggrieved citizens, local journalists, trade union organizers and politicians, accepts that criticisms should be directed at the ministry or the minister and that the anonymity of the manager should be preserved. This tradition is clearly an important part of the British system of responsible government, though it cannot be legislated for and some African and Asian countries have found that it cannot easily be established in a new Parliamentary democracy.

Another tradition of British political behaviour is what may be called a tradition of discretion. This manifests itself at various levels and in various ways. There is, for instance, a strong tradition that official secrets should be kept, and not divulged either by leakage or by evidence before a committee of enquiry. Government departments guard their secrets with what many critics regard as excessive zeal. In some situations consultation with representatives of affected interests requires the disclosure of confidential information, but when this occurs a gentlemen's agreement to respect the confidence is invariably effective. Ministers themselves are extremely discreet at Press conferences and normally take care not to mention new developments until these have been announced to the House of Commons. Even journalists appear to be discreet in this respect: certainly political gossip in London is much less likely to contain advance information of impending changes than it is in Washington or Paris. The tradition is that developments in Whitehall need not be divulged to any outside body except Parliament, and even Parliament's rights to information are closely restricted by

convention. Naturally a tradition of this kind is occasionally breached, but when this happens drastic steps may be taken to re-assert the tradition. Only in these terms is it possible to understand why Hugh Dalton had to resign from the office of Chancellor of the Exchequer for divulging a detail of the budget to a journalist a few minutes before he divulged it to the House of Commons.[1]

Another aspect of this tradition is the general agreement that it is better not to probe too deeply when things go wrong. British governments make disastrous mistakes, some of which have been discussed in Chapter 11, but these are rarely followed by any kind of official enquiry or even by a public or Parliamentary demand for an enquiry. There is hardly ever anything in this country to parallel the American enquiries into the U.2 episode; the somewhat analogous (though less explosive) episode of Commander Crabb was passed over without any enquiry at all. It was typical of the British attitude to those matters that the American government was criticized by several British commentators who thought it would have been more discreet of the State Department to have denied all knowledge of the U.2.

Occasionally, but not very often, this tradition is also breached. In the months following the Suez expedition it was breached by members of the Parliamentary opposition who demanded an official enquiry into the allegations of 'collusion' between Britain and France. But it is noteworthy that no enquiry was held, and that it was in France, not in Britain, that someone published the 'inside story' of the expedition, which was apparently based partly on information derived from official sources. Characteristically, the only occasions on which it is easy to breach the tradition of no enquiries are when it is alleged that someone has breached the tradition of discretion in some other way. Thus, the Labour Government had no hesitation about establishing the Lynskey Tribunal when it was alleged that a junior minister had accepted favours from business men, and the Conservative Government showed no reluctance in establishing the Parker Tribunal when it was alleged that there had been a leakage of information about an impending change in the Bank Rate.

Another and most important tradition of British political behaviour is the tradition that the government of the day should be given all the powers it needs to carry out its policy. The Parliamentary opposition does not normally make any attempt to obstruct

[1] It is true that Dalton was not popular with some of his colleagues in the Cabinet, who may have welcomed the opportunity to get rid of him. But this does not explain why his resignation over this trivial slip was accepted as necessary by the entire Press as well as by politicians of all shades of opinion.

legislation, to prevent the delegation of legislative powers to ministers, or to reduce the financial appropriations for which the government asks. The parties expect to take turns in governing the country, and each expects to pursue its course without undue hindrance when it has the reins of office.

It is evident that the general public both expect and desire this tradition to be observed. As Quintin Hogg (now Lord Hailsham) noted: 'The British on the whole prefer to see a strong government of which they disapprove, rather than a weak government whose political structure is more complex and whose power to govern is limited.'[1] All practical experience in the twentieth century confirms this view: it is clear that decisive action by a government is nearly always approved of, and that there would be widespread concern if for any reason a government were to experience obstruction in the implementation of its policies. This attitude is reflected in the reluctance of people who vote Liberal in municipal and by-elections to do the same in general elections, for fear that a Liberal revival might result in the election of a Parliament in which no single party had a majority. It is also reflected in the almost universal British feeling that the ability of the U.S. Congress to reject legislation proposed by the President is a serious defect in the American constitution.

Another aspect of this tradition is the belief that a government should not be deterred from pursuing policies which it thinks right by the fact that they are unpopular. L. S. Amery laid great stress on this, saying that a British government is 'an independent body which on taking office assumes the responsibility of leading and directing Parliament and the nation in accordance with its own judgement and convictions'.[2] Nigel Nicolson (a man of very different political outlook from Amery) said that 'British Democracy has hitherto emerged successful from its most important test: unpopular decisions by a government are, in general, accepted; and popular clamour weighs no more than an ounce or two in the scales of its judgement'.[3] There can be no doubt that many Labour leaders, for instance Stafford Cripps and Ernest Bevin, have taken the same view.

The public themselves do not appear to object to this assumption that their leaders know best. In 1845 Sir Robert Peel made the following comment on this topic:

'I would not admit any alteration in any of these bills. This was thought very obstinate and very presumptuous; but the fact is,

---

[1] *The Case for Conservatism*, pp. 303–4.
[2] *Thoughts on the Constitution*, p. 31.
[3] *People and Parliament*, p. 11.

244

people like a certain degree of obstinacy and presumption in a minister. They abuse him for dictation and arrogance, but they like being governed.'[1]

All the evidence suggests that the British people still like being governed. Statistical support for this generalization has been provided by a recent enquiry into voters' attitudes. In a survey sponsored by *Socialist Commentary* after the 1959 election a representative national sample of persons aged 18 or over were asked to pick four out of fifteen characteristics which they thought important in a good party leader. The two characteristics which led by a large margin were, first, that he should be 'a strong leader', and second, that he should be 'strong enough to make unwelcome decisions'. These characteristics were put first by people of all political sympathies, and it is interesting to see that among Labour supporters 53 per cent thought it important that a party leader should be 'a strong leader' compared with only 36 per cent who thought he should be 'in touch with ordinary people' and 23 per cent who thought he should be 'progressive and forward-looking'.[2]

This tradition that the government should have both the powers and the ability to provide strong leadership plays a major part in determining the nature of political responsibility in Britain. Together with the traditions of administrative impartiality and anonymity and the tradition of discretion among office-holders, it ensures that when there is a conflict between the desire to be responsive to public opinions and the desire to pursue a consistent policy the government usually comes down on the side of consistency. If the three kinds of political responsibility distinguished in Chapter 1 had to be placed in order of priority, the British political tradition would clearly determine the order as, first, consistency, prudence and leadership, second, accountability to Parliament and the electorate, and third, responsiveness to public opinions and demands. It is this tradition, and not the doctrines examined in Chapter 9, that explains and supports the system of disciplined party government that the country now enjoys.

Important as it is to realize this fact, it would be a grave mistake to under-rate either the extent to which the government is responsive to public opinions and demands or the complexity of the relationships and channels of communication which influence its responses. It was the Liberal error to suggest the responsiveness depends simply on the administration's accountability to Parliament, and it is an

---

[1] Quoted in Lord Rosebery, *Sir Robert Peel* (London, 1899), p. 67.
[2] See Mark Abrams and Richard Rose, *Must Labour Lose* (London, 1960) p. 25.

error of some Whitehall spokesmen to imply that it depends simply on the discretion and sense of duty of ministers and civil servants. The British constitution is not easily understood, and it cannot be adequately described unless some account is given of the people who engage in politics, the patterns of communication between them, and the values and doctrines and traditions which shape their behaviour.

# INDEX

247